BREAK DOWN *to* WAKE UP

ALSO PUBLISHED BY DAWN PUBLISHING:

Slave Boy – Book 1 in the Democ-chu Series
by Nath Brye (2020)
Unlocked – Discover Your Hidden Keys
by Carmelle Crinnion (2020)
Moana – One Woman's Journey Back to Self
by Dawn Bates (2020)
Becoming the Champion – V1 Awareness
by Korey Carpenter (2020)
Becoming Annie – The Biography of a Curious Woman
by Dawn Bates (2020)

The Trilogy of Life Itself:
Friday Bridge – Becoming a Muslim, Becoming Everyone's Business
by Dawn Bates (2nd Edition, 2017)
Walaahi – A firsthand account of living through the Egyptian Uprising and why I walked away from Islaam
by Dawn Bates (2017)
Crossing The Line – A Journey of Purpose and Self-Belief
by Dawn Bates (2017)

BREAK DOWN *to* WAKE UP

Journey Beyond the Now

A collection of journeys by some of the world's most influential voices

Curated by
JOCELYN BELLOWS

© 2020 Joceyn Bellows

Published by Dawn Publishing
www.dawnbates.com
The moral right of the author has been asserted.

For quantity sales or media enquiries, please contact the publisher at the website address above.

Cataloguing-in-Publication entry is available from the British Library.

ISBN: 978-1-913973-03-2 (paperback)
        978-1-913973-04-9 (ebook)

Book cover design – Miladinka Milic

All rights reserved. No part of this book may be reproduced, stored in a retrieval system, communicated or transmitted in any form or by means without written permission. All inquiries should be made to the publisher at the above address.

Disclaimer: The material in this publication is of the nature of general comment only and does not represent professional advice. It is not intended to provide specific guidance for particular circumstances and should not be relied on as the basis for any decision to take action or not to take action on any matters which it covers.

*Dedicated to
my beloved son, Chase*

"One day you will tell your story of how you overcame what you went through, and it will be someone else's survival guide."'
~ Ehraz Ahmed

CONTENTS

Foreword – Marcia Martin xi

Gratitude xiii

Introduction 1

Chapter One – Jocelyn Bellows: Strike a New Match 5

Chapter Two – Dawn Bates: The Scotland Saga 25

Chapter Three – Stephan Neff: A Phoenix First Must Burn 43

Chapter Four – Tomas Garza: Reconditioning 59

Chapter Five – Dannie-Lu Carr: Loving the Baby Rhino 75

Chapter Six – Paul Honeycutt: Bearing Witness 91

Chapter Seven – Patrick Cooke: Jungle Awakening 119

Chapter Eight – Renelle McPherson: Tantric Tantrum 137

Chapter Nine – Jason B. Kendrick:
Those Who Can 'Do' Those Who Can't 'Teach' 149

Chapter Ten – Geoff Laughton: All Is Not As It Seems 171

Chapter Eleven – Lisa Berry: The Hormone Debate 185

Chapter Twelve – Brice Hancock: Last Call for Alcohol 197

Chapter Thirteen – Kevin Lockwood: On a Magic Carpet 213

Chapter Fourteen – Gurleen Khokhar:
The Inner Calling – Wings of a Passionate Lady 235

Chapter Fifteen – Arlene Wallace:
Breaking up with Being a Broken Parent 257

MARCIA MARTIN
USA

The most prolific pioneer behind the scenes influencer on the who's who in the Human Potential Movement. Marcia is one of the most innovative minds in thought leadership over the last 40 years. Global speaker, corporate executive coach, transformational thought leader, and change maker extraordinaire.

Marcia Martin has trained over 300,000 people around the globe how to look in a very direct way at the prison they have created in life that limits them from reaching their full potential.

Dame Marcia (knighted in 2008) spends her time consulting entrepreneurial and corporate companies in leadership, communication, collaboration and championship performance.

As one of the Founding Members and Sr. Vice President of Erhard Seminars Training – est – (later known as Landmark Forum), Marcia Martin was personally mentored by innovative academic thinker Werner Erhard for 10 years in the art and technology of Self Transformation and Human Development, and helped take the est organization from inception to millions of graduates worldwide.

She has consulted, trained or coached some of the greatest thought leaders and authors of our time including Jack Canfield, Tony Robbins, Lynne Twist, T. Harv Ecker, and Robert T. Kiyosaki.

Foreword

What a magical and transformative book you are about to read and on a subject that is important to all – *Why do we stay in untenable situations and how do we get out faster and easier?*

I've been in many of these kinds of situations – that many people have – where we feel at a loss to move forward or break away from what is not working, and what is not good for us.

The difference between me and most is that from a very young age, I had guidance and training in what to do in such dilemmas, and so, as I experienced these kinds of upsetting breakdowns in life, I also had the blueprint of how to move forward and to succeed in the face of desperation, depression, abuse, addiction, betrayal, and the like. I was lucky to have such information and guidance at an early age.

I consider myself an expert in this domain, having trained and coached over 300,000 people around the world in championship performance, communication excellence, relationship building, and extraordinary leadership.

My life has been blessed with amazing mentors by the time I was 20 and beyond: I was trained personally at the knee of Werner Erhard, Buckminster Fuller, Warren Bennis, Peter Drucker, John Denver, Jerry Weintraub, and Marianne Williamson.

Many people do not have the luxury of this knowledge and this practice to overcome and maneuver in such incidents in life. And so, I am overjoyed to have such a book as *Break Down to Wake Up* be available to us all. This book holds the answers (and guidelines) to how to get through the dark spaces and how to reach the promised land of personal power and abundance.

The power of this knowledge is in the personal stories shared within this book, from real people, in real situations, who give all those who are up against a seemingly insurmountable circumstance, the road map and courage to get through the darkness and to take the steps into champion action to the light.

I have been there. I lost a child to suicide; I had a divorce from a man I thought would be my lifelong partner; I was betrayed by a lifelong friend; I lost millions of dollars in a business deal gone wrong; and I have loved someone fiercely who did not love me back.

I was able to handle these events in such a way that I came through the experiences in a more powerful way to move forward and take the next step to success. This book will give the reader the guidance to have that same powerful outcome.

The stories in this book are authentic and powerful. Do not despair. Just enjoy and receive the knowledge of how a human being can, in fact, *Break Down to Wake Up*.

Apply what you learn here and enjoy a new future.

Marcia

Gratitude

An enormous thank you to the incomparable Dawn Bates. Through the laughter, the tears and a few kicks in the rear – thank you for seeing this vision and believing in me. For sticking through the ups and downs – for it all – for bringing this book to life.

To Marcia Martin – thank you for your insightful words, for bringing shape to this compilation, for your wisdom and understanding of the human spirit.

I wish to thank each and every author who bore their soul and poured their hearts onto the page. By bringing your depths of emotion forward, you give permission for others to heal, so thank you to Lisa Berry, Dannie-Lu Carr, Renelle McPherson, Stephan Neff, Paul Honeycutt, Geoff Laughton, Tomas Garza, Brice Hancock, Kevin Lockwood, Jason Kendrick, Patrick Cooke, Gurleen Khokhar and Arlene Wallace.

And, finally, to my friends and family who have supported throughout this amazing journey called life.

Introduction

Have you ever felt so alone, at the bottom of your barrel that NO one could possibly understand the depth of your despair? Living in your own muck, hating your day to day existence though not really knowing how or what to do to shift yourself, to shift your perspective?

I have.

And that is exactly why I am sharing my story, my journey of bitterness and pain to living a life of peace and joy.

Let me be very clear with this, I still have my moments of darkness. I still have moments of self doubt. Anxiety creeps up from time to time. And, even with all of this, I also know what happens on the other side, when I allow the energy to pass through and see the clarity and beauty within.

Why this book? Why now? I have been asking myself this a lot through this process. It is my journey, it is my greatest lesson. At 40 years old, I found myself at the lowest darkest point in my entire life.

I had moved across the country, walked away from a prolific career, and just months after settling into this next chapter of what I thought was going to be this fantastic adventure, I was in a deep hole. I found myself in a drought of my entire life. I was miserably unhappy in just about every single aspect of my entire way of being.

And, in the months to come; through this journey of healing, I found myself.

I found the essence of my being. This was not a one stop, quick fix, oh no, not even close. It was begging and sobbing and shaking, on my knees, it was digging in to learn about who I am. It was about who I was being.

Why this pain?

Why this sorrow?

Why me?

I was crippled, so afraid I will never truly feel connection or love. I believed that I was not good enough because no one loved me. Yes, these are words that I have said to myself more than once – lacerations to my heart, to my soul.

And in the midst of this, I transitioned into walking with some lightness, to eventually radiating in my light – living wildly beyond anything I could have ever imagined.

But let's be real – I just summarized years of my life in a few short paragraphs.

All that said, I am more like you and you are more like me than we are different. Our journeys may twist and turn in different ways, our experiences and how we experience life may look, feel, taste and sound different. However, at the base of it all – you and I really are alike.

I want you to know that you are not alone.

And this is why I have chosen to curate this book with my fellow authors. Sharing moments of darkness of pain, of despair, of self-hatred of ugliness, each of us have felt it all.

Collectively, we are sharing our own journeys through alcoholism, relationships, leaving a cult, reinventing what it means to be a family, seeing our bodies as beautiful and strong, recognizing toxicity in the workplace and even more important – toxicity within ourselves. Each of us has been there and I promise that you are not alone.

The more we share our stories, both publicly and privately, the more I realize that there are so many of us out there who have hit the darkest depths of hell and the lowest of lows.

And, in our own personal strength, of embracing ourselves, finding our own fire, striking a new match, each of us have the ability to create a life wildly beyond anything we could possibly dream.

In the chapters to follow you may see yourself in one or more of these journeys, you may find yourself relating to how one of these authors may have felt.

I promise you; this is temporary and that is why we call it journeying beyond the now because The Now may feel infinite, and yet it's just a fleeting moment. When the light returns there will be another dark cave, and there will be light again, and know that this is all connected and with each journey we get stronger and more brilliant in our way of being.

Because by sharing your journey at your lowest of lows, you found yourself. It was this path you bravely crawled, walked and ran into your own personal freedom. Finding yourself, your joy, your love and thriving.

You are not alone
Your story is valuable.
You are loved.
Always remember that.
Lovingly,

Jocelyn Bellows

Break Up to Wake Up Coach
Podcast Host: *Leap*
www.facebook.com/jocelyn.bellows24
www.anchor.fm/whatsyourleap

JOCELYN BELLOWS
USA
Break Up to Wake Up Coach
Host of *Leap*, The Podcast
www.facebook.com/jocelyn.bellows24
www.anchor.fm/whatsyourleap

Jocelyn Bellows is a Break Up to Wake Up Coach, Author, Podcast Host and Motivational Speaker. In the wake of the ending of her marriage in 2017, she began a journey of self-discovery, learning and expanding on understanding why she was the way she was and took actions the way she did.

During this intentional journey, she uncovered the truth of who she is and her continually evolving life's purpose.

Jocelyn works with men and women, allowing them to discover their deepest and truest selves. Together, they uncover the layers of stories and untruths that each of us have told ourselves, getting to the roots and re-writing the story. By understanding those base layers and removing the weeds, one then gets to create room to plant a new story line that nourishes the soul and allows us to live a life of purpose. As the host of *Leap*, Jocelyn interviews life coaches from around the world about their own 'leap of faith' in creating a life of purpose and fulfilment. Jocelyn currently resides in Colorado with her son.

Chapter One
STRIKE A NEW MATCH

I am a co-dependent. There, I said it.

Wow!

I don't think I've ever said that about myself before. And when I finally understood what that was, I truly began to understand the patterned behavior I had throughout each and every one of my romantic relationships, my friendships and every personal relationship I have ever created in my entire life.

This has been a key in unlocking the truth of who I am, how I love and how I relate to my being in this experience called life.

And I only truly understood this when I finally broke down to my lowest point of my being, feeling that I had lost everything and found myself.

~~~~~

Here I was again.

Sobbing, crumpled on the floor.

This as a result of what most might consider a simple conversation between husband and wife. This scene had become a common occurrence throughout my marriage. Conversation over finances, grocery shopping, plans for the week, you name it, a mundane non-confrontational communication became a sparing of words and often ended with me cowering. This has become my defense mechanism as a way to transition out of the conversation right here in front of us. I wrapped myself very tightly in my victimhood.

Forty years old and no backbone, no ability to stand up on my own and speak my power, speak my truth. And I was SICK of it. I was sick of the situation, of this scene I watched – no played part in – for the last decade plus of my life. Oh, wait, who am I kidding, for my ENTIRE LIFE.

I was angry. I was angry at my partner. I was angry with myself. No, anger isn't quite enough. I was sad, depressed, rageful, sorrowful, empty, lifeless, challenged, confused, lost.

What the hell was I doing here? How the hell did my life get to this point? Do I even remember what it was like to feel an ounce of joy? Of life? Of peace?

Surely not at this moment. Blinking through the steady tears rolling down my face – I recognized this as the only standard in my life. Unable to communicate my needs, my only defense was to play victim. Victim of the conversation. Victim of my marriage. Victim that I was never 'good enough', never pretty enough, not a good housekeeper, cook, wife, mother, friend.

Was this true? Well, it sure felt like it as I lay on the floor unable to move. The weight of my burdens so heavily laid upon me. In this moment, while my son sat in a chair across the room watching his mother beg and plead for the words to stop piercing my frail skin. I didn't know what was real or what I created as my reality.

I couldn't bear to look at my son. I didn't want him to see me in this state – weak and small. I wanted him to leave. I wanted to leave. I wanted to run. Inside my head, there was this ranting dialogue, *What the hell are you doing here? Stand Up for Yourself* and yet no words left my lips. The salt water of tears, an all too familiar taste on my tongue.

I held a tremendous amount of shame for what my life had become. I felt abandoned, unloved and loathed just about everything in my life. And worst of all – I blamed everyone else around me for what my life was.

I trusted someone else with my heart. I trusted that I wasn't going to get hurt even though I fell so hard for my husband. I ignored my own intuition when I knew I had to leave. I loved him. I loved him in the only way I knew how to love another.

I relied on someone else to love me. I relied on someone else to take care of me. I relied on someone else to make me happy. And, none of that – not one ounce of that did I feel. I was bereft. I was an empty shell. I was a plastic bag being blown in every which direction the wind wanted to take me.

Fall of 2017, I truly knew that my marriage was over. I was checked out. I'd finally put very heavy boundaries around protecting and shielding my heart from the man that I had chosen to spend the rest of my life with. And in the darkest recesses of my being I was emotionless about this knowledge.

He loved me. He loved me in the best way he knew how.

And, he didn't fail my marriage either.

I did.

I failed my marriage because I didn't love myself. Even writing this, it is an excruciating pill to swallow.

Once I made this decision to leave, I knew in my heart it was the absolute right decision I needed to make for me. I couldn't explain it, I just felt it.

Because I felt as if I had been hurting for so many years. I was heavily armored, protecting my heart from damage and attack from anyone outside of my being. Wearing this layer was the only thing I knew how to do.

All that I knew was that I wanted ME back. I didn't even recognize myself anymore. I was a shell of a human. I didn't know who I was, what I enjoyed or even liked about myself. FORGET loving myself. That wasn't even an option.

Looking in the mirror, I didn't recognize the person staring back at me. I was hollow. I was a shell. I was gaunt, but not the physical sense; useless, directionless.

Moreover, I HATED myself. Yes, I hated myself. How did this happen? How did I allow myself to go this far down into a deep dark sullen state? It was not depression, not this time. It was a TOTAL LOSS of my distinction of being.

In the days after filing for divorce, the grayness, the flatness, the inability to see anything clearly – I truly do not remember how I flowed through those early days. The pockets of memories, which seem like horrific nightmares were of me listless in my home, tears flowing, endlessly, no energy, no ability to get up, to move.

For weeks on end, I sat alone in my five bedroom home in silence. Sometimes weeping softly, sometimes screaming and sobbing, sorrowful for all of the errors in my ways of being. Not honoring myself, not loving this person that I was.

I spent days on the sofa and away from all technology. It was devastating for me to even acknowledge that life was moving all around me – people laughing and loving and the world spinning on.

I was not.

I was still.

I was paralyzed.

Only a few of my friends had been through a divorce – however, each of them had moved forward and were in new, fulfilling relationships. And, yes, while maybe they had walked this path, I still didn't think for a moment that ANYONE could possibly know this despair – this brokenness, this mess that I had been.

For the first time in my life I really truly felt all alone. I stopped communicating with my friends, I turned my phone off for days because it was too painful to never have any messages from anyone inquiring about my well-being.

The loneliness was all that filled my days and it was by my choosing. I had to understand why I ended up in this marriage that I had felt so alone in for so long, I had to understand why I felt so unfulfilled in my career, why I felt so unfulfilled in my relationships with others because I had no idea.

I remember in the early days after I made my decision, having lunch with a new friend who had been divorced many years and was now remarried. She shared very wise words with me at that moment and loosely she shared with me the fears that I couldn't put to words, "When you are faced with making a decision of this magnitude that is revolutionizing your life, it is if someone had torn the landscape off from your purview, the dreams that you once had are now no longer, and it's all been smoke, all just fire. And what is left is a blank slate. Dreams are dashed. It is just a blank canvas."

And I often reflect on those words because they were so powerful to me. At that moment, I thought to myself then well now what? What does my future hold? Because there's nothing on it.

With tears rolling down my cheeks as I shared with her, this is exactly how I felt. Only the canvas at that moment felt dark and heavy. What I failed to see in this conversation was what were the possible opportunities to craft an entirely new life – create a new picture, a new scene.

It took several months for me to even pick up any writing utensil to create a new mark on my blank canvas because I lived in such a paralysis of fear. I knew somehow I was always going to survive financially. I had come this far – supported myself and my family – so that fear was eradicated.

My biggest, most overwhelming, kept me up at night, inability to breathe, inability to be present in the moment – was when was I ever going to love again? Who could possibly love this broken mess of a woman. This woman who ended a marriage without a job who was just hanging by a thread most days. How could anyone want to be with me?

You see, the words echoed in my mind – I am not, nor will I ever be good enough because no one loves me. Yes, this is exactly how I felt for most of my life. My validation was only believed if I was seen and valued by another, no, specifically, by a man.

The judgements were harsh – far and wide – and unrelenting at times.

I failed. I failed at marriage. I failed my son. I failed my parents. I began beating myself up for not being fulfilled and for being weak and small. Believing that I was a complete, total and utter failure because no relationships to this point had actually worked. Self-loathing at its finest.

Begging and pleading, when was I going to love myself enough to live a life that I wanted to live?

I began asking myself where did I go wrong? I began asking what was my role in this? What was I bringing to the table? Who was I being in this marriage? Who was I being in my life?

But even in my deepest darkest points of bleakness, of greyness, listlessness – there was still a spark – something deep in my belly that kept saying, *Press Forward. You will be okay.* Maybe for only a moment today, but I am okay. I still had an ember left inside of me and that ember was what kept me going.

Even with that defiance of the self-doubt and leaning just ever so slightly into the idea that I am going to survive, I still had a major inquisition with myself.

What is it going to take? What will it take for me to let go of my victimhood, my sorrow, my anguish, my self hate?

Did I have it in me?

I had no idea what was to come.

I didn't take some magical trip around the world or escape into a false reality.

No. I dug in.

I dug into getting to know me.

Over time, I transitioned from a self loathing perspective to a self loving perspective. It was in this transition when I began to really understand what it meant to love myself. That canvas that was white and blank and empty began filling up a little bit of color and warmth and brightness.

I began to uncover that my part in this marriage no longer working was because I did not ask for my needs to be met. I showed him how to love me by not loving myself. I didn't love myself. I didn't even know

HOW to love myself. Was I too nice? Did I not establish boundaries? Did I just allow myself to be beaten down with words? The answer for me was YES to ALL of it.

I came to learn that the love that I needed to find was the love for myself. That's when I start to transition from an external love to an internal love.

The ending of my marriage went deeper than that relationship and I knew it. I had seen this roller coaster of love pattern around my romantic relationships in general.

This gave me even a further platform for me to explore who I was being and how was I showing up in all of my past romantic relationships? And even bigger, how was I showing up in life? Was I playing on the court or simply watching from the sidelines?

Early in my separation, I made a few key decisions. I decided I was going to detoxify my life. I gave up drinking and began a nutritional cleanse program. I also began deleting people from my life. With the little acuity I had, I began evaluating the people in my life. Those who didn't make me feel good or felt that they were negative or brought me down – I literally deleted them from my phone, my email and all social media.

Additionally, I was absolutely going to seek out support in a healthy and positive manner. I was NOT going to give up on myself. I have come this far. I am going to continue forward. I have to. I have to for me. I have to honor that little girl whom I'd promised my life was going to be spectacular and amazing.

Having battled anxiety and depression throughout my adult life – I was quite familiar with therapy. I had bounced in and out of therapists offices for years – starting in my 20s. However, I had always noticed that I felt little relief in those practices. I committed to going to sessions weekly for months on end though had not received any true and lasting changes.

So, realizing that I wanted to radically change my life, I investigated alternative ideas. First with business coaches because I was out of work. And, then, through a force much larger than my own, I crossed paths with a life coach. I figured, what do I have to lose here? So, I booked my first consultation with only a glimmer of hope that something might possibly be helpful here.

And, so off I went. In that first session, I shared a very broad overview of my life – about to divorce, out of work, parent to a young son and that I felt utterly lost, directionless and that I simply wanted to feel better about anything. Sitting in a wooden chair in the middle of the office, my coach asked me to close my eyes. He walked through a simple exercise that calmed my nerves and quieted my mind. As I shared the scene that was unfolding in my mind, a dark cavernous cave, I was invited to walk to the darkest corners, recesses of that space.

Of course I didn't want to because that was terrifying to have to look at the spaces of my life that I was most scared of – however, I complied. Again, this was only an image in my mind, not reality and I had nothing left to lose at this point. I sat in the dark corner, the recesses of my being and began uncovering my deep seeded pains that were inflicted over stories I had crafted in my mind.

What was true, was that I was healing deeply planted wounds. My days were filled with two to three hours at the gym, moving softly – this was my usual, and only outing. I was meeting with my life coach twice a week – diving deeply into the core of why I had shown up in this way. I began learning yoga and started a weekly practice. That weekly practice became a daily practice. Yoga was my reason for leaving my home. I didn't want to reach out to ANYONE because how could anyone truly understand my pain, my loss, my discomfort in my own skin?

Day by day, coaching session by coaching session, my inner confidence grew. It was a slow ember deep in my belly. Every day, that ember grew only a touch stronger. I envisioned sitting at a campfire, talking with past lovers and friends – making amends with whatever pain I had felt had been inflicted by them, only to understand that the pain was only mine and all that I spewed in their direction was only poisoning me. I carried a mentor to this vision – this started as someone near and dear to my heart. And with each passing visit to this campfire scene in my mind, that mentor was replaced with dancing monarch butterflies – those butterflies were my intuition, my inner guide.

The transition from an external source to the butterflies became my transition from trusting another to trusting me – my inner being, my knowing of me.

I began journaling more regularly – working through my emotions, what the flow was going through me at that time. This became cathartic and a beautiful way for me to release all that was pulsing through my being. I was inconsistent with my writing, however, every time I did, there was another layer peeled back. I began to see myself and experience myself in a whole new way.

This once very meek, very insecure woman who always seemed to feel a void in my life began to write beautiful words to the person I was blossoming into. No, the person I always knew I was but could no longer see.

~~~~~

ACTUAL Journal Entry:
Dear Jocelyn,
Live in the moment. Enjoy the stillness of being. When you start to doubt, come here – in the space of calm – after falling through the cracks. It's okay to be vulnerable. Believe in yourself. When you feel yourself starting to fall, keep going. Follow the movement, slowly and intentionally and deliberately. You are guided by your heart. You can let go of control. That was then (the head) and this is now (the heart). Again you say come here. Embrace the dark and wash it away. Let it all in. My gates are open.

Forgive yourself. Embrace the pain. Acknowledge its existence and know that you are stronger, and light, and love. Trust yourself. Allow yourself to trust those who your intuition says it's okay to. Release those who no longer serve you. You are a whole being. Trust your gut, your intuition.

There is a guide deep within, a compass that provides direction and clarity. Feel into your feelings, all the good, and all the flaws. You are perfect just as you. You attract the light because you are the light. Remember the calmness within. This is your strength, your full being.

There is a force compelling you forward down a clear and open path. This is your path to take. Relinquish control of the movement and allow your body to be glided and guided on this journey.

Heal yourself, knowing that the scars are there as a reminder of how far you have come. Live in the lightness of the being that you are today. The being that you have created within you. Embrace this magnificent woman who you are. Who you always knew you were and are truly living.

When trust is interrupted by a bolt, listen to your intuition and let it guide you. There is a pull within, that will again serve as your guide. Trust it. Love it. Appreciate your wholeness of being.

Your life is a kaleidoscope of emotions, feelings, love, experiences and people. Take time to see the colors, feel the emotions deeply, experience the light that shines from deep within. This is your innate wisdom. Believe it. It is yours and it is all within you. Open those gates, allow others to see your beauty and radiance. Share this wisdom, embrace the beauty and faults of others. We are all perfect just the way we are.

Lovingly,

Jocelyn

~~~~~

Yeah – I really wrote that about myself.

And

I

Believed

Every

Single

Word

Reading these words back to me, even as I pen this chapter, there are quiet moments of disbelief that it took me 40 years to really see my beauty.

As a young girl, I yearned to be part of the crowd, to be invited, to be welcomed into that group of popular kids. As I aged into my teenage years, that void grew even bigger – an inner begging to be loved by another. Pining to have a boyfriend, to be seen, to be accepted by someone else. This desire was debilitating. The depth of this void was so deep and completely unfulfilled. It was tied to some false belief that I was only ever going to be important if someone else was going to love me.

The inner work continued.

One of the early lessons I played in was learning about vulnerability. For so many years, I was wearing this very heavy armor, thinking I was protecting myself, my heart, from injury, from heartache, from heartbreak. In fact, that armor was only separating me from the greatest love that I could ever feel. It was in fact, keeping me from loving me and opening myself to receive love from the world around me.

So I played with this idea. To drop my armor and embrace me, I did, in my opinion at that time, some very bold things.

It started with posting on Facebook. Yeah, I know how that sounds. Everyone posts on Facebook, right? Nope, not me. I was a voyeur watching everyone around me sharing their highlight reels of life and I was on the sidelines, still waiting for MY life to get better. So, fuck it, I was going to put some skin in the game. Here's the catch though:

I didn't care one ounce of what anyone shared, commented, posted – it meant nothing to me.

I played with this toy. I began sharing exactly where I was. If I cried all day, I cried all day. If I had a moment of breakthrough – that went up. If I went for a short run that made me feel good – up it went. And steadily, those stories of despair were replaced with stories of triumph.

But it wasn't about anyone to have pity for me or look at me. This was my public journal. And that was the best part because I was completely unattached to anything that came through.

Why?

Because It Didn't Matter.

I now understood that I was good with myself. Good, bad or indifferent.

I was good with me.

The more I played in this arena, the more I got curious. Who do I Get to be now? I have shifted so much of my being, removed a great deal of toxicity around me. By changing my eating habits, by changing my drinking habits, by removing people in my life that brought me down, by leaning into things, and activities, and conversations, and people who made me feel good.

As I began to really take a deep dive into WHO I was, the scene of the blank canvas did shift. It did become brighter, lighter and whiter, and a clear canvas where I could explore and expand. As I began to heal through my journey I started to pick up a pencil, began to sketch what I wanted my life to be.

And through this maze of uncertainty, the clouds lifted and clarity set in. I AM my own lover. I am my own best friend. I am the one who gets to save me. I am the one who gets to honor me. I am the one who gets to determine my worth. Egoless – because I am not my ego. I am a beautiful, omnipresent ray of light.

As part of my self-dedication of bi-weekly coaching sessions, changing my diet and regular exercise, I began attending a spiritual center. Growing up, I was raised Jewish, though truly never identified with the religion. My parents were very gentle about religion, it was available to me and my siblings, not force fed. However, I felt like an outsider looking in, it didn't resonate, it didn't feel good.

So since I was experimenting with new ideas, this was an opportunity that presented itself. My first experience was attending a guest lecturer – a transgender woman of color took the stage to share her prolific journey of self-discovery.

Before even entering the dome shaped building, I could feel a shift within me. I felt more relaxed, at ease, welcomed, loved, embraced. I couldn't explain it then because it was something I'd never felt before. It was as if there were arms open to receive me and wrapped me in a beautiful loving embrace.

I entered the building and took my seat. There was lively chatter all around me. I had come alone and was a bit nervous, but knew that once the show began, my inner chatter of self judgement of being on my own was going to disappear because all eyes and ears were set to be on stage. To my surprise and joy, both of my seat neighbors, neither knowing one another struck up lively conversation and actually embraced me with hugs. What a beautiful welcome. The stage lit and the evening program began. I was enthralled by this prolific, confident, steady voice who had been through deep anguish and pain triumphantly echoed her journey and radiated. Enraptured by her words, the evening was over in what felt like a heartbeat. As tears rolled down my cheek – I felt something new within me.

What was this? My body felt like it was in a full blown vibration. I looked down at my hands and they were steady, but my body, my extremities were pulsating. And that continued until I arrived at my car which was in an outer parking lot. I met a friend at my vehicle who was onsite and unable to attend the actual event. By this point, my body had calmed and was in flow – so me being me – immediately asked, "What was that? What the heck am I feeling?" Grinning from ear to ear he sweetly replied that was the energetic vibration of the container of everyone in that space.

What???

This was a new language to me. And, yet, was incredibly comforted by these words. So much so, I began attending this spiritual center. The messages contained words of love and acceptance and oneness and conscious collective. The words were melodic and peaceful. They warmed my soul. And so I continued to dedicate my Sunday mornings to this space that made me feel welcome and whole. About two months into my weekly visits, I was stopped at a traffic light in a trance, soaking in the beauty of the Colorado Rockies. It was an out of body experience. I knew where I was, yet I was so present to the beauty of nature. Pivotal as I had never seen this landscape as I did in this moment. Eventually, someone honked as apparently the light turned green. This, by the way, rarely occurs in the gentle Colorado climate. So my guess is that light has probably been changed for several moments. And I had no idea.

Affirmations began appearing all over my home – on my bathroom mirror, every corner of my bedroom, my family room and front door and in my work space – reminders of what I can be and where I wanted to head.

I began reading the works of Byron Katie, Gabrielle Bernstein, Jen Sincero and other spiritually and consciously minded authors. Diving into these books became comfort. When I would squirrel into spiraling negative thoughts, I picked up a book and read the words. I devoured them. I began to really understand that the world was much larger and greater than my little worries that used to keep me locked in my head and frozen with fear. In this perspective, I felt safe. I felt loved. I felt the love of the universe all around me.

I set goals for myself and began achieving them – completing six hour hikes in the Colorado mountains, running my first half marathon at elevation, returning to the soccer field to name just a few. I began hiking – going out for four to six hours – solo on trails. I began doing less and feeling more.

I focused on being present in the moment I was in. I first remember this when spending an afternoon with my son in a local park. We packed up our things for the day and took a 1.5 mile walk to the park – planned to stay for lunch with no plans of how long we were to be there or what else we had to do for the day. Sitting in the park that day, he went to play in the splash park and as I sat in the grass, soaking in the sun, I began to feel free – free from the anxiety that had long haunted me. The anxiety of what is next, how do I entertain him? Does he know that I really don't know how I get through my days, that I hold the tears back because I don't want him to see me in this tortured pain?

Instead, I lay in this grass with a smile spreading across my face and felt lighter and free. I was just there. Delighted in his laughter as he ran through the various water jets. I got up and joined him. We laughed and delighted in the moment.

As hours passed, we had lunch and just sat in the grass with not a care in the world. Reflecting on that day, I know that a switch was hit. This woman who spent her 20s in New York City always running from thing to thing to fill her time, who was SO uncomfortable in her own skin who hated having 30 minutes of downtime because I felt unimportant – was joyfully in just being. This is when I knew I was turning a corner.

I embraced this idea that I was going to do things I had never done before. While continuing to explore and expand in pushing my physical boundaries, I played with new employment and income streams. I drove Uber and Lyft – indulging in learning about my passengers and their life journeys while safely transporting them to their desired location. And I loved it. I loved meeting new people and exploring new conversations and even befriended a few along the way.

I had a few spare bedrooms, so I began renting them out on AirBnB. It became my side hustle. I had been a part owner of two small businesses with my former spouse and loved the idea of running a business and treated this as my business.

I found myself loving to be in my own company. I was free from the need to have a partner at all. What filled in, was my own personal internal happiness. I was free from the pain of anxiety and depression that had long been constricting, holding onto me. I settled into my life, became more relaxed and joyful. New people, new opportunities and a deeper sense of inner completeness within me began filling that area that I once saw and felt as a void in my life. When I finally gave myself permission and surrendered to this knowing, my life radically transformed.

My happiness is my responsibility. For so many years, I hung, no clung to this idea that I was only ever going to be happy when I had that perfect partner, or had a child or had that 'job' that I worked for years to attain.

And, as I transformed into someone who is beautifully content and truly happy, I began living my life with enthusiasm and passion. I shifted into becoming a super attractor. I became a magnet, drawing in new people and new opportunities into my life.

Over time, I picked up my pens and colored in the white and before I knew it, I had my crayons, my markers, my paint and that blank white canvas became this vibrant beautiful piece of art with the color of life, joy and exuberance.

Moreover – I became unbusy. Intentionally. I created space in my days – to daydream. To just be in my own company. No phone, no computer, no TV, no music – just blank space. And what I began to notice was that when the TV was on, I felt under attack from the outside noise. I preferred the silence. I preferred my own company. THIS BLEW MY MIND at first. For so much of my life, I had longed to be a part of something bigger, a group of friends, truly loved and supported by a lover and now, I didn't even fathom the need. And I knew it. I felt full from within. I felt vibrant and loving and light and happy. There were days I felt such immense joy from within that I wanted to crack my body open and let that joy beam out. My skin was too much of a container for this sense of love.

On the rare occasion I listened to music, love songs sounded different. Instead of hearing that love was an external love, or love from another, the words were being sung to myself. I was the center of love. I was the one to love me fully.

I learned what I can do and ask for. I learned that I can speak my mind and when I do, I can get what I desire and deserve.

And while I do not fashion myself to be a writer or journal on a consistent basis, I did pen myself a mission and vision of the person I was becoming and choose to live into daily.

I am a beautiful being and I give myself permission to receive the love that pours into me. I pour love into others. I choose to receive, and be still, and love myself for the person that I am. I am fallible and have learned bad habits. I limited my growth by staying in situations that no longer served me. I learned. I learned how to love myself and what I chose to tolerate and what I CHOOSE to have be better for me going forward.

I radiate my light, be open to receiving love from myself, from others and to lead with love. To be at peace within my being. I am a sensual goddess. I am enveloped with love; my heart is full, and warm, inviting and radiating; its full power from within, creating a warmth that radiates beyond my being. This feels like a pure state of bliss. It feels easy and light, boundless, radiant, joyful, inviting, calm, strong and confident. Most days I am oozing with self confidence and balance and gentle, flowing with the air and water and with the currents of mother nature. This state of beingness feels natural and loving. I feel this sense of peace, calm and serenity in my being. It is flow and easy. I support this by loving myself in kindness, getting proper rest, eating a balanced diet, drinking plenty of water and staying hydrated and nourishing my mind, body and soul.

I have so much gratitude for having experienced all of it – the depth of the sadness, inability to literally pull myself up off the floor – sobbing and living in this dark, cold space. To cocooning in safety, allowing deep emotions to be felt and healed. And, in time, blossoming into a butterfly, floating free and light, softly gliding as an observer of life blooming all around me. And, then, landing on my feet and stepping into new experiences again, and again, and again and again – solo – building an inner strength of knowing who I am, and exploring the wonderment of life to be explored.

My former spouse and I continue to co-parent our son. And, while our journeys have taken us on different paths, he is a wonderful father. I now understand that the more I love me, the more he can and vice versa. This is a continual learning process.

Reflections

Reflections

DAWN BATES
LOCATION FREE

International Bestselling Author, Author Coach and Strategist,
Publisher, Freelance Writer and Ghostwriter,
Molecule Shaking Speaker and Sailor
https://dawnbates.com

Born in the UK, Dawn is best known for her profound wisdom, 'molecule shaking' truth slaying and high energy, not to mention a trademark giggle which is as infectious as a flu epidemic.

As well as being an international bestselling author, author coach and strategist, and ghostwriter, Dawn is an online entrepreneur, specializing in brand expansion, developing step change strategies and global visions, underpinned with powerful leadership and profound truths.

She writes for various magazines, and when not sailing around the world on yachts, she appears on various media channels highlighting and discussing important subjects in today's society.

Her first trilogy *The Trilogy of Life Itself* is powerful, as is her current series of nine books *The Sacral Series*. Both compilations bring together the multi-faceted aspects of the world we live in and takes you on a rollercoaster ride of emotions, whilst delivering mic dropping inspiration, motivation and awakening. Both bodies of work capture life around the world in all its rawness.

Chapter Two
THE SCOTLAND SAGA

The pain I felt rise from deep within me no physical injury could ever deliver. This was a raw pain from my soul, like the very core of my being was being ripped from me in the most horrendous, most destructive way possible.

Watching as my children walked out the door, not knowing when I would see them again, I had held it together, for their sakes; but the moment that door was closed, my legs had no power in them. I fell to the floor and screamed a soundless scream, pulling my arms into my body, fists clenched as if I was ready to fight the fight of my life, tears streaming down my face and a white noise so loud I couldn't even process my own thoughts.

They didn't care about the games they played, so long as it was another court case they could add to the winning streak for their career progression, for the firm, for the statistics of the government. At the end of the day, they would leave the courtroom, go to the pub, raise a glass in celebration and then go home for dinner and sleep soundly. They didn't care about the lives of those they destroyed on the way to the top. Why would they? They were lawyers, legalized thieves of people's lives, futures and as I was finding out, the souls of those who felt deeply.

Finding it hard to breathe I started to see the silver rain drops. Knees pulled up close and tight to my chest, head into my knees, the raindrops were the only light in this dark tunnel of fear. I could feel the wetness of my jeans as my tears fell with ease, cascading with the mucus from my nose. Not a pretty sight, but then none of this was.

A simple choice made from a place of purity, insights and experience, twisted beyond recognition into an image even I would be afraid of.

But it wasn't the truth, it was nothing near the truth and so help me God I was going to prove it wasn't the truth.

My mind was lost in the vortex of confusion. How had I got here? Becoming a mother had always been at the top of my list of dreams to achieve.

Pretending to walk down the aisle with my mom's net curtains over my head when I was just a little girl, because there was no way I was having children without being married. Good girls didn't do that. Respectful women didn't do that, and I was a good girl.

Sitting in class being given our list of options to choose from for our GCSE's the very first one I ticked was Child Development. The second Drama. No hesitation and within seconds of being given the list, I had already handed my form back to the teacher.

She looked at me, a slight frown and then a smile on her face. Mrs Collins knew not to question my speedy response. If I wasn't in the library, then I was reading, unless I was at netball, rounders or hockey practice. Or maybe choir, if I liked the songs Mrs Wells had chosen.

Yeah, I know each and every teacher I had, and they knew me. They knew that when I set my mind to something it was already done; and it didn't really matter what happened along the way, I always came up smelling of roses.

For me learning about how a child developed both inside of me and throughout life, combined with how to bring out the different methods of storytelling and confidence in a child through drama made perfect sense. I was going to be a mom, and the best mom ever. Like my mom, but not.

I didn't want to be the mom who got to a certain age and wished she had done this, that and the other.

I wanted to see the world, and I wanted my children to see it too. I wanted them to experience different cultures, eat more than meat and two veg, with roast potatoes, because potatoes weren't really a veg, they were a food group all of their own. Mashed, chipped, roasted, baked and made into crisps.

The next on the list was to learn as much about as many different subjects as possible and learn to cook healthily. If I was going to be the best mom ever, I had to know how to cook healthy and tasty food. I wasn't going to be one of those moms who heated stuff up from a box, jar or plastic packaging.

Head swimming I was back in the kitchen with my boys, laughing, dancing and cooking together. Hearing them laugh and debate with me, with each other, the best sounds in my auditory library; except the sound of them sleeping peacefully.

Their faces flashed and created a kaleidoscope of images behind my eyelids. The pain raged through the depths of my soul once again. My dog Kelt, at my feet, wondering what on earth was going on, gently tapping at toes, pushing his way onto my lap. I held him tightly, and rather than wriggle his way free, he stayed and hugged me back.

The avalanche of tears came thicker, then the wailing. A wailing I didn't even know I was capable of making. Kelt jumped down, looking at me as if I had been possessed; looking at me tilting his head from left to right as if to ask me what was wrong.

I could only just see him through my tears. My sleeves were wet through from the wiping of my tears, slimey from the snot that ran from my nose, and yet I didn't care. I had just watched my children walk out the door, to go live with their dad, whilst I fought the biggest fight of my life.

Feeling the acidic bile rise up from my guts, I tried to get up off the floor, but I couldn't. I had nothing. I crawled my way to the bathroom and lay there, just in case I was sick. But nothing came. Except more pain. More tears and instead of fear, a rage was building up inside of me.

How dare they tell me I was a bad mother!

How dare they tell me I had neglected my children!

How dare they accuse me of abandoning the two most precious people in my life!

Who the hell did they think they were!

They didn't know me.

They didn't know the life we had led.

They didn't know the education I had given my boys, both in one of the very best private schools and life outside of the education system.

They didn't know of the work I did in the world.

They knew nothing!

They simply put on a uniform, clocked in for shift, called themselves a police officer and then went around looking for reasons to arrest people.

They were despicable.

Racist.

Ignorant.

Judgmental.

And who the hell did they think they were to destroy the lives of others just because we made different choices from them?

Choices based on living a full and adventurous life, a globally educated, life full of rich cultural diversity.

As the rage built, the sickness rose, and before I knew it, I was heaving my guts up… with nothing coming out.

What was there to come out?

I had not been eating, in part because the turmoil and anxiety of what lay ahead of me was making my stomach tight and the thought of food repulsive; and because the court case had drained my finances to a point where I couldn't even afford to feed my own children.

What the hell had happened to my life?

Our life?

How the hell had we got here?

How had it gone so badly wrong?

He had come into our lives.

He had blinded me.

Distracted me.

And here we were.

The boys no longer with me, but with their dad.

A good man.

A kind man.

A good father.

And here I was with my soul consumed, with regret at ever having invited this new guy into our lives.

But for me to win this court case, he had to stay.

I had to believe it wasn't him.

I had to believe it was just a coincidence.

But I didn't believe in coincidences.

Never had.

So why now?

Tired, and exhausted I had fallen asleep on the floor.

Yet again I had cried myself to sleep, with my dog curled up beside me.

My shadow, my fur baby.

If only he was a man, he would have been perfect.

So loyal, so loving, so playful, always excited to see me, and always there when I needed to go for a walk to breathe in the fresh air, move my body, and gain clarity.

And here he was, tapping me gently on the shoulder, waking me up to tell me it was time for a walk.

How long had I been asleep?

What was I doing on the bathroom floor?

And then the memory of the boys waving goodbye, the door closing, me sliding down the wall in pain returned like a banshee on steroids to ignite the fear and the pain all over again.

But this time I wasn't going to allow it to take over.

My boys needed me to be the mom I had always dreamed of being.

The best mom ever.

The one who rose even higher with each new day, each new challenge and did it was style and grace.

Picking myself up off the floor, I washed my face.

Walking through to the bedroom, I started to take my clothes off.

This was the moment I chose to fight.

Fight the fight of my life, and no police officer, no lawyer and no judge was going to take my boys off me or tell me I was a bad mother.

No fucking way.

I grabbed my combat t-shirt from the draw, pulled on my jeans and pulled my hair back in a ponytail.

Moisturized my face, applied my mascara, eyeliner, and my lip gloss.

Added a couple of bangles, put on my trainers, and it was time to go for a walk.

Refocus.

Re-energize.

And re-group.

Head held high and a smile of determination on my face.

Walking the dogs I had to put my game face on. I was too well known in the local area to even consider being anything but cheerful.

It was almost as if I needed to be the person they all needed me to be just so I survived.

And I wasn't going to survive.

I was going to thrive.

And those involved were going to wish they had made smarter choices.

They had picked the wrong woman to mess with.

They had picked the wrong Mama Bear to fuck with, and now they were going to hear me roar so loud my fellow Mama Bear's in Alaska would hear me.

This was a fight I was not going to lose.

No way.

Not now.

Not ever.

And in the process of winning my fight, I was going to help every other mother, father and child going through something similar to win their fights too.

This wasn't just my story this was the story of so many and they had no right to do what they were doing, no right whatsoever.

Kelt and I must have been out walking for hours, because by the time we got back to the apartment it was already almost dusk, and the boys had left earlier that morning.

Arriving back at the apartment I was hungrier than I had been for a long time, but with no money to speak of, it was a bowl of rice and a dash of tabasco all over again.

A meal I had taken to eating to make sure the boys had all the veggies and nutrients they needed.

I had even gotten to the point where I had started to tell them I had eaten late so would not be eating with them at the table, something which was easily believable as I had been working so hard since their dad and I had divorced.

I worked hard anyway, but since becoming a single mom, things had ramped up even more. I had to provide, and I couldn't rely on anyone else to provide for me and my boys.

This was all on me.

And I was not going to let my boys down.

Ever.

With all the documentation following my arrest laid out on the table, I went through it all. Letters from my solicitors, statements I had given my lawyer but not the police as they still had not questioned me, still haven't to this day.

I had started to print off documents regarding the Child Protection Act and grabbing my highlighter pen, I went through this with such laser focus I could have burnt a hole in my dining room table.

I cross referenced what I was reading with ideas and gaps I was making on my note pad. I drank more tea than I ever thought possible, because we each cup another thought, or insight would come.

Arriving back at the table, I would do another search on the internet in family law, then criminal law and then Human Rights Law.

My printer was on full speed, and all the paper I had put into storage after closing my last business had now come in very handy.

Cross examining all these different aspects of law, and the different laws in Scotland to the ones in England, I began to realize just how different England and Scotland were, and how each area of law negated the other.

I began to realize just how dangerous the law was, how corrupt it was, and how it would be near impossible for someone who had no idea about the law could end up serving time in prison, or being convicted at the hands of a lawyer who was only allowed to practice one area of the law.

The more I learnt, the more I knew the public needed to know about what I was learning.

The more I cross referenced what I knew as a Police Assessor and as a Human Rights activist, the more I realized the massive mistakes the police officers and my first lawyer had made.

The more I studied the more I became angry at how the public were being duped, lied to and how little protection we actually had from the law and legal systems there to protect us.

I had always joked that I would become Dr Dawn one day, but now I was reading all of this, the more I knew I had to study the law, not for a degree but for the purpose of speaking out and empowering others.

I began to see that this situation hadn't happened to me, it had happened for me. For me to serve humanity at an even higher level than I already had been.

Beginning to feel tired, I looked at my fitness tracker. It was already 3am, and I needed a walk. "Come on Kelt, let's walk!" Springing off the couch, his little tail wagging, we prepared ourselves for our walk.

"You need a little friend, you do. We need to get you a wife, what do you say, hey Mr Man? Fancy a wife?" With the smile that spread over his face, and the speed at which his tail started wagging, I knew he knew what I was saying. "We'll get you a wife my darling, just let Mommy get this sorted and we'll find you a beautiful lady to make magic with; what do you reckon?" With that he barked his yes, and we headed out the door.

It was a really fresh autumn morning and dawn wasn't far away. The silence of the morning was always my favorite time of the day. Being outside when no one else was around was always perfect. I had often wanted to just explore the world with no one else around. Just me and my dogs, walking and exploring woodlands and beaches, and sitting on the beach with a fire, looking out at the ocean, the horizon, one day sailing across the wide expanse with nothing and no one but the ocean and marine life itself.

One day. One day that would be so.

As Kelt and I came to the brow of the hill, I looked out over the city of Sheffield, silent and beautiful. It really was a beautiful city, and one that had been my home for almost seventeen years, minus the four the boys and I had spent living in Egypt with their dad. I realized I was smiling. I felt peaceful. A feeling I hadn't felt for a long time. It felt nice, and then I noticed I had a solitary tear rolling down my right cheek.

I let it fall, continued smiling to myself and looked out over the seven hills of Sheffield. Taking a deep breath I turned and called to Kelt who was sniffing and marking his territory in the bushes. He ran back to me and as we walked around the bend, he ran up ahead, always slowing just slightly to look back at me to make sure I was still coming, to give him the smile of approval. God I loved this dog. He had been with me through everything, a rescue from our time in Egypt, and now we had another Uprising to live through, another kind of civil war, one that no one saw coming; not even me.

But this time it wouldn't be a civil war of military tactics, water cannons and Mossad Style flyovers by the air force, this would be the kind of civil war that was a slow burn, the kind that civilians would wake up to slowly, one by one, drip feeding the messages they needed to hear, the majority who were not ready to hear it, and for many who did hear it, they would be able to grasp the complexities of what they were hearing.

Those who heard the call would be activated, inspired to act, but these would be few and far between, until the right stone was turned and the ripple effect from that one stone created a tsunami across the globe.

But the first battle had to be won first, and I needed my boys to see their mother win. I needed to win. Not just for them, but for me; and for every other single parent out there who was being unfairly treated by our legal system and those put in place to serve and protect us. Those who put on a uniform to fool us into thinking we were protected, they needed to be held accountable. They needed to have that chip knocked off their shoulder before the police forces around the world were even more rotten to the core.

Climbing into bed, Kelt at the foot of the bed already snoring, I offered my gratitude up to God. I had two beautiful children. I had a home, in a beautiful city, with a gorgeous dog who just knew when and how to be my rock. I asked God to cleanse my fur baby of all the negative energy he had absorbed, asked Him to help me and the boys through this challenge that lay before us, and I asked Him to give me the strength I needed to fight this fight. I fell asleep in the middle of my gratitude, feeling and hearing the sentences becoming staggered as my tired mind tried to piece together the sentences.

And I slept.

Slept like my life depended on it, because quite frankly it did.

I had slept so soundly into the afternoon, I hadn't even woken up to walk Kelt, who was now sitting next to me pawing me to wake up and take him to the toilet.

"Hello handsome," I said, stroking him behind the ear. "Are you ready for your walk are you?" Leaping off the bed, he went and stood by the back door. "Hang on a minute Baaba, Mama needs the bathroom."

Even to this day, I see these memories as if they happened just a few hours ago. So much of what happened back then is all a blur, but these moments, these defining moments in the haze of the trauma, they shine brightly like a beacon at sea reminding me of the journey taken.

Fighting the fight to clear my name of the charges brought against me, some would say illegally, and then fighting alongside my lawyer so the powers that be would not add me to a list of people who were a danger to children and vulnerable adults was a long three year battle.

It cost me dearly in many ways, but it also showed me what I was truly capable of.

So many women wear the badge of honor as a single mom, many as a 'poor me' label, and others wear it as a protective barrier to prevent themselves being hurt, or as a way of holding themselves back.

Being a single mother, or father, isn't a disability, nor is it something that should hold us back. It is a phase in life, a gift for us to receive so we can grow into the parent, and human being we were born to be. It is an opportunity to understand our strength, to get to know ourselves and to show our children that it doesn't matter whether we are in a relationship or not, we can thrive regardless.

For decades, centuries even, single parents have been looked down upon in society, mocked and eyed with suspicion. We have been blamed for the breakdown of society and yet we are, the parent who remains with the children providing them with everything they need, including not giving them everything they want.

Each child raised by a single parent learns to become resourceful, respectful and organized much more than many children of dual parenting families, if allowed by the parent in question.

Being a single parent isn't something that should be made shameful by our politicians, by married couples in society, and nor should it be worn as a badge of shame by the single parents. By allowing ourselves as single parents to become the victims or the scapegoats of society we are dishonoring ourselves, our children and the opportunities which come from stepping up and being the very best version of ourselves.

Focusing on serving others, focusing on the goal in hand, rather than feeling sorry for myself, allowed me to fight the system with confidence. With this confidence there was still fear, there was still a lot of 'What ifs'. But turning those 'What Ifs' into new avenues to explore for solutions helped me lead my children effectively, allowed them to see that it didn't matter what others thought about you, so long as you knew your truth, and you turned negatives into positives, greatness can happen; even in the darkest times in your life.

My boys got to see their mother study hard, build a business, write an international bestselling book, fight a corrupt policing, and education system, with a smile on her face. They got to see that when we set our sights on a goal, and we play full out on achieving that goal, we truly do get to become the very best version of the person we want to be.

My goal of being the very best mom I could be came true in the most surprising of ways. Our family may have been torn apart by divorce and then by events unseen and certainly unimaginable in our world, but we rebuilt ourselves and our family in a way that serves us all.

The events that happened in Scotland in 2015 may be unbelievable, they may have shaken me to my core and left me feeling as though my soul had been ripped by my body, but they happened, and no amount of feeling sorry for myself was going to help matters.

Following on from my wrongful arrest in July 2015, I was offered a fully funded PhD in Criminal Law and Social Justice, mainly in part due to the questions asked at many of the symposiums and lectures I attended. I didn't take the PhD, it wasn't going to allow me to fulfil the goals I wanted in life. It would have been an anchor, maybe even a prison of a different kind to the one I may have ended up in had Police Scotland, the lawyers and the Judges in Scotland had their way.

The lessons learnt along the way for both my boys and those surrounding us, and of course the lessons I learnt, have made us all wiser. My boys saw their mother fight for them, saw me give everything I had to bring us back together. They saw the depth of a mother's love for her children that many children will never get to witness. Is this a good thing or a bad thing? Well, it depends on how you look at it.

It's sad that many children never see their parents fight for something so profoundly powerful, that they never see the true potential of what it is to fight for yourself and those you love, but it is also a good thing that others haven't experienced something so life shattering that they have to fight.

Our children are more resilient than we give them credit for. We are more powerful than we give ourselves credit for, and when we feel like we can't go on anymore, there is always more within us.

I knew I loved my children, but the lengths I went to for my children, for my family, and for others showed me a side of myself that I couldn't help but fall in love with and admire. I am a much stronger woman than I gave myself credit for, and my desire to serve humanity and help others took on a whole new level of existence.

The depths of self-belief I have, the courage to fight back against the bullies and my determination to get my PhD in International Law and Social Justice was clarified and strengthened.

In some ways I would never wish what my boys and I went through on anyone, but when I feel the fire and determination within me, when I see the awareness and wisdom my children have learnt through this whole experience, and I receive messages from parents from around the world once they have read the full story in my third book Crossing The Line, who have been inspired and protected by what I shared, it makes the whole experience worth it.

My business may have been put on hold in many ways, I may have lost £100,000's in lost revenue, and had to take out an Independent Voluntary Agreement, one step away from bankruptcy just to clear the debt the court cases created with all the legal fees, travel and accommodation expenses, but the lessons learnt, have been invaluable.

The police never issued an apology, nor did my case get taken to an independent investigation, because sadly the lawyers in England cannot try a case which happened in Scotland, and vice versa. There is no such thing as UK law, and there was not one law firm in the UK willing to take on my case. So another fight began, the fight within myself to let it go, to focus on sharing my story and building myself up so the boys could see another way of succeeding against all odds.

The Scotland Saga brought with it pain and suffering, but it also brought with it an awakening like no other. The relationship between the boy's father and I is greatly improved and his support throughout the whole saga has brought the four of us closer together. As parents we may not be married, but the four of us are a family, and will always be a family, regardless of the dynamic of marital status.

We've all learnt what we are all truly capable of, and of course what the governments, legal and so-called justice systems are really truly made of. The boys have learnt to take negative situations and turn them into positives, to dig deeper, to get creative with the 'What Ifs' to find solutions for every outcome and to keep the end goal in mind.

We've all heard that phrase "everything happens for a reason" and whilst I agree with this, I would also add that the reason everything happens is because there is always something for us and society to learn, to gain awareness of.

We may not like the things which happen, and we may not understand them at the time, or like the feelings which rise up from within us, but when we step outside of ourselves to focus on how we can use the situation to serve others, that is when we truly embrace our power and our wake up moments.

So here's to embracing our breakdowns, because with every breakdown, there is always a beautiful breakthrough waiting on the other side ready to wake us up, individually and collectively.

With love and gratitude to you, and for you, wherever you are, and may you gain courage from this chapter and the other chapters here in this book to help you move forward towards the person you wish to become, for yourself, for your family and for humanity.

Reflections

Reflections

Reflections

STEPHAN NEFF
NEW ZEALAND

Anesthetist, Alcoholic in Recovery and Author of *My Steps to Sobriety*
https://stephanneff.podbean.com

Stephan Neff is an anesthetist, author and alcoholic in recovery.

After studying medicine in Heidelberg, Germany he travelled and worked in Europe and Australia before settling down with his family in beautiful New Zealand. As a retired pain physician, he developed a specific insight into human psychology. As a man trying to drown his sorrows, he found out the hard way that the critters can swim. But over the last seven years he made every day a little bit better than yesterday.

Today Stephan is an expert in living a life so fantastic, that alcohol has simply no role to play. He shares this passion through his podcast, YouTube channel, and other social media (all titled My Steps to Sobriety). In his book *My Steps to Sobriety* he shares the lessons he has learned as a doctor and as a man. And the truth is simple – the past does not equal the future. Every alcoholic can turn his life around, one little decision at a time. This book shows how to do it.

Chapter Three
A PHOENIX FIRST MUST BURN

> God, grant me the serenity,
> To accept the things I cannot change;
> Courage to change things I can
> And wisdom to know the difference.

The words penetrated me like a laser beam. How could they possibly know how I feel? I had only just arrived here, yet, the words spelled out the existential question hidden deep in my tormented soul. The first time I ever read them was my first day in rehab.

I was literally the proverbial deer caught in the headlights. As an anesthetist I was a specialist in my field. Type A personality, perfectionist, idealist, empathic, a heart the size of my home town – the works. But deep inside I was a broken man. The evil twins of shame and guilt were constant companions. And they had a knack of replaying 'The Best of Stephan' at 3.30 am: everything I could have possibly done wrong over the last 40 years. But guilt and shame paled into insignificance when it came to resentment and anger. Oh boy, now we are talking. After all, I had gone through some hard times. I had stood up to the powers in charge to defend the patients in my care. I was the fighter, the knight in shining armor who was rescuing the damsels in distress. Well, I guess at the end I was more like Don Quixote fighting windmills. But I guess that is a side effect of a liter of vodka a day (and then some). Nevertheless, I would have loved to whistle-blow and tell the truth to the world as I saw it. But guess what, as a doctor you are forbidden to speak negative about the institutions you work for. The little bit of fine-print in the contract that you never read before signing. Another source of bitter resentment in my life.

"Hi, I am Thomas, I am an addict."

"Hi, I am Beatrice, I am an alcoholic."

Suddenly – silence. Looking up, it was my turn to introduce myself to 20 complete strangers. Where was the hole to hide in?

"Hi, I am Stephan. I am an alcoholic." Boom. There it was. I only said the words in order to fit in. After all, surely I wasn't an alcoholic! I am a doctor. And yes, there have been huge psychosocial stressors and more pain and trauma than I cared to remember. Surely, it was absolutely normal to have a drink or ten to numb the pain.

But that moment something changed in me. It was as if the dam started to break. Speaking out those words changed me forever. Hearing those words come out of my own mouth caused a flood of emotions that made the world's scariest roller coaster look like a baby swing. Shame, guilt, elation, freedom, embarrassment, joy, surprise – hell, how many emotions can you possibly feel in 10 seconds.

I don't remember too much of the following hour. I was too engrossed in the emotions that were washing over me. Emotions… those pesky little things I had tried to drown for the last 20 years. Guess what – the critters can swim. And here I was, suffering the onslaught without a crutch to lean on. No music to play, no film to watch, no bottle of wine to alter my state. Simply me and my emotions. Damn, I did not sign up for that!

Oh, yeah, okay, I did not sign up at all. It was my wife who had signed me up for the holiday of a life-time. Four weeks, full board and entertainment, for the cheap price of $27,000 dollars. For three years she had begged me to stop drinking. Talk about the kettle calling the pot black. Before that she was hitting the bottle as badly as I was. Surely she must understand how hurt I was.

Leave me alone! my inner monologue screamed. *Look what they have done to me! Now I will show them! I will drink three bottles of wine, that will teach them a lesson!*

But one day the co-dependency had run out. Lisa had found Jesus Christ and with the help of her church and some counseling had stopped drinking. Me, well I kept going like the 'man' I was. Or shall I say 'emotionally retarded numb-nut'? But that was all to change now.

And change it did. For the next week I was not just talking – I was singing like a canary. Not only was it okay and safe to speak out – no, people actually seemed to be interested. My case worker asked me to write a letter to a certain institution that I had focused my anger and resentment on. She asked me to be detailed, to the point, not to leave anything out, to tell it warts and all. And I did go to town. Well, I went to my room since in the first two weeks of rehab you are cut off from the outside – no leave and no phone calls or messages. And I wrote late into the night until my fingers cramped. The next day, I arrived at my one-on-one counseling session poised like a snake. I was ready to share it all with my caseworker. I was willing to go into immense detail to make her understand why I simply had to drink. The counselor briefly looked over the many pages, then folded them neatly in half and placed them to the side.

I was dumbstruck by her next words, "Let's put that to the side for a moment and talk about you!"

"But, but, but…" since when did I stutter?

"Let's talk more about you. And by the way, I have a good book for you to read…"

Again, these bloody emotions. I was angry with her. Why did she make me write all the shit down and then not even give a damn?

I left the interview bewildered and resentful. "Stupid cow! How dare she treat me like that?"

Against my better judgment I started reading the book she suggested. The story of a woman whose estranged and deranged husband one day killed their children and the woman's father in front of her eyes in their driveway. The story unfolded within the first few pages of the book and I felt sick to the stomach just reading that. How the hell could this woman continue to live? But that was exactly what this book was about. *Rise* told the woman's transformation through loss and grief, anger and depression to ultimately find peace. I stopped reading. The sun had set outside. I had been lucky, the rehab hospital was not completely full and I had no one else in the double cabin living with me. The silence surrounding me allowed me to think. My brain automatically compared her plight with mine. I knew this was no pissing contest. But she had won hands down. Who was I to talk about suffering, compared with her. But, if I accepted that as a fact, what could possibly justify my drinking? I closed the book and tried to watch some television. But just as much as you cannot un-hear words I could not undo the change that affected my thinking.

By now I was in the second week of rehab and my head started to clear. Turns out, when you drink like a fish for years and suddenly stop drinking, your brain does not like it. Whilst I never showed the full symptom complex of a withdrawal I had a mild tremor and my blood pressure was through the roof. But things started to settle quickly and a new me started to rise from the ashes of the old me. I can say that now – seven years down the line. At the time it was far from obvious. I did not burst into flames like a mythological phoenix. I did not have a magic revelation where the sun shines through a crack in the clouds and wise words are whispered from angel's tongues. No majestic software upgrade that gets it all over and done within a few hours.

No, the revelations came in drips and drops and the angels wore clever disguises. Some had tattoos on their body and initially didn't smell so good when they started rehab. Turns out that we addicts come in all shapes and sizes. Alcohol is the great equalizer. It doesn't care if you are a boy, a girl or in between. Rich or poor, chocolate or vanilla, important or a nobody. And more importantly, alcohol is a great solvent. No – it does not solve problems. But it dissolves relationships, marriages, jobs and bank accounts. Which makes for pretty good stories around the campfire. Or in our case, the smokers corner where we all debriefed and licked our sores like the wounded animals that we were. It was here that honest words were spoken which even our closest friends would never hear. It was here that a bond was formed and a band of brothers and sisters emerged. It was through the haze of the cigarette smoke and the steam of coffee that you looked into the eyes of fellow travelers that were all on the same path. We had used drugs and alcohol like band aids to cover wounds that were festering. And now was the time to rip off those band aids and lance that pus. Oh yes. It bloody well hurt.

But come on, was it really so bad? After all, I was holding down a job, was married with two children and never had a run in with the law. True. I was a high-functioning alcoholic. But how long would that streak of luck have lasted? I didn't get into trouble every time I drank, but every time I got in trouble I was drinking. You know, the best email you have ever regretted? Yet another time when you broke a promise to your children? Yet another time when you made your wife cry with your words or your actions?

I had come to the point where even my marinated brain recognized that I had to change. That I could not continue as before. That the old me had to die and that I had to reinvent myself. But how? And who should I become?

Turns out, I was in luck. The rehab hospital was exactly the right place to show me what to do. Funny that is! I knew what had not worked. Now, rehab pulled my head out of my ass and I no longer lived in a world of shit. Amazing what happens when you start following the advice of others who have been successful in managing their own addictions.

My rehab was based upon the 12 steps of Alcoholics Anonymous. In a nutshell:

The first three steps show you how to give up.

Four, five and six teach you how to own up.

Seven, eight and nine reveal how you make up.

Ten, eleven and twelve make you grow up.

It sounds easy, doesn't it? Reality is, each and every step is as painful as peeing glass shards. Rehab at times feels like that. The crowd of counselors, fellow travelers, psychologists, psychiatrists and addiction specialists looking after me would have given the Spanish Inquisition a run for the money. Was it worth it? At the time I had no clue.

Anyhow, *What actually happens in reality in rehab?* I hear you think.

Well, the only thing that changes in recovery is everything. Yes, you read that right. Everything changes, and in a weird way the change is both immediate and yet incredibly slow. The first thing you learn is that keeping a strict daily routine is a life-saver for any addict. In my rehab the daily routine started with a 7 am wakeup. By 7.30 you made your own breakfast and at 8 am you received the first motivational kick up the ass.

Then came a mixture of lectures and activities that were all designed to show you right here and now that you can actually live a different life. The days were busy but good busy. There was flexibility in the system – as long as you made progress you could to a degree choose how you wanted to spend the flexible times. But the things that were impossible to change were the regular communal meal times and the mandatory sober fun.

For most alcoholics this is an oxymoron. 'Sober fun' – impossible! Teetotalers are boring! Where's the fun in that? After all, our brain recognizes that we are drinking far too much which causes guilt. What better to do than surround yourself with other people that drink at least as much as you do (or better, even more!). This way you can live under the illusion that nothing is wrong with your lifestyle. And your whole language changes to accommodate your addiction. But of course, you rephrase the problem.

"It's wine-o'clock somewhere!"

"To me drinking responsibly means not to spill it!"

"I used to think that drinking was bad for me. So I gave up thinking!"

Sounds familiar? Welcome to another characteristic of a high-functioning alcoholic. And like so many comedians over the ages – on the outside we wear the funny and joking mask, whilst on the insight the light has gone out and we are committing suicide in installments.

But it is here where a good rehab system starts to shine. How do you convince someone to change when they see no hope? How do you implement change in someone who has thought many times about simply ending it all because they felt so helpless? There is only one way – you have to walk the walk and stop talking. Live the life you want the addict to live! Show them those qualities that have been missing for so long in their lives – honesty, transparency, authenticity and integrity. That is where the magic happens. It is said that 95% of communication is nonverbal. Oh, how true these words are when it comes to rehab and later recovery.

So far so good, said the man falling out of a skyscraper with every level he was passing.

"I get it!" you say. Simply implement good habits and everything will be fine. Hmmm… about that…

The new habits I learned and practiced were fun. But I had barely started to scratch at the surface when it came to what matters most. Do you really believe that simply taking away the only thing that gave the alcoholic some sort of relieve, whilst not addressing the real reasons he was drinking, would be anything but senseless torture? Attend any mandatory court-ordered AA meeting and you will see the white-knucklers. Those alcoholics that have not addressed the problems in their lives and who live in the constant purgatory of wanting, needing and yearning for that one drink that is too much and the thousand that are not enough.

Don't get me wrong. You need to stop drinking/using before you can get better. But only stopping will not get you anywhere. That's the reason that 80% of alcoholics relapse in their first year of sobriety. Alcohol is a mighty foe who should not be underestimated – ever!

In order to live a life full of joy I needed to address the pain in my life. And for that I needed help. In my opinion it is simply impossible to somehow undergo therapy alone. Even the best book or the best course cannot replace a skilled person listening to me and reflecting on what I was saying (or not saying for that matter). And of course, I had to develop trust in such people. In my rehab, that was not difficult. To start off with, I had to realize that every person treating me (bar a few of the doctors) was actually an addict. The yoga instructor who in the past turned up drunk to her clients was now leading a class for the inmates. The counselor who runs the dreaded 10 am 'emotions' meeting had been sitting in my chair a few years back. The smirk on my case-manager's face said it all. *You can't bullshit a bullshitter!* She had been in my shoes in the past. Her brain had fought tooth and nail to hold onto the old destructive coping mechanisms just as much as mine did right now.

But there was one big difference between 'us' and 'them'. Our guardian angels were well-groomed, relaxed in their confidence and displayed an aura that was palpable. They clearly had their ducks in a row. Me, I at best, had squirrels that were hosting a rave.

By the end of week two I started to develop more insight. The first time in my life I worked through my emotions in the same way that I would approach a difficult case at work. I would look at the facts, rather than assumptions. What could I ascertain as the truth, not just a version that I had liked to believe.

Fact is, we have got supercomputers between our ears but no one has given us the user manuals. End result? Like so many others I had been dabbling a bit here and there, pressed a few buttons and suddenly found a behavior that in my mind was positive and made sense. Like the beautiful dopamine rush I got when I wolfed down half a cheesecake after a shitty day at work. My brain knew that this is not good for me in the long run. So it quickly came up with a smoke screen to distort reality and perception. My brain is clever like that. It will lay down memories and it takes artistic license to change the 'truth' just that little bit to make it less painful for me to remember.

The good thing is that the people looking after me knew this. Having lived through their own transformations they can see clearly the obstacles that I put in my own way. And they have found ways to get rid of them.

For me, resentment and anger were the two biggest challenges, followed in no strict order by hopelessness, helplessness, frustrations, fear of existence, financial struggles, anxiety, low moods, the fact that my kids were not behaving, shame, guilt… you get the picture. Where to start? Where to start?

Shrek said it best in his first film in 2001:

Shrek: Ogres are like onions.

Donkey: They stink?

Shrek: Yes. No.

Donkey: Oh, they make you cry.

Shrek: No.

Donkey: Oh, you leave 'em out in the sun, they get all brown, start sproutin' little white hairs.

Shrek: No. Layers. Onions have layers. Ogres have layers. Onions have layers. You get it? We both have layers.

Donkey: Oh, you both have layers. Oh. You know, not everybody likes onions.

Shrek was onto something there. Rehab is like that. It strips back one layer at a time to reveal all the trauma and negative emotions one tried to hide so cleverly behind the myriad of masks one was wearing. And as alcoholics we will do everything to numb the pain. The absolute last thing I wanted to do is to address the issues that are really at the core of the problem. For years I buried my head in the sand. My main focus in life was to numb those feelings with alcohol or in fact anything that was available to me.

And now, after decades of hiding, someone wants to shine an ultra-bright spotlight into my soul. After years of denial I was suddenly supposed to open up and talk about my emotions. Yeah, right. Fat chance for that!

That's where Shrek and his onions came in. I couldn't address all the things that were wrong at the same time. I had to focus on one, and make a start. Once I started peeling back one layer and dealing with the bad things I uncovered, life was never the same again. Once I started changing, I started an avalanche that I couldn't stop. I was sliding down the mountain and I assure you, it was a bumpy ride. The moment I dealt with one trauma, I found two other things that had held me back. I had barely opened one wound when I realized how much that pus has influenced other parts of my life. This journey was painful and difficult, and because of that, I realized there is no person walking this Earth who shows more courage, honesty, dignity and integrity than an addict in recovery.

Change doesn't happen overnight. It doesn't happen in one session. There is not one magic meeting. For me, the pus had drenched my whole body and soul. Sometimes the stink was obvious, sometimes it was cleverly hidden by mental constructs I had created to deal with emotional trauma.

For example, in my youth I was the victim of gang violence. The attack was unprovoked and the guys just wanted to have some fun. I carry the mental scars to this day. But in the immediate aftermath I reframed the experience and made it the reason to train hard in martial arts. The fact that I put the gang leader for three years behind bars and he swore he would kill me on release might also have had something to do with that. Training four hours a day, I became quite a fighting machine who was constantly aware of his surroundings and who would not be caught out ever again.

Later on, the same trait also made me quite a good doctor. I excelled in emergency settings and became a passionate teacher for junior doctors who wanted to learn a structured approach to chaos. So, all peaches and cream, isn't it? It would take me quarter of a century to finally accept that these 'positive traits' were actually signs and symptoms of post-traumatic stress disorder. 'Losing control' would be the constant theme of those pesky dreams that make you wake up at 4 am on the dot, sweating and hyperventilating.

But rest assured, there was so much more. There was so much pus hidden in my body. And it needed to be drained, one pustule after the other. That was a hard pill to swallow for me at the time. But by now I had learned to trust the people I had paid to make me better.

Rehab is like starting a big jigsaw puzzle where you never know how many pieces there are. And guess what, there is no picture to guide you. And so you keep working on the puzzle, one piece at a time. You address one problem at a time until you are content that you have either sorted the problem or that you truly cannot do anything about it. One way or the other, you are ready to move on to the next puzzle piece.

And the journey never stops.

George Carlin said it best: "Only because you got the monkey off your back does not mean that circus has left town."

Alcohol was the poison of my choice. But until I addressed the reasons for my drinking I would never succeed in changing. Every new self-discovery revealed new aspects of my previous life. I began to appreciate the impact of childhood trauma and the scars that bullying and adolescent anxiety had left behind. I suddenly appreciated the post-traumatic stress disorder as the demon chameleon that it is. And it took me some time to put one and one together and accept that at times I had suffered from depression. All of those things are potent drivers to drink.

And if an addict simply white-knuckles it and decides to stop drinking without addressing the underlying reasons? There are myriad other addictions that will creep up on him. The cheesecake at 11 pm, the frequent visits to the fast food joints, the fact that you need to buy larger clothes – yes, Sir, welcome to the wonderful world of eating disorders.

Eating is not your thing? How about gambling? Or working every waking hour of the day? Or working out four times a day in the gym? Or smoking? Cross-addiction is a very real thing for all of us alcoholics and addicts. Because we simply jump onto a new horse that is running in the same race.

Addiction does not last forever. You either get clean or you die. And that's a choice. We alcoholics don't know that whilst we party with our demons. But there is no shadow of a doubt that we can and should be able to get clean! Addiction is simply a disease that alters the functioning of the brain. And like any other disease there are ways to treat and manage addiction. Yes there are challenges. There is not one approach to treatment that will work for everybody. And many addicts are not yet ready to change. Therefore treatment interventions need to be available when the individual needs them. As a society we increasingly recognize the impact of alcohol and demystify addiction in our daily lives. Mental health campaigns have started to change the way we think about depression, PTSD and anxiety. And finally a new generation of youngsters are growing up who are to be taught that it is okay not to be okay. All that should make it easier for you or your loved ones to access treatment. But at the same token our lives are irreversibly changed by COVID19, climate change and a myriad other challenges. Life doesn't get easier, that's for sure.

When I left rehab at the end of the 28 days I was a different man. The old me had died and was buried under a ton of new habits. Or so it seemed to me then. Needless to say, there were no fanfares and parades when I came home. Whilst I had made huge progress in a few short weeks my family had kept their noses to the grindstone. When I wanted to talk about my achievements no one really showed any interest. It took me a while to accept that they had heard it all before. The lies, the promises, the thoughts of a new life. That was the first inkling that I was far from the finish-line. That this was not a sprint but an ultra-marathon. And I had only just left the starting blocks. I remember the fear that overcame me at that moment. The wave of anxiety and doubt. Would I be able to keep my promises this time? Was the old me really dead? Or was I kidding myself? Did I just spend a huge chunk of money for nothing?

Well, my life is not a Hollywood romance, it always was and is a horror film with an admittedly awesome cast. I was neither 100% successful nor was the journey easy. Like a zombie, the old me tries to come back from the grave now and then.

"What a beautiful sunset – would it not be nice to enjoy that with a glass of Chardonnay?"

"Come on, you did just publish a book! Let's celebrate with Champagne!"

"You had a bad day – I know the answer: A black Sambuca, flambéed with some coffee beans. That will cheer you up!"

Yeah right! That's the addiction speaking. Clever and convincing as it always was.

But today I know that if you don't work on your sobriety you work on your relapse. These words are not just motivational quotes. They are brutal in both simplicity and truth.

Heading this advice I have learned to look after myself. I have found the triggers that make me want to self-destruct. HALT is all I need to go off the rails. When I am hungry, angry, lonely and tired – oh boy! Give me three out of four! Even today I get thoughts about alcohol and sugar. Give me four of the triggers at the same time and I can guarantee you that my addiction wants to come out to play. But instead of getting hit by one self-inflicted broadside after the other I have learned to look after myself. Why? Because I have learned to love the new me. The new dude is cool, warts and all. I carry my scars with pride. I no longer get upset by those things I hated in the past. When I have a desire to drink I greet this thought like an old acquaintance.

"Hello, old friend! It has been some time since I last saw you. What is it that you want to tell me?"

I no longer feel guilty and shame-ridden when my brain suggests a drink. I rather see it as a message that I have slipped in looking after myself. In the same way I have learned to surf waves of anxiety and deal with deep dark mood holes. As a master of procrastination I have learned ways to turn chores into things I do want to do. "A stitch in time saves nine" is an age-old adage I learned to follow whenever I can. I will push through fatigue and assure that I get at least one or two of those things done which I really don't want to do. Daily, no exception. At the same token I have no hesitation to roll up in a fetal position when my brain demands it. From now and then I throw a pity-party but I no longer pitch a tent over there.

When people remind me of my past I remind them that I don't live there anymore. On the contrary – what was once my mess is now my message. The old phoenix had to burn for the new phoenix to rise from the ashes. And instead of being ashamed about it, I nowadays host a YouTube show and podcast to raise awareness and discuss addiction and mental health problems. I am still an addict. But nowadays I am addicted to having my shit together, and I truly love the new me!

Reflections

Reflections

TOMÁS GARZA
USA

Author, Podcast Host and Producer, Creative Facilitator,
Meditation Instructor
https://tomasgarza.com

Tomás Garza is a longtime practitioner of meditation, Author, and Host of the podcast *Decide to Transform*.

He is a Councilor and Founding Faculty Member of the International Academy of Universal Self Mastery (IAUSM,) and together with business partner and co-author Lisa Berry leads the IAUSM Media Department. As an Interviewer, Show Host, and Podcast Producer, Tomás enjoys giving people a platform for expanding and expressing their message. An avid hiker and lover of hot climates, he and his wife Cindy live in Phoenix, Arizona.

Chapter Four
RECONDITIONING

All I can remember was the pain. That covered everything else: the lights, the orange walls, the ugly white gown, and the tubes – lots of tubes. I didn't know where all the tubes came from or were headed, but I assumed they were attached to a needle stuck someplace inside me.

"You're in the hospital," they kept telling me. "You were in a horrible car accident. Do you remember?"

"No."

"Yes, you were in a car accident and your hip bones are shattered. We're getting you stabilized for a couple of days until you're ready to be transported for surgery."

I understood that much. The next few weeks saw me live through a six-hour surgery, three days of I.V. morphine for the pain, the hideous detox and night sweats, then learning to walk again. As in all over again. Starting from zero.

How did I get here? Well, I got in a car accident, but it goes much deeper than that. This all happened because I needed to break up with myself, but I kept refusing, and getting T-boned at 60 miles per hour was the wake-up call. Sometimes waking up begins in dark places. I'll explain.

You could say that the car accident had its roots in my childhood, decades before it ever happened. Even at a young age, I learned to stop showing up for myself. Even at a young age, I learned to live somebody else's life.

People learn all kinds of things from their families, helpful and unhelpful. Because as human beings we are always teaching, we are always learning, too. We always put out energy, a vibration, and others learn from our vibration, from how we show up and relate to the world. We could say absolutely nothing and people would still learn from our vibration. A person does not have to be a child to learn actively and immediately; we all do it, all the time.

Let me list what I learned growing up, the lessons of a well-educated, semi-aristocratic family that seemed on the surface to have it made. As a child who enjoyed school and generally excelled, the 'family pressure' fell more heavily on me than it did on others. These lessons got even further reinforcement.

First, *life is not about happiness*. Rather, it is about status, looking good, having the right career, the right education, having the appearance of being an "upstanding person." Happiness is overrated, for fools. Only certain professional occupations (doctor, lawyer, politician) matter, and the rest are beneath you.

Second, *life is a sacrifice*. You have to give things up to live correctly, like your happiness, like yourself. Buck up and do it.

Third, *the first two lessons are your duty*. This is an obligation, and just the way life is.

Got it? Good!

People learn about life in many different ways, and unfortunately many of us grow into adulthood believing we neither deserve nor can ever attain happiness. We learn through repetition that while such a state may exist, it is not for us, so why bother trying?

Well, despite this conditioning, I resisted. I wanted to live my life differently. Unfortunately, this resistance was almost always met with strict forces of control, with reinforcement of the perceived unhappy order. When you are always punished and shut down for insisting on yourself, at some point it is tempting to go inward and keep quiet on the surface, to play along. This served as my strategy, effective at avoiding conflict in the short term but in the long run highly detrimental. I say it wound up detrimental because I reached young adulthood with all of my family's conditioning intact, with an angry, dour attitude that in no way matches the person I am today. It is easy to see now that I needed to break up with the person that I was, but I did not see it then. Because it was all I knew, I just kept going.

That is what most of us do, isn't it? We just keep going. We put our heads down, our blinders on, and spend every ounce of our energy rationalizing, telling ourselves that the situation isn't all that bad, that it's just the way it is, that it will get better one day. Well, what if 'one day' never arrives? What then?

We find ourselves in darkness, toxicity, and dread. We find ourselves in bad relationships if we don't believe we have a right to feel happy. I found my darkness and toxicity in my career choice. I found the dread, too, and plenty of hostility, but very little happiness.

My path to darkness literally followed the weather, from the desert Southwest of New Mexico, where I was raised, to rainy, dark, and cloudy Portland, Oregon. Following my obedience to family duty, I found myself matriculated in law school. I was not happy; in fact I was numb. The first week of school showed me all I needed to see of the prevailing attitude, one of competition, preoccupation with status and 'reputation', and the predominance of a system that uses the word 'versus' far too often for my comfort and satisfaction. Legal case names all bear the mark of an adversarial system: *Garza v. Garza, Human v. Human, Self v. Self*. Opponents everywhere, and very little in the way of cooperation, all in a dark climate under the tyranny of a slow, steady drizzle that falls from October to May.

One might rightly ask why I didn't cut my losses and withdraw during the first week of school. I could have, but I kept going. I slogged my way through the gloom and the mud every day to class, read hundreds of pages of appellate court opinions every night as homework, and spent the dark days not dreaming of tropical beaches but rather in a state of ignorance and dullness, numb and aware of my suffering, but not energized enough to do anything constructive about it.

These were three long years.

At the end of these three years, I arrived at a crossroads, a decision point that I knew was coming, but which I dreaded. Dread being up to that point a lifelong theme. Upon completing law school and receiving a degree, every graduate must decide whether to sit for a particular state's bar examination. Only a successful passage of this exam renders one an attorney and allows the person to practice law. For most, this decision is automatic. They have come this far, and sitting for the bar exam is simply the next step.

For me, too, this decision was automatic, but not in the way you might expect. Toward the end of my second year, to my surprise – and also pleasure – something snapped. The train of my upbringing flew off the rails. I decided that under no circumstance, in this lifetime or any other, could I ever put myself through the hell of sitting for the bar examination, much less the practice of law. While some of my friends understood, I knew none of my family members would. So, why did this bother me? Because I had allowed them to mold and shape my mind and my self-concept.

As I had feared, this decision not to become a lawyer was met with incredulity and hostility by some. Years later, as I worked in a completely unrelated industry and having utterly moved on in my life, some family members still had the gall to ask me if I would ever reconsider and sit for the bar. At one point, I can remember saying, "If you want a lawyer in the family so badly, why don't you go to law school yourself?"

That was the last time this person ever asked that question.

You would think that this big decision represented some sort of turning point. It figured largely, no question, but what the next few years showed was that it takes time to get rid of negative conditioning. As human beings, we gravitate to what feels and even smells familiar, so making one step in an overall process – no matter how huge – does not represent the end. As much as I would love to say I served as an exception, I did not.

Having never decided fully in favor of happiness, the old mentality of life-has-got-to-suck-and-suck-you-dry continued to prevail. I had allowed myself to avoid the practice of law, but I found myself guilt-ridden and unable to avoid a related profession, namely mediation. People's voices of, "Well, you'll have to put that degree to some use, won't you?" and, "Well, I suppose you have to do something to justify all that time and money spent," saw me stop short of leaving the legal profession completely. I settled on what in criminal law people call a 'lesser-included offense'. This for me meant Alternative Dispute Resolution. While not a bloody lawsuit, it still involves conflict, often heated conflict. While I found myself naturally able to hold space for parties in dispute in my role as mediator, I still found myself mentally and emotionally brutalized, sucked into a vortex of creeping dread. This vortex moved more slowly, but it was every bit as thorough and every bit as effective at bringing me down. If life isn't about happiness, after all, let's throw a little conflict on there! How about some drama?

No, you haven't had enough – that isn't possible!

We can really clobber ourselves as humans sometimes, can't we?

The field of Alternative Dispute Resolution aims to give decision-making power back to the parties. In court, a judge decides the outcome. In mediation or a negotiated settlement, people can control the outcome themselves. This can lead to happier results. One can see this as a positive.

Mediation also involves heated disputes, drama, and fighting. The same person who was drawn to law school and the attendant drama gravitated without thinking too much to this conflict arena. The toxicity crept up slowly, but creeped up it did.

As a mediator, I specialized in the arena of family disputes, which most often meant divorces, separations, and child custody battles. People commonly refer to a custody dispute as a 'battle' and this is quite correct. A battle it is.

The combatants – my former clients – came from all walks of life: doctors, homeless drug addicts, winemakers, drug dealers, and every type of person in between. Every person alive is capable of dissolving a marriage or a partnership, and each one is in pain – sometimes extreme pain – at the time.

The pain of a breakup or divorce can hit extraordinary highs. It causes ordinarily nice people to become mean and twisted, to say things or do things they would never say or do under different circumstances. Divorce brings out the worst in people, all too often, and the behavior I saw and subjected myself to on a daily basis confirmed this.

Now let us all be clear: I was subjecting myself to this. I put myself in a room with high-stakes combatants and their toxic relationships. I kept scheduling the cases. I kept getting paid, and while I could have made money doing almost anything else, I had not done the work on myself to break up with my habit of unhappiness. I still found myself drawn to conflict, bitterness, and ritualized drama. That was life, right?

Deep-down I yearned to get out of this, but I couldn't yet. For years, I put my head down, went back to the office, and sat with grieving people who projected their own fear onto each other – and sometimes me – and dealt the verbal brutality.

For reasons of confidentiality, I cannot mention names or certain circumstances, but if you're wondering if this would make good theater, it most certainly would. Just when I figured nothing could shock me, something always did.

As the years wore on – having spent 13 of them as a mediator – I found I needed more frequent and longer vacations. I began to actively seek a different path, because this one was not fulfilling. I felt resolved on this from time to time, but whenever it came to writing out and sending resignation letters, I never could complete the last step. I never sent them, even though I wanted to. My conditioning still had a hold on me, so I would rationalize that I couldn't walk away just then, that I needed the money too much. Besides, I still had the status I expected of myself as a reputable professional. In short, I was still working for my grandparents and my parents and their ideas about life, even into my early forties. I couldn't leave. I just couldn't.

You might ask why I never seemed to have the courage to leave this negative career behind and dump the toxicity completely. Seriously, why couldn't a grown man just say, "Fuck it, I'm moving on from this." – why is this so hard?

Let me answer this question with a question: is it easy for anyone to move beyond their past conditioning?

No, it is not. Because as human beings we are always learning, we constantly absorb messages from all around us: from family members, friends, television and internet ads, also from the spinnings and gyrations of our own minds. Other people talk to us, billboards talk to us, and we talk constantly to ourselves. Bombarded with this stream of information, we formulate opinions about who we are, what is possible for us, even what we can and cannot do. These opinions become entrenched with this never-ending reinforcement, forming our self-concept, a completely conditioned existence that we live with and accept as our 'reality', our lot in the world, just the way things are.

With this much conditioning working against us, is it any wonder it is such an effort to change it?

And yet we all retain free will. We each hold at all times the power of decision. We may not be aware of it, or we may choose not to exercise it, but each and every one of us can decide to transform our lives. We can decide to flip the script of our conditioning and become the person we really are, who we were meant to be. This power of decision can lie dormant for years before we exercise it. Once we do, our lives can change rapidly. We can go to bed at night as one person and wake up the next morning as someone else.

In my case, I hadn't yet decided to live my life happily. Opting not to take the bar exam represented a start, to be sure, but it was far from a final, unequivocal decision. Mediation was the lesser of two evils, and not happiness. Toxicity still governed my work life. Without a real decision, the concerted effort needed to change can never gather momentum. In business, we see this as various starts and stops. In relationships, we see it as a string of short-term couplings where one is unwilling or unable to commit. Without deciding to really, truly live in joy and happiness, one starts on the road to fulfillment but turns back, again and again, for ostensibly different reasons each time but for the real reason that he or she has not decided to.

Not having made the decision, then, I dreamed of life after custody mediation. I envisioned scenarios, and I wrote resignation letters, but I never sent them.

December 3, 2013 started out as just another Tuesday. I dragged myself out of bed, ate breakfast, showered and prepared for work, a slate of mediation appointments and an appearance at a neighboring county's courthouse to teach a Parent Education class for divorcing parents – I was never the most popular person in the room. The last thing I remember was buying gas for my car, then pulling out of the gas station and heading off to another day of professional nonfulfillment.

They, whoever 'they' were, told me I was lucky to be alive. Not everyone who gets t-boned at 60 miles per hour lives to tell about it. I did not remember the accident; I still have no recollection of the time from when I left the gas station to waking up in the hospital stuck with tubes and writhing in pain, with a blasted left acetabulum, the bone that wraps around the hip joint. Consciousness came and went, the result of heavy narcotic pain medication. When I was aware of lying in a hospital bed, I found myself knowing – not thinking, but knowing – that mediation was over, that I would never go back. I also knew that as bleak and as dark as everything seemed, that I hadn't hit the absolute depths yet, that more was to come. I did not want to think about this, but it all hit me quite clearly in those rare lucid moments when I awoke from a trance of pain, extreme fatigue, and the rush of morphine or whatever other pain medication kept pouring into my body from a needle stuck someplace where I lacked the strength to find it and rip it out.

I could not quit mediation on my own, so the Universe quit it for me. The price? Well, several thousand dollars of medical expenses not covered by insurance, months spent learning to walk again, and the excruciating hell of physical therapy. The surgery to repair my acetabulum was successful, and miraculously the hip joint sustained no damage, so these days I have a full range of motion and actually find myself stronger and more flexible than I was before the car wreck. I never worked another day in mediation; since I was incapacitated and unable to serve my clients, all of them were transferred to other mediators. Left with a clean slate, I ended all my commitments immediately.

It is weird, I think, that sometimes we are so reluctant to let go of unhealthy conditioning that the Universe has to smack us – in my case, literally – to get us to shift gears. If conflict, drudgery, and toxicity are all a person knows, experiencing life on the other side can be shocking and disorienting, even if the person had yearned to have this experience for a long, long time. And so it was with me. I stood closer to a breakup with my old self, but had yet to take the plunge.

Things still had to get worse before the breakup could finally occur. Like many breakups, this one was gradual. You would think the shock of the car accident would have ended everything, but more growth lay ahead.

The end of mediation brought the end of ritualized conflict to my work life, but not the ritualized conflict within. I had gotten rid of one, now the other faced me down with no intermediaries between. As I recovered my physical health and mobility in a slow and frustrating process, the question, *What the hell are you going to do next?* resounded.

On the surface, there is nothing wrong with this question: it arises naturally during any transitional period. Where I allowed it to brutalize me was in my conditioned attachment to doing something 'big' or 'worthy of status in the eyes of the community', and doing the sensible thing and giving myself grace and time to heal and chart my course for the next steps did not enter into the picture. The same inner voice that rejected happiness before in my career choice rejected health, wellness, and sanity now. I heaped pressure on myself to figure it all out.

This proved too much. Short of the spiritual practice that had always sustained me, and walks in the fresh air, I did not know what to do with the oppressive voices that came down on me. I felt lost; I sank. For several months, I spiraled.

A few more things about the old me – and you may have already guessed – because I put my head down and sucked it up all the time, even when something like law school or my career choice was killing me, it makes sense that I prided myself on self-sufficiency and rugged individualism. I didn't need anybody. I could do everything alone, and I didn't need help.

I had dumped the ritualized combat, but I hadn't yet dumped this.

The day I accepted my depression, and that I had been depressed for a long, long time, was a dark one. My wife and I took a walk on the outskirts of town, and I remember feeling miserable. That was not, unfortunately, a new feeling for me, but what really stood out was what I saw, literally. I looked around me and instead of seeing green fields and trees, I saw blackness. Blackness had literally clouded my vision. At this point I made the decision to seek help. I admitted that I could not do any of this alone. When the walk ended, I made a phone call to the doctor's office for an appointment to get on antidepressants. I needed them, and I needed the help of other people, as well.

At this point, I broke up with the old me.

The breakup was clean. Well, more or less, because they're never fully clean; there is always a mess somewhere. Let us just say I never went back to my self-imposed drudgery. I never went back to my steady diet of misery. People go back, you know, but I am happy to say I didn't, and I wound up going off the medication two years later.

So what did I break up with, specifically, and how am I different? It is tempting to answer, "Well, how am I not different?" Instead let me offer a summary of the transformation, because happily there is fulfilled and abundant life on the other side.

I broke up with my anger. I never considered myself full of rage, but pent-up frustration from years of choosing someone else's ideals can leave a person surly, even mean sometimes. Since I no longer pursue someone else's dreams, I have less frustration. Someone who is fulfilled and not frustrated treats people nicely.

I broke up with my rugged individualism. I did this when I asked for help. I am now a part of a thriving partnership; even working as an entrepreneur is something I do not do alone.

I broke up with judging people. I used to do this; my family did it, so I learned it, too. People who didn't follow our expected norms were 'less-than'... 'stupid'... 'losers'. Passing judgment takes too much energy, emotion, and time. I have given it up; I now accept people for who they are, because you never know the struggles a person has had to endure, or may be enduring right now.

Also, *I broke up with my defensiveness.* I once knew only attack; judgment is attack, and I found myself on the receiving end of a lot worse than judgment. A person under threat – whether it is physical, emotional, psychological, etc is always defensive, always expecting the next assault. This person often misinterprets people's words and behaviors as attacks, and I did for years. Not anymore.

People look at me now, and they don't always see the scars. They don't see what used to be depression. They instead see the silliness, they see the smile, the calm, the person that creates and holds space for people and gives them a platform to express their truth and shine. They ask to appear on my podcast. They ask my partner and me to produce shows for them. They take my meditation classes. They see and feel the relaxation. I am glad, because it was not always this way.

Like any worthwhile path of transformation, this one took time. This was a process. It began with a decision to suffer less and not sit for the bar exam after law school.

It continued with a decision to go deeper into spiritual practice while breathing in my clients' drama as a child custody mediator. It ended well after the car wreck when I decided to seek help, accepting that I couldn't do any of this alone. Many people called me. The Universe called me. The Holy Spirit called me. Finally, I answered.

If I had to say one thing it would be this: I learned to trust the process. A journey to fulfillment is indeed a process, and it never truly ends. We can be fulfilled, but in order to remain fulfilled we must show up every moment of every day and decide once again in favor of our happiness. We can choose happiness or the old path of frustration, bitterness and pain. Each and every moment we choose, and when we choose happiness, it is enough. We can then rest assured that happiness will find us, and even though the path may be filled with many twists and turns, each of them is part of a larger plan. We have only to show up, teach, and lead, playing our part.

When we go against this, as I did, the Universe will smack us. I suggest, of course, that you not wait until a vehicle smacks you at high speed. We receive messages again and again, and in different forms, until we get it. I was stubborn, but you don't have to be.

I make the decision for happiness every moment of every day, and having made that decision, I act on it. Head in that direction, even when I do not know the outcome. What I am sure of is that I am happier than I was before.

Reflections

Reflections

Reflections

DANNIE-LU CARR
UK

International Coach & Consultant in Leadership,
Personal Impact & Creativity. Author. Speaker.
Award Winning Theatre Director. Singer-Songwriter,
StrongWoman Competitor
https://dannielucarr.com

I'm an experienced, successful training consultant and coach who works, predominantly, with women and those who feel they have less internal permissions to get braver, find their power, purpose, use their voice and embrace fearless leadership in all areas of their life and work.

I give others the tools to stand up and be heard, provoke important thought, create new narratives and realize change by effectively galvanizing others into action. I have 15+ years of experience in coaching, consulting, designing and running training as well as being an experienced pubic speaker.

I'm the founder of three signature online programs: Flaming Leadership, Warrior Women and 28 Days of Defiance and am also a Published Writer, Award-Winning Theatre Director, Singer-Songwriter as well as the founder of Creative Wavelengths™

Chapter Five
LOVING THE BABY RHINO

"A cultural fixation on female thinness is not an obsession about female beauty but an obsession about female obedience. Dieting is the most potent political sedative in women's history; a quietly mad population is a tractable one." – Naomi Wolf

2020, AGE 45

I felt as if my body was going to buckle and with only five or so meters left to go, I had to put the yoke down. I could hear the shouts of, "Don't give up," "Get your ass under it," "Get it over the line." I dug deep and attempted another lift. It wouldn't budge. That usual doable 150 kilograms felt like it suddenly had doubled in weight. A few seconds later I tried again. Nope. I had to give up. I walked away from the yoke, deflated. Then something inside me kicked back, and I got under it a third time. Using every ounce of strength in my body and in my mind, I pushed as hard as I could. With the force of a baby rhino it came off the ground and, despite the lift being completely off-center, I managed to move forwards to get it over the line.

1978, AGE 3

My earliest memories are of being a carefree, curious and rambunctious child. At age three, a man at the local petrol station handed my sister two dinosaur badges saying, "Give one to your brother."

I was horrified and chipped back without missing a beat, "I'm a girl!" I assume my short wavy hair and dungarees confused him. That's not how a girl should have looked.

I wasn't born thinking that I should be anyone other than who I was. None of us are. But society seems to have different ideas for so many. Particularly when you happen to be assigned the label of 'girl'. Little did I know that this was the beginning of so many comments and criticisms about how I looked and that my living hell had only just started to open its enormous mouth to consume me bit by bit.

That petrol station moment is one of my earliest memories. That and being patted a lot on my bottom, accompanied by the comments:

"She's solid as a rock."

"Strong as an ox."

…and suchlike. I didn't mind the words so much. As a child of that age such words don't really equate to much. There isn't context. They are meaningless. But, like most children with a strong sense of self and a sensitivity to the outside world, I was acutely aware of the judgmental tone in which they were given (unasked for, I hasten to add) and the continual comparisons to my sisters. I was aware of being touched objectively. Patted and commented on. Which I hated. My impulse was always to push them off and run away… but I never did. I pushed that down deeply inside myself instead and smiled, as girls are taught to do.

I was always the one (I'm the youngest of three sisters) with the wayward wavy hair and the most 'built' and 'solid' of the three. At least that was the script I was handed from very early on from the majority of the adults. That and "your sisters are so pretty" which, at such a young age, I took to mean that I was not. That I needed to 'reel myself in a bit' if I was to stand any chance of also being given that label of validation from so many of the people that I barely knew.

It's interesting isn't it, that if I had been a boy, these things would have likely been considered so much more of a positive. The word 'feisty' would have most certainly been replaced with something like 'confident' if it was being used for a boy. I also suspect that the judgmental tones would have felt much more like I was being 'approved of' than 'disapproved of'. Amidst the landscape of skinny 1970s models, a robustly built girl was very unsettling for people. I didn't fit the mold. I didn't even know the mold. I would learn what it was quickly enough. Part of the mold certainly involved the 'pretty' meter, which is most certainly reserved for girls alone to be judged and ranked from the get-go.

SUMMER 1983, AGE 8

I was 'tall for my age'. This was commented on almost daily by teachers, other people's parents and relatives alike. I wanted to shrink and blend. As extroverted as I was, this was just too much attention. I remember feeling like a showpiece; a weirdo; a freak. I wanted peoples' eyes to be anywhere other than on me.

Things really took a turn for the worse for me when my period started early. Precocious puberty. I only found out the term for it in my early 30s. Having a name for it is extremely helpful, nevertheless. You realize *it's* a thing and that *you* are not. You are just a small human who was unfortunate enough for 'the thing' to happen to them. That's all.

It was a crushing day. It was a day which it would take me decades to heal from, although of course I didn't know that at the time. I was so ashamed. I actually thought I had crapped myself because the blood was a kind of brown color and I didn't have a clue about periods. I hid in the bath and dunked my pants in the bathroom sink, hoping to clean out the evidence but luckily was interrupted by my mother and given a concise period talk which was, of course, necessary but I felt anxious and sad.

Going to school the following day whilst bleeding into a sanitary towel made me feel deeply scared and alone. When I needed the toilet, I waited until all of the other kids were playing outside during the break and then went back in, thinking I would be alone.

One of the girls made sure it was her job to follow me in and climb on top of the loo seat of the cubicle beside me. She leaned over and gasped. I looked up horrified to see that she had seen my bloody knickers. Before I could register any more, she had run outside and spread the word about it like wildfire around the playground. By the time I walked back outside there was only one girl who would still talk to me whilst the others stood in their huddles, whispering and giggling.

One of the boys kicked a football to me and it bounced off my chest. I went red faced and rage-like. It was only much later on, and with an adult's hindsight, that I realized this was actually an act of support. In their own way they were trying to get me to look elsewhere; away from the judgment. 'Come and play' was the call. I took the cue soon enough and it became a regular thing for me to start hanging out with the boys and playing football in the playground with them. You didn't need to be thin or pretty to play football.

At that moment I broke up with the bitchy girls' circles. I broke up with my childhood. One was a choice. The other was not. Both were my new reality.

1985, AGE 10
Football, sadly, didn't last long. Running became increasingly uncomfortable as my body decided to keep growing and growing. It's incredibly confusing for a young person to be in the mind of a child, wanting to run and kick a ball about, but to be ovulating and developing hips and breasts. Some kids called me 'fat' and laughed; others tried to grope me. Many of the moms talked about me to each other at pick-up time which, of course, I endlessly overheard. Many of their dads would look at me in a way which felt scary and wrong. Having some of your school friends' dads stare at your chest and leer at you whilst you play chase, football and other games in a desperate attempt to cling on to the last shreds of your snatched away childhood, is a vulnerable and unsafe place. It made me feel so much anger, which I turned in over on myself.

One afternoon, my friend's mom told me to step on the scales. She then proceeded to declare that I was way too heavy and that she was putting me on a diet. She showed me her shelf full of diet shakes and told me that they'd be a good idea for me; I should try them! My chest and face went red and my head began to spin. This was my first experience of body dissociation – something which became a regular practice for me in the many years that followed; it became my failsafe for damage limitation.

I was convinced that I was repulsive to everyone who saw me. My carefree and excitable nature was quickly replaced by one of melancholy and worry. I was walking on eggshells endlessly and expecting any comments in my direction to be on my appearance before I had revealed anything about the person I actually was. I became apologetic and self-deprecating about how I looked. I developed dark depression. I stayed hidden in my bedroom as often as I could. I didn't want to go outside, no matter how sunny. In fact, the sunny days were the worst. That was when I felt the most alone.

My solace was writing songs in my bedroom and listening to music. And I loved to read. These things gave my head a distraction from everything else that was going on around me. And if I started to feel anything at all, or re-associate with my body, I ate to numb the pain instead. It was then that my weight went up rather than down. I couldn't look at myself in the mirror anymore. I was repulsed by the person looking back at me. I didn't feel like her. I felt trapped in my own body and I wanted it to disappear. I felt like I had been born into the wrong shell.

My comfort eating went from bad to worse as did my self-consciousness. My shoulders came up to my ears and my eyes went to the ground. I walked around shrouded in shame about how I looked and who I was. I wasn't good enough. I was a disappointment. I was there to be laughed at. I was there to be talked about. I was there to be mocked and teased. I was there to be sad, alone and uncomfortable.

1986, AGE 11

My first day at secondary school and my sister was just starting her third year. She was very popular with the boys. On my first morning break, a group of third year lads came running over because word had gone around that her younger sister was now in the yard. As they stood around me one commented loudly that I was "a bit of a pig" and another laughed and said "yeah, Porky Pig" and made an oink sound.

The all too familiar red face and neck ensued, and I stared across the sports field, pretending I hadn't heard them, but my heart was racing, and I choked back tears.

1988, AGE 13

My sister had started dating a monster. A boy who hit and shouted and treated her like dirt. He would only do it when they were alone or when I was around. It was down to me to protect her, which I often attempted to do. For the first time in my life, I realized that my short and stocky frame was actually quite strong when I was determined enough.

One day when I had managed to push him off her, he grabbed my right arm and pulled it to a dislocation point at my shoulder, locking me into place. At this point he leaned over me and whispered into my ear that I was "fat, obese, repulsive, ugly, disgusting". It became a regular occurrence and the words stayed with me, running through my brain at what felt like a constant. It became a torturous tape long after he had gone home.

1989, AGE 14

I wasn't the only one with boobs and periods anymore. I wasn't the only one who needed the permission to get changed in one of the private cubicles before PE. I wasn't so different from some of the others now. It felt like a relief.

I began to kick back and express myself through my appearance. I pierced my own nose on the sports field – that hurt! I shaved off the sides of my hair, dyed it blonde, then yellow, then pink and then dreadlocked it. I continued to eat in secret to keep my feelings numb and to keep my loneliness at bay.

I got into trouble at school for how I dressed and had one particularly horrific experience with a female teacher who declared, to the rest of the corridor, that my 14-year old's legs were far too fat to be seen in such a short skirt. I ran home, with that now familiar red face of rage and humiliation. I sobbed all afternoon, refusing to go back into school for the rest of the day. I comfort ate a whole box of cornflakes covered in cream and sugar and hid the evidence. I sat numbly staring into space for a few hours, my stomach swirling.

By this point I absolutely loathed secondary school. The pain from those comments and criticisms were so endlessly emotionally painful that the only way to process it some days was to hurt myself physically. At times I would slice at the tops of my 'too fat' legs and at one point I tried to hack my left breast off, which still bears some faint scars. I still hated my body so much.

Music became my salvation yet again. Many weekends were spent hanging out in the city center, listening to live music in a bar or slamming around to vinyl in some club's mosh-pit, immersed in the wonders of early 90s indie and grunge with a bunch of people who were a few years older than me and firmly took me under their wings. I had finally found my fellow misfits and creatives and felt, for the first time in a long time, like I belonged somewhere. Amidst the ones who were always judged. I found black baggy clothes I could hide in. And every gig venue was dark anyway so nobody could really see what I looked like and nobody, quite frankly, gave a damn anyway. It was escapism at its best and I loved it. I began to get a weeny bit of confidence back as I realized people might not like what I looked like, but they did like who I was. In my mid-teens it was a revelation to realize that I mattered beyond my appearance. Who knew?!

1991, AGE 16

I had a few 'boyfriends'. Nothing at all serious, although they felt it at the time. I remember some of the chat up lines I had being along the lines of, 'you'd be really pretty if you lost weight', 'I'd give you a ride home on my bike but I don't think my back tires could hold you', and 'I love a girl who has plenty of flesh to grab'. I craved every crumb of external validation I could get, every piece of being good enough and was so utterly thankful for every pathetic piece that, had I been remotely religious in any way, I would have dropped to my knees and given prayers of thanks there and then. Instead, I gave up the boundaries to my body, my heart and my self-worth almost entirely. And I gave them the power. I let other people write my life script and dictate how I should feel about myself.

Nevertheless, I pushed through my GCSEs, doing pretty well, ironically apart from music. They had judged the guitar to not be an instrument worthy of any attention and with a basic knowledge of sheet music, coupled with lazy teaching, I got very left behind. Totally deflated, I turned to the theatre. And the gym.

I fell in love with plays, playwrights, the intelligence, the truth, the articulation of the emotions I had never had words for before or felt allowed to express. I fell in love with the honesty of my classmates and my teachers; the permissions to discuss real life with grit, humor and anger.

And when I wasn't immersed in plays, I was immersed in the gym. Lifting heavy things and making myself sweat helped me discover the beauty of endorphins and for the first time in my life, since puberty, I understood what a natural high felt like. I became addicted to the combination of that with regularly starving myself. The weight fell off. Suddenly I was noticed for something 'good'. I had lost weight. The topic of conversation had switched. It wasn't about how much weight I had on my frame but how much I had lost. It felt great. I was finally getting some validation from the outside world. I was on a serious high.

It is worth noting at this stage that I had failed to realize that it was actually the same conversation as had always been. I was still looking outwards for the validation. I was craving acceptance. I was starving my body into submission. I was obeying the rules that had been written for me without my request for them. I was still accepting other people's version of me rather than identifying my own.

1993, AGE 18

Keeping the weight off was incredibly tough. Before long I was in the classic ABC cycle of eating disorders: anorexia, bulimia, compulsive eating. In addition, I was spending two to three hours a day at the gym, obsessively sweating out and burning off as much as I could. It had become an addiction; a torturous cycle of simply existing for the acceptance of others. 'My body will be good enough; I will keep pushing until it is perfect!' I pushed my body to its limits. Externally it was getting there but internally it was far from it. I was becoming more and more removed from myself.

1995, AGE 20

Having received a 2:1 honors degree in performing arts, I was told by my tutor that I would have easily been given a first if I hadn't lost most of my second year to toilet visits and stomach upsets. She told me this in a private room, firmly holding my gaze. Her eyes were telling me to stop. These toilet visits and stomach upsets were entirely self-inflicted by my nightly potion of the hot chocolate laxative I hid under my bed. I would sneak downstairs after saying goodnight and spoon 8–10 times the amount recommended into hot microwaved milk. My stomach was crippled with pain most nights but to me it was worth it. I would also sleep with my window open so the cold would make me burn more calories. Some nights I barely slept at all. My body 'rebelled' by holding the weight tenaciously anyway and I endlessly hovered at pretty much the same on the scales whatever I did.

Of course it was holding the weight! It was fighting its hardest to protect me from any more damage. But I didn't see that, nor did I thank it. Disgusting, I told myself. Far too heavy for someone my height (I can't remember when I stopped growing, just that one day everyone seemed to overtake me and most of them kept going). Short AND stocky. Like a rhino. Not 'nice' at all, I would taunt myself. Ugly, ugly, ugly.

1996, AGE 21

I attached all of the judgment and pain to the place where I grew up and decided that I needed somewhere fresh with new people, new adventures and new beginnings. By September of 1996, I was headed south to London to train professionally at drama school. And I was so excited. No weight history there. I needed to break up with the northeast and I needed to break up with who I had been there.

After arriving, it wasn't long before the comments from the other students began. 'Big boned', 'a bit chubby', 'a definite character actress'. There would never be a romantic lead for me. I fought through but my mental health was a mess. It was too much, too raw. London seemed cold and heartless. Big and scary. My binge-eating returned tenfold. To try to compensate, I began cycling everywhere.

It felt like my life had become the merry-go-round from hell. In the theatre bar after my final showcase, one agent said those same horrific words I had heard so many years before, "You'd be really pretty if you lost some weight. A few stones and you could almost be a lead."

A few *stones*? *Almost* be a lead? I'd worked so hard on my performance, wanted so badly to be wanted, to be good… and yet here I was, still not good enough. Never good enough.

2003, AGE 28

The acting profession was tough and more judgmental than society had ever been. Out of the frying pan and into the fire. Years of jobbing, some of it fun and some of it not so fun. Lots of 'between jobs' temping, bar work and waitressing. By now I had settled in London and discovered that directing and writing were much happier places for me. I began to realize that I didn't mind my brain and ideas being center stage but I didn't want my body to be there. Or at least, not all of the time. The final straw had come when a producer decided to feedback that he thought I'd get more work if I dropped half a stone. This producer was working with me on a radio play! I broke up with acting and decided to only work on projects I wanted to do, more for love than for money. I decided to center my work on writing, directing, and other things, which I did.

2008, AGE 33

Boyfriends and dating had been a mixed bag. I had found it hard to be fully present with men. I was far too busy worrying about when they would judge me, hurt me or leave because I wasn't good enough and they would find someone thinner and prettier which often became a self-fulfilling prophecy. My latest break up had been with my boyfriend of nine years. He left me because he wanted to travel more. It was at a time when I was desperate for a baby. I started comfort drinking home alone in the evenings. I comfort drank a lot. My weight went up yet again.

2011, AGE 36

I hooked up with an actor I used to know for a while, but following a tumultuous relationship, a heart-breaking abortion and miscarriage, we broke up. I stopped eating properly and my bulimia returned. My weight dropped yet again. I was in grief and depression for three years, although still highly functioning both at work and in my life. Eventually, I found some therapists. I started, bit by bit, to unpack what my life had been.

I woke up to the fact that I hadn't been living my own life, but one I thought I should be living. I woke up to the fact that I was trying to shoehorn myself into the mold that had never fitted and never would. I woke up to the fact that I was stronger, both physically and emotionally, than I had ever given myself credit for. I woke up to the fact that I was more than okay as I was and that other people's opinions about my body were not mine to hold. They didn't belong to me. They belonged to them. I woke up to the fact that I had allowed myself to be coerced into an abortion by someone who didn't have my interests at heart. I woke up to the fact that I was allowed to be angry about the mind-fuckery and abuse I had endured through my life. I woke up to the fact that I could say ENOUGH. I started to break up with the judgements of others and society's limitations about how women 'should' look. I started to break up with the abuse I had inflicted on my own body for the last three decades.

WAKING UP...

It wasn't a sudden wake up. It was a slow and steady one with occasional moments of enormous revelation.

I started doing Crossfit. The first time I did a class I was in pieces. I could barely do a thing. Two years later, I was making big lifts and celebrating the fact that my shoulders were bigger, stronger and better. I was celebrating because my arms and legs could lift heavy things. I was celebrating going against the 'thin is better' concept and embracing the 'strong is better' one. It felt right. It fitted me. I felt like I had finally come home.

I went on to compete in team events, open water swimming, running through trails, lifting atlas stones, logs and other awkward objects.

I discovered Strong Man, or more specifically, Strong Woman. There has been nothing more motivating for me than to train and compete in this sport. It was made for me. I'm a small and strong woman and it fires my belly when I go into the gym and get new personal bests with my lifts. I've been scooped into the community with support and people pushing me all the way. Most lifters are the kindest people you could ever meet. Every one of them has their story, their struggles, their reasons for lifting.

I am small, but strong and compact and I humorously label myself a baby rhino. There is still a bit of self-deprecation going on. I feel akin to the rhino; people take away the strength of this creature for their own personal vanity and gains, trying to make themselves feel better. Rhinos love to get into the mud, throw their weight around and play. I am waking up to loving the baby rhino inside me and living the game of life by my own rules, finally.

I lift.

I lift heavy.

I don't buy into being reduced to a number on the scales or the dress size that I may wear. I don't buy into the concept that women should be 'nice and slim' anymore. We come in all shapes and sizes and we are not objects to be approved of or be disapproved of. We are human beings. Every one of us is beautiful and unique. We need to celebrate that and create the space for women to blossom and grow in whatever direction they want to. Not to shrink and take up the smallest amount of space possible in order to make everyone else feel better. Or superior.

Does my body offend you? Does my strength offend you? It's no longer my issue!

In addition to those who I have met on my journey of strength training and lifting, there are three women who have been key to my wake up call. Firstly, Linda Anderson, a transformational Emotional

Freedom Technique (EFT) coach, who through her practice worked through my tears, identifying the childhood trauma that was playing out like an old tape repeatedly. Through her work, I can see it for what it was – old beliefs that had never belonged to me but that I had held onto anyway. I learned how to parent my own inner child and give her what she had needed back then – reassurance, the script that she was a loveable child and she had never done anything wrong. Bit by bit, I was able to release that old trauma and start to see myself with fresh eyes.

Secondly, Diane Goldie, an artist and maker of wearable art. Diane's quest is to tailor clothes for people – to fit their real bodies and to celebrate taking space and being seen. I learned so much from her and the first time she made a dress for me I burst into tears. It was the first time something had fitted me so perfectly and it was the first time I felt truly beautiful. I love her garments and now have many of them.

Lastly, Naomi Wolf and her writing. Her books have changed the way I see the world forever.

I'm still waking up. Every day I wake up a little bit more. The old scripts still sneak in and it is ongoing work to turn down the volume at times or challenge it head on. I am doing the work. I continue to do the work. Not just for me, but for every person who endures the body dysmorphia, the eating disorders, the depression and anxiety and for everyone who has ever been given a cruel remark because of how they look.

It was when I finally started to embrace my strength, my powerful compact frame, my true self as a woman in my own right, with zero apology, that I began to reconnect to the essence of that happy, driven, girl who didn't let anything stop her. It had taken me 42 years to fully break up with society's ideas about what I should look like and connect back to my own truth about who I had been all along, which I had buried and lost deep inside of me for all those years. This baby rhino is precious.

She is strong.

She is valuable.

And she is awesome just the way she is.

Reflections

Reflections

PAUL HONEYCUTT
USA

Self Exploration Guide, Queer'd Up Podcaster
https://www.facebook.com/paul.s.honeycutt

I left the corporate world to pursue the dream of entrepreneurship. Having gone through some tough lessons I'm now utilizing my skills in finance to help people through homeownership.

During that process I also discovered myself and have become aware of a true passion in helping ones discover SELF. I'm kicking off a podcast, retreat business called Queer'd UP.

Focusing on uniting, uplifting and inspiring the LGTBQ+ business & entrepreneurs. I grew up in a large family and was raised in a cult, which will be the focus of my story and breaking free from the loss of self. I enjoy spending time outdoors in Colorado and recently spent 30+ days camping alone and being with SELF. It has propelled me to go after the life I want to live and pursue my passions.

Chapter Six
BEARING WITNESS

Sitting on the sofa of my Airbnb in Santa Fe New Mexico I have this sense of strength, resolve and finality. In less than four minutes my mother and I had a conversation that for many when I told them set their heads spinning and yet for me years of anger, fear, uncertainty had left me grounded and at peace.

For the better part of seventeen years she and I had not spoken more than a handle full of times and had only seen each other maybe three times. Our relationship had been close when I was younger. My older sister would always say I was my mother's best friend. I would tag along as she went shopping, garage sales and in the kitchen. She was always so warm, hard working and driven in many ways. The best of cooks and the consummate host.

You know that pit of the stomach, nagging feeling when there is something you really feel you need to do but having the guts or courage to seem out of reach? It had been a constant companion. I had so much to say to express to her authentically. I needed to do this for me.

This is my letter to her.

Mom,

Your life to me is a mystery in many ways. You rarely ever shared personal things about yourself. I don't even know your birthday. Here is what I know. Being a young mother moving across country with your first husband to be abandoned with three young children must have been scary, difficult and exhausting. To have someone knock on your door sharing a beautiful story of a paradise full of abundance and perfection, it's easy to see why one would be attracted to it. Then finding a sense of community of others that had your back and were so helpful with your kids anyone would be sucked in.

What made you suddenly decide that everything you knew was not worth it or what you believed anymore? What was it like to leave all of the traditions of the holidays, birthdays and to have your family be upset with you?

Did they really come up with a plan to introduce you to dad in hopes that meeting him would possibly bring you back to Michigan and leave the Jehovah's witnesses? He was your brother's best friend. Had a good stable job as a sheriff, stability and was a solid man. But how did you convince him to start studying with them and to convert?

Why was it such a secret about how you met, when you got married or anything really to do with either of your past. What trauma or hurt had you both gone through to walk away from a stable job, family, his two sons and move us to Texas?

For some odd reason I'm embarrassed to even tell people I was born in Texas. I think I hated it just as much as you did. The stress of such a big move, pregnant with me, one can only imagine how difficult that was.

Was it really so wrong dad being a sheriff and forcing him to leave a job he loved just because of the beliefs of the JW's? I know it was hard for the family being from the North and Yankees. Southerners didn't quite like you and on top of that you were in this odd religion.

I'm writing this letter because I have so many questions and also wanted to express what your choice to raise us in this cult impacted me.

Did you really feel I was capable enough to take a stand my first day of kindergarten against celebrating birthdays. Handing me a piece of literature to make the point that I was not allowed to have a cupcake, be in the room or celebrate with my classmates. Instead I had to sit outside against the brick wall, knees pulled up to my chest while they had fun. Did you ever have to take such a stance at that early of an age? How was I to really understand all of that.

This memory has stuck out so plainly as the first time feeling on the outside, weird and not good enough. I did not fully understand that belief but I followed the direction you gave me. That was the foundation of just doing as I was told and to not ever question authority. I have forever felt that way and I often wonder if you knew how much that sucked to be the odd kid in class. Then came the pledge of allegiance and in Texas that was a big deal. I could feel my skin redden and I would get so nervous, sick to my stomach would I stand and salute or follow the order of staying seated. No one ever understood and then to explain that we don't believe in earthly governments, only the government of Jehovah. You could see their eyes go wide or just glaze over and most of the time I wasn't even sure of what it all meant. Memorization was the key, not true belief just be able to repeat.

Like most children, I just wanted to make you proud. I loved spending time learning to cook, bake and going shopping with you. I knew that meant towing the line and being a good witness.

I don't know about you, but were you exhausted with the full weekly schedule for the witnesses? Monday family study, Tuesday having people over and it was book study, Wednesday prep for Thursdays two hour meeting, Thursday rushing to get there in time for the meeting, Friday was Watchtower preparation or preparing to go out in the ministry on Saturday, Saturday getting up early going out knocking on doors in the hot weather dragging us kids along, Sunday the public talk and Watchtower study. I mean I'm just exhausted writing this. It sucked. I mean homework wasn't even important enough if it got in the way of this schedule. I'm not sure whether schooling even matters. You both never seemed to care truly about grades as long as it was a pass. Forsake everything for 'The Truth'. Imagine if your parents woke you up every weekend to go knock on the doors of your neighbors, classmates. I'm confident you would have hated the long hours dressed up knocking on doors on the weekends. And the meetings were so boring. It only got worse as I got older.

Here is the deal. We did get to do some kid stuff but the lack of encouragement to learn music, sports or anything that wasn't regarding the cults beliefs baffles me. Gymnastics was the first thing you enrolled me in and I loved it. I started to get good but suddenly I was pulled out. Too much time away from 'The Truth' Really?! This carried throughout the rest of my schooling and into early adulthood. School sports, nope!! Orchestra and band were okay until I had to miss meetings. The Student Council absolutely not, that was a form of earthly government. I wanted to fit in and I loved those things. I always had a musical ear. You knew that, it was noted in my baby book. But anything that I desired unless it had to do with serving righteously was out the question.

How mad did you get when my third grade teacher Ms Massey would take me in the hallway and paddle me for no reason and I would come home upset and crying. I started to withdraw not understanding what I was doing wrong. I always wanted to be a good kid. What did you do to protect me? Did you sympathize with me on what that was like? Being punished because of a choice in a belief that you made and I was forced to take a stand on.

For me the move to New Mexico was the most exciting thing. I couldn't wait to get the fuck out of Texas. I was too young to know why but getting out was all I remember. The move to the mountains was the best thing and today I still am so relieved we left. What was it like to finally not seem to be struggling financially and to have a nice home? Life started to seem easier, however the pressure pot of middle school, puberty and becoming a teenager put into motion so many more challenges.

That was about the time I started having severe pains in my stomach. I would get so stressed and worried about the littlest of things. You took me to the doctor and he said I was just stressed. I wasn't even twelve and suffering from severe stress. Did you have a clue what was happening in that little brain of mine? I think you did. Just pray, focus on your bible studies and go preach it will all work out. Trust Jehovah. Well that was BS and you knew it.

Be responsible and the good one was always the running theme in my mind. I knew that I would only make it or be accepted if I was perfect. Perfection though was something we would never attain until we had been tested and proved worthy. When would that happen, way off in some story book future.

Coming out of the water after having been baptized in a pool in Amarillo I had arrived. I was going to make things better. For some crazy reason I felt the need to make up for the hurt and loss I saw you and Dad go through when my older brother ran away and got married to an unbeliever. He was cut off and suddenly out of our lives. I damn sure didn't want that to happen to me. So forge through it and be a good trooper. Would it fix me? Would I not have to ever worry about those fears and doubts I had about myself. Did it make me clean and pure?

The drive to be perfect solidified around that time. I knew I needed to show up a certain way and man did I want to please and be the best person in the room. Competitive in nature is something you passed down to me. I'm fiercely competitive. I wanted to be baptized before any of my older friends. I wanted to show that I was more spiritual and smarter. Truly I didn't care it was all about the appearance. I was learning if I acted, spoke and did certain things I would be recognized, and you and Dad would actually pay attention or give me praise. I wanted nothing more than that.

Sneaking into Dad's office and breaking into his briefcase to get the Elder's secret book that had the answers to the three part interview with elders to get baptized felt so wrong but I simply couldn't fail. To be honest I was never really paying attention or learning the things they wanted us to do. It was simple memorization. I was going to impress and in my own way I think I did but I knew I had cheated. SHAME.

I ate birthday cake once and thought I would be taken by the devil.

I kissed a friend that was staying over wrong, wrong, wrong. Cheated on that test. I struggled to always be perfect but I gave it my hardest effort and even if I couldn't I would fake it. Then I would sit in tears praying for forgiveness, begging to not make feel this way, protect me from Satan. SHAME.

School became torture. Prison possibly was a better description of what was happening in my mind. Everyday having to take a stand and be different it was exhausting. SHAME again with my classmates, I was the freak, I didn't fit in and I tried so hard to find ways to cross the line but remain okay or not get caught. Every holiday would come and I would try and figure out some way to either get out of school or participate in a way that I wouldn't stand out. Eyes were everywhere. Other Jehovah's Witness kids in school would be watching and we all knew it was the righteous thing to turn someone in. It was the Christian way!!

I wonder if you hadn't been a popular girl in school if you would have known what it was like to be the loser in class. School pep rallies, sporting events, plays, dances all over the table. I knew not even to ask because bad associates were at those events and it took away from meetings and could potentially harm us. Everything in the world was there to test us, try and make us sin and to prove that evil lived on the earth.

Yeah we did some fun things: road trips, hiking, skiing, camping. All with JW's. Picking up the phone to call an approved chaperon pleading a case to come spend their evening or weekend with my group of teenage friends was humiliating. I was a good kid and they were all nerds as well. But nope couldn't go anywhere without one. Sin was always a moment away. No dating that was only for marriage and simply unacceptable.

I had never felt so captured even within the congregation my friends all knew you and dad were super strict. Where did that come from? Why did you want to control and not allow us to do things? Were we paying for the mistakes of our older siblings? What did you really fear?

From an early age the FEAR of Armageddon and the end of the

world was instilled in me. You reinforced in me daily, the worry and fret about not being good enough. It was slowly layering brick upon brick of a small inner prison within. What I had to look forward to was not graduating or living life. It was that I would never see that day because this world will be destroyed. If I'm not perfect I would go down with it. That is so fucked up!!

Puberty was in full swing and the odd realization was creeping into my body. The attraction was just so natural, yet I knew this was the devil. He was after me! He was out to tear me away from my family, friends and 'The Truth'. I couldn't let him get me. I couldn't stop the urges, the thoughts, desire. It was so wrong. What had I done to deserve this. Was it because I slipped something and pledged allegiance to the flag? Maybe it was eating that birthday cake or singing happy birthday to someone at school. Could it have been because I lied about why I wouldn't celebrate or I would lie that I wasn't a Jehovah's Witness. I was for sure going to not pass the test. Gross, disgusting yet so thoroughly natural. This was my test. Jehovah was allowing me to go through this so that I could fight it, overcome it and be declared a righteous servant.

Fag, I remember the first time I got called it. I'm not sure I even knew at that time what it meant but I got the message. Again I was the freak. Fuck! So I had to deal with being a JW and now this. Why was I attracted to boys? God, how could I make this work? Disappear, go within, do not draw attention to yourself at school or meetings. How did they know and I couldn't even figure out what it was and what it meant.

Then it kept being thrown in my face. When I would get on stage with the assigned topic to discuss how masturbation was bad and had to explain through the scriptures why. Or that time I saw my assigned topic was 'Homosexuality and how it is wrong'. I had to go up and speak about how terrible, deprave it was and I WAS. I WAS A FAG!! SHAME.

To this day I'm confident those were assigned to me on purpose. A subtle way to shame me into obedience and to solidify the fear of death because of it.

I went to bed with tears drying on my face every night. Praying the gay away. What a joke. My body couldn't resist. Yet how could this be? It was the devil's influence. Surely I wasn't born this way, that message had been beat into me. I felt suffocated. Suddenly I became so vigilant about how I acted and portrayed myself. I was not going to give my classmates or the congregation the opportunity to suspect. I thought I was beating him, I was winning the fight by acting, lying and putting on a good face. He kept after me that damn devil.

I lied to you that's when it started in earnest. I couldn't be myself, I knew it. I had to hide it. Be the perfect kid. Schooling and my grades never were truly of importance. I remember if I passed that was good enough.

The perfect family. I got that message loud and clear. Show up to the meetings prepared to answer, take on extra responsibilities, go in the ministry as much as possible. Be set out as a good example. I wanted to be the best of the best. Inside I was eating myself alive.

What did I want in life? What was I interested in? Nope that was never a discussion. My life was laid out clearly for me. The path, preach, work to preach, go to the headquarters and serve maybe get married. But never a thought to what I wanted in life. So I figured I didn't deserve that. It was selfish and ungodly to be focused on oneself.

The moment I got behind a wheel I felt such a freedom. Now you and dad did trust me to drive myself around and I loved the exhilaration of it. It was the safest space I had. I could be in the car listening to the music I wanted and just be me. It was my sanctuary. And still is to this day.

I explored and one day found a gay coffee shop and bookstore. Man did I think I was in heaven! I remember walking thinking would they know? I was terrified and so excited. Soon I learned what cruising was. This will be hard for you to hear and when I look back it was so dangerous. At the time it was my only outlet and so I started to get picked up by men. Not teenagers but men! I did things that only compounded the shame, guilt and fear within. It was like a drug I couldn't resist. Moments of pure bliss and I got hooked. I knew I was doing something so terrible in the eyes of Jehovah and 'The Truth'.

Eating my soul away I had to confess and I did. You and dad betrayed me. I was broken in tears, afraid and what did I have to do? Sitting in front of three grown adult men as they asked me in detail what had happened. My confession was a lie. I would not tell them about the men I made up a story that it was a friend from school. But they pressed me to ask how he touched me, how did I give him a blowjob. I mean we hadn't even had a sex talk outside of how boys get erections.

Humiliation to the deepest degree. They asked me such explicit questions that I broke down and I couldn't even respond. I sobbed. That was it. I was the worst person ever. I wanted to die. Get me out of this room and yet that went on for over two hours. Pure torture, shame and humiliation set in as my go to emotions.

Lying at that point was the only means to survival. Shove who I was down and press forward. Put on a good show and you will not have to deal with that again. Or so I thought. Fear of death and the end of the world kept me ever vigilant of my sins.

On top of that everyone in the congregation knew that I had been privately reproved. All responsibilities suddenly removed. That was the key signal that someone was not a good associate during that time. Just more reinforcement of not being good enough.

As it came closer to time for gradation my desire to go to college and travel wasn't even a consideration. You and dad squashed that telling me the college would corrupt me and isn't appropriate for true Christian believers. How was that? Why did you just say you didn't want me to open up my mind to other possibilities? To the potential of life. To think and dream for myself. Never once did you ask what I wanted or desired. It was simply put forth the option of being a regular pioneer (knocking on peoples doors 90 hours a month plus working), Bethel (go volunteer take a vow of poverty and work in the headquarters), or go to where the need was great (essentially poor areas or underprivileged areas to try and convert).

The end was nigh!! The end was nigh!! Was I going to survive? That is what drove the decision to pioneer. Plus I needed to make up for continuing to have homosexual thoughts and feelings. I had zero passion for it. All I wanted to do was go travel, but that was simply unacceptable.

You were given the opportunity to explore what you wanted. You had freedom as a teenager to play and enjoy the time of life. Yet suddenly you had restricted me so much it was miserable. Questioning the organization or you and dad was out of the question. We did not question 'The Truth', The Elders, The faithful and discreet slave, and I was not to question you. Trust in them, knowing that I certainly didn't know what was best for me or could form an opinion.

Escape to Colorado at 18 was my plan. I moved there with such excitement for being an adult and the chance to start living my life.

I did my best to be the best servant I could. Meeting on time and participating. In the ministry, I was there and ready to go convert. I marked those little boxes on the time card that was due and I lied. Why were they so worried about how much time I spent I couldn't figure out it was just what you did. I had to look good though so I marked my hours up, the amount of publications handed out and time spent studying with others. Just reinforcing that the truth was worse than the lie for me. It saved me to look so good. It made me feel important, looked up to and I was praised. Again just reinforcing that the facade was far better than being myself.

It worsened for me. I was working full time and putting in 90 hours a month preaching door to door. I was becoming exhausted, however being so busy and focused I thought would make up for the continual slips. The gay bookstore coffee shop I found, or just about anywhere I knew they hung out. I was so curious. Yes, I was choosing this. I thought against all of my training and let's be honest brainwashing. Again I was not born this way that was out of the question. It was just not natural.

Up until then being single was a badge of honor. Yet when I stopped pioneering the pressure started to get married. Everyone was doing it, and you, I think, knew it needed to happen. I never wanted to get married. I didn't even know what it was like to date or be in a relationship. That was never taught, it was to pick a girl, date (of course with a chaperon) and get married. I knew that once I started dating I essentially had chosen my wife.

You hated being second to men. The way the sisters were less than the brothers bothered you. Maybe you wouldn't admit it a lot but it was so apparent. I paid attention. Yet that is what you wanted me to do. I did not want to get married. I couldn't imagine even kissing a girl let alone wanting to be with her initially or married to one.

Again putting on a show was better than being honest with myself. Okay fine! I will find a girl to date in 'The Truth' and just get married. Ugh! But I wanted to travel. I wanted to explore. Not be tied down working to support her and our activities in the cult. Yet another prison that seemed inevitable for me to visit.

History had proven to me that you would easily cut out a child from your life if they didn't remain faithful or left the organization. The severity of my baptismal choice hit me in the face like a bitch slap you never expected. Todd, didn't get baptized, so you always found a way to be there for him. Your actions showed you proved that you could justify that. Tracy though, she had been baptized and thus you turned your back on her. I lost one of my closest friends when you did that. I towed the line but it hurt like hell. So I wasn't going to do that. By this time my younger brother and sister had both left as well. I felt I had to hold on. It would break your heart and I couldn't do that. I was dying inside of self hate, shame to the point of wanting to end it all. If I did that it would only bring shame and disappointment again to you. I couldn't win either way.

It's like a zebra suddenly seeing it is surrounded by lions on the hunt. It's pure fear and the reaction is to run like hell, but they must know it's over. There simply isn't a chance and to just give in. I was that prey. I knew it was over. I was going to die somehow. Either getting married and killing myself within or leaving to a death at the hands of Jehovah at some point and losing you and the only people I knew.

I did my best to try and yet I just shriveled up inside. I put as much effort into work as possible and did what I could to fake being a faithful servant.

Suddenly I was around people through work that were so kind, open and wanted me to be part of their group. It felt so good to be accepted. It was this odd time of showing up to the meetings but wanting to hang out with them. To enjoy life. You had lied to me about worldly people as we called them. They were far from bad people. They worked hard, had families, sure they celebrated holidays, birthdays and enjoyed hobbies and extracurricular activities. However they certainly never tried to come after me to turn me into some evil bad person. They were the normal ones. I was again the odd man out. With open arms though they accepted me.

They didn't watch every move to catch me breaking some rule. They didn't shame me for who I was. They asked me my opinions and wanted to know what it was I thought and believed. Now that I couldn't answer truthfully. Who was I? No clue and that didn't matter because I didn't matter was what I believed.

I started to wake up to a different world and way to live. I couldn't handle celebrating a holiday and I hated when my birthday came up. They all wanted to celebrate and the guilt and shame I had made me so sick I bailed on the parties even one they wanted to throw for me. I turned my back on people that wanted to honor me because of some stupid outdated unsubstantiated belief that birthdays were so bad.

You did teach me to respect women and I'm thankful for that. Five women became a savior to me. Amanda, Kandice, Tammy, Lourdes and Karen. I so wish you could meet them. You would love them. If it wasn't for them I'm not so sure what would have happened to me.

Have you ever had a time when you had a feeling that you couldn't escape? A feeling that something big was about to happen or you suddenly became aware of a thing you could no longer run away from?

As I was leading a double life, I was transitioning from somewhat faking being a good servant to flat out knowing I was simply doing it so I didn't have to deal with the pressure and being called out for not doing what was expected of me. My truth was coming out to me more and more. Or should I say I was meeting up with guys, going to bars, creating a group of friends gay and straight. I was building a life. The shame was still there. I hated what I was doing, however that train was picking up steam and I didn't want to put the brakes on. I would deal with the shame and depression but no way was this stopping.

Keeping two lives straight and all of the lies is a full time job. I did whatever I could to seem like a good JW, and with my friends I was acting as if that was never a part of my life that I was all good.

Under the stars on a trampoline in the Black Hills of South Dakota, a conversation with myself was to be had. I simply couldn't take it anymore. The clarity of the choices before me were undeniable. This wasn't going away. I owned it. I was GAY. It wasn't the devil after me, it wasn't a choice, it simply was me. So I had two options as I saw it Mom.

Option one: Accept it but get married and just push forward with the hope that I would be able to stay faithful and just live with the guilt and shame.

Option two: Accept it knowing that when I came out that would be it. I would lose you, family and everything I had known.

It was the first time I didn't even have to hesitate. I trusted some deep feeling inside that the second option was really the only option. I took it!!!

The next day I had never felt this inside. There was a small space of lightness I had never felt. Yes I was scared as fuck. But the excitement and resolve were for once stronger than the shame and fear. I knew the outcome. I would lose everything. I was okay with that.

My first time standing up for myself.

Well you know the story. Somehow someone found out I was gay in and it spread like wild fire. Suddenly the phone would not stop ringing. The elders try to get me to talk to them. Oh they wanted me to come in and confess. NO FUCKING WAY!! I had done that once and it was not happening again.

My oldest brother saying I was so disgusting and that I could no longer have a relationship with my nieces whom I had spent so much time with. That hurt the most.

And then that phone call I finally answered from Dad when he said either I speak to the elders, repent or that was it.

That was it. I hung up and in my mind I thought, *I'm going to wrap those 26 years of my life up, tuck it away, ignore it and blaze into this new life. I've got this. It won't impact me.*

Love was always conditional. Yours, God's and everyone I had grown up with.

Up until then we spoke multiple times a week. I loved you so deeply, yet so quickly you cut me out. Anger is a funny emotion. It can creep into your life so subtly. Impacting in the smallest of ways. I started to resent others that had great families. The holidays sucked even more. Sure I didn't need them but now everyone was celebrating them and I had zero tradition or idea on how to behave. I would constantly stand up for others when they couldn't understand how a parent turns their back on a child.

Self hate was actually something taught to us in almost every meeting. It was directly stated that way but when you are told you are constantly not good enough and to live with a deep shame, you learn to hate, and hate turns to anger and self loathing.

I was a fake. I didn't fit in again. Not a Jehovah's Witness, and not a worldly person. Being gay still put me on the outside for many. My other behaviors deepened. I didn't know how to date or have a relationship. I found solace in many one night stands. Random meetings felt like a warm blanket of comfort. I could hook up, explore and not have to be accountable or even wait for feedback. They didn't know me nor did I them, and I liked it. Of course I wanted a boyfriend. Lying, being fake and certainly not revealing your true self just doesn't work.

How could I show up for someone else when I couldn't even be honest with myself still? SHAME

Fifteen years had lapsed when I got the call that October that Dad was in the hospital. By then I was well into a successful career, bought a home in San Diego, had a group of amazing friends, was traveling around the world, experiencing new things. I felt proud of what I had accomplished and loved myself in many ways.

I hadn't spoken to him in over ten years. I didn't know how to handle it all. He had chosen to not pursue treatment. He was given weeks to live. Now this part is something I'm not sure I can say without getting angry. It was decided we would all come in the end of November. This was the first time seeing him and you in a long time. I wasn't surprised how resolved and calm you both were. As he stated his faith allowed him to be at peace. However here is the bullshit I couldn't get past. Here we are trying to spend a few days with him and the damn brothers and sister kept showing up. And when they did, they wouldn't even acknowledge us truly. We were pushed aside for them. Hmmm I see it was so clear they are more important than his own children.

What happened to seeing your kids as humans? You would treat a stranger that walked into the Kingdom Hall with more kindness and grace. My younger siblings were crushed. Yet there was no consoling. It felt like you have to be here since he is dying, but couldn't wait for us to leave.

It was the first time when I got a few minutes with Dad alone that he told me how proud he was of me and loved me. It was genuine and brought me to tears. It took this to get that one simple sentence out of him.

I was in New Zealand for a month when he passed. I flew back over New Years to be with the family for the memorial of his life.

We had a brief moment alone and you choked up and said, "I'm so sorry Paul. Life must have been so hard for you, having to deal with being gay (you said it out loud for the first time to me) I wished I had done more to be there for you. I should have done things differently. I knew you were gay from the time you were a child."

Had I died? What the hell is going on? What was happening? You always knew? You felt bad? You had remorse? I was blown away. It was the first time I felt you really saw me and I saw your love for me. I was elated, maybe this was the turning point. You knew I didn't choose it as you had said before. I mean mom, you've always had gay men around you. So many undercover gay men in that organization. It allowed a bit of my anger towards you to subside. You knew and you just couldn't do anything because of the truth. That was okay. I'd take any little piece of love.

Dad's passing opened up a door to everything I had shoved down. Suddenly I was wrought with fear of the future. I was going to die young. I had no passions. What was I doing with my life? I had worked hard to get a job I thought I wanted and suddenly I thought, *Shit! If I was to die tomorrow, am I living for myself?* I couldn't reconcile god, religion or spirituality. Even who I truly was behind a long list of lies and facades. I didn't know myself.

My deep need to please others, to at all cost put on a show of being perfect and having it all together; coupled with extreme shame regarding my own sexuality and sex. Having put forth lies that I felt protected me but couldn't keep up with. A vehement hatred when I felt people were trying to control me. I would lose it when people would simply ask what I was doing for the weekend or where I was. It felt like an invasion of my privacy. I was extremely secretive. Unsure of how to voice an opinion or thought and when I would it often came from a place of extreme frustration of having not spoken up that I would insult or hurt people. It felt like an invasion of my privacy. I still hated myself. I was angry. It was unraveling. I thought I was good but all of the patterns kept showing up louder and louder in my life.

Looking back I went through a series of relationships that all ended for the same reasons. I didn't know myself, I wasn't deserving, couldn't speak up afraid that if I really started to acknowledge who I was they would leave. When I got super stressed I went to my old comfort of random sex and feeling so unworthy.

I was in a relationship hoping it would bring comfort and a sense of family. I didn't want to die alone. I knew very early on that I wasn't happy. We got along fine and had similar interests, yet I again wasn't listening to myself. I wasn't being truthful. Going back to that fairytale I was hoping for, ignoring all of the signs. Most of all denying myself.

Feeling weak, unloved, put down, but hey this was as good as it was going to get. I can compromise. We traveled, lived large and had a beautiful home yet I hated myself and in turn began to resent him more and more. Had it really been fifteen years of a new stage of self denial, self hatred and shame. I started to feel lost, it was a darkness that entered my life.

I had been denying myself for my whole life. Sure I did things for myself. However when you do not acknowledge and accept them for what they are, it's yet again another lie to yourself.

'The Truth'! Oddly that's what I grew up believing in. Centering my whole life around that concept of one group of people holding the truth and that we as individuals could only know that by following such regimented steps to righteousness.

My Truth wasn't that.

I was angry and it was directed at you, dad and the cult. Damn! That is so hard to say, but I was pissed off and it was impacting my whole life. I thought it was behind me. I had to actually question what happened and why was it affecting me so deeply. I was highly successful at work, I had the coolest home that I just loved, I had money, no debt, retirement, great friends, enjoyed good food and drink and had the ability to travel when and where I wanted. To so many that was a great life. Empty, unfulfilled, unhappy, fake, unaware, depressed that was my truth.

Darkness started creeping into my mind and body. It felt like I was swimming up class five rapids on a river and getting pushed further and further down river. I could see where I wanted to go. The force was so strong that I started to tire and give up. Distractions became my focus. Smoking weed, drinking, eating, the gay apps that I would drain hours upon hours of my day and night on. Pointless endless conversations that lead to nowhere. Cold, aloof and indifferent were my constant.

Feeling unaccomplished. I was staring down a life of half starts, unfinished dreams, unfilled experiences. Denial of things I wanted to try and learn. No pursuing as perfection seemed out of reach and control of the outcome was unknown so why even try. I would fail and what was the point. Was I living my life waiting for the end of the world? I dared not look deeply at myself or even think to ask what I truly wanted.

When something piqued my interest I would not give myself permission to try it. I would fail or waste time. If I did try it, I would find a way to tear it apart. Break down what I should have done better, or find a reason to be upset about taking time for myself.

Turning 40 was a trip. never truly imagined or thought about by my life much past high school. I was living with a deep seeded belief of an impending world doomed to destruction. Remember you told me I wouldn't even graduate high school?

What happened in those years wasn't all bad. I've had a lot of ups and downs and fun. But that daily guilt that was installed in my brain as an app from an early age held a grip on me that I couldn't understand or grasp.

Salvation always was in the form of someone else telling me what I should do or be. I looked for answers that would just make me feel moments of relief from such an inner hatred of myself. What I wanted was always wrong, surely somewhere inside I was capable of loving myself right?

Do you love yourself Mom? Do you torment and eat yourself up daily for your life and choices?

Oh how my hatred for you grew and I hated that. The other thing I wondered was why did you take us away from your family? I didn't even know my aunts, uncles or cousins. You had judged each child unworthy that I didn't even have a relationship with them.

You gave me a deep appreciation for travel and exploring. I loved the road trips we would take. Cooking... it's a passion. I love it and I'm good at it. I think you would be proud. I love to read. Remember you told me to read and it sparked my imagination and still does. The cult gave me a few things as well. The ability to speak easily in front of crowds, I can go into any group and fit in quickly and get to know people, I'm good at sales I mean what could be tougher than selling the bible door to door on a Saturday morning when people just wanted to sleep in?

I wanted so badly out of the situation I was in with work and my relationship I would do anything. I wanted out of my skin, my life and my brain. If I could just cut that little voice out and flush it down the toilet I'd be so happy.

So I got a call from two former colleagues and they wanted me to join them in building a company. You know some of what happened but I won't go into detail outside of this. I walked away from a great career into something that I knew almost right away was a mistake. But I didn't trust myself and that inner app saying don't do this. I walked away from a hard earned bonus because it was what they needed. I believed in a paradise story I was told and never verified, just like I never verified anything I was taught. If someone I thought was smarter than me told me something then it must be true.

I moved back to Colorado as you know and it got worse. I could see it happening, the frustration, the loss of money, the stress and yet I just wanted to focus on the paradise idea I had formed. Reality wasn't even something I wanted to acknowledge or was capable of. I was losing money, everything I had worked hard for, my current relationship was starting to suffer. I couldn't look him in the eye and share how deeply worried I was. I felt like crawling into a cave and just curling up, and so I did. I stopped fighting. I just took what was coming and didn't stand up for myself. This time the shame, guilt and self hatred was too much to handle.

Over this bullshit!! It happened while watching a documentary about the Jehovah's Witnesses. I had joined a Facebook group of ex-JWs as well. In both of them I saw the devastation this cult had done not only to me, but to countless others. Every time someone commented or posted it was as if they were in my brain and had lived my life.

It was time… I had to look at this.

My therapist, by the way I could never understand why JWs said you can't go to one. Well I went to a cult recovery specialist. Our first session mom was a breakthrough. I cried most of the time and even in writing this I don't remember everything we covered. However I learned very quickly how they controlled you, and thus you me. It was a realization that I wasn't crazy. I had been programmed from an early age with these issues and challenges.

The anger and resentment welled up and yet also I felt myself coming to shore. Understanding that I had been brainwashed. I could barely afford to pay for the sessions but I had to. I had to unlearn all that I was told and to realize the beauty within myself that I never saw. That I was an individual and not just a number in the cog of the cult. I actually had value, self worth and I could create a purpose for myself. Of my own choosing, desire and strengths.

Awareness… meaning to listen, to observe what is going on within and around you. I had a curiosity within me that wanted to know more about the world that I was told was dangerous, evil and ending. What did I believe if what I was told and assured was 'the truth' and the only truth? I abhor and still do hate organized religion. I get why you and others do it, but it's not for me. I cannot do it. But spirituality now what was that? It certainly wasn't seven days a week going to meetings that you just memorized things. It wasn't feeling shame every day. So maybe I should explore this.

It was time to break the rules and I was excited to do so.

Have you ever had those moments when things just seem to be coming into your life and you can't explain why? I was running into people through networking that were speaking about awareness, spirituality, or these very open minded ideas. Feeling a call to explore more, so I did.

One was a book called *Awareness* by Anthony De Mello. I would suggest you read it but I know you won't. That would be too scary to even look at after 50 plus years of 'The Truth'.

He writes: "We don't want to look, because if we do, we may change. If you look, you lose control of the life that you are so precariously holding together. And so in order to wake up, the one thing you need the most is not energy, or strength, or youthfulness, or even great intelligence. The one thing you need most of all is the readiness to learn something new."

WOW! I wanted to learn, so I dove in. Not only into reading but exploring thoughts of others, teachings, people that had different ideas and beliefs. Shut this voice off is what I wanted and yet I started to see I could by stepping outside and actually acknowledging reality.

For the first time spirituality had a meaning to me. I felt it in nature mainly. It was when I felt the most calm, peaceful and that voice had shut up. Spending time out there and starting to have conversations with 'Source' I found peace within. Something for myself that I created, wholly unto me. This was my belief. Energy is around us everywhere I always felt it, but to acknowledge that it brought a freedom to the oppressed mind of before.

The next book I would line up for you to read is *The Untethered Soul* by Michael Singer. This would trip you out at almost 80, but I sure wish you would read it and maybe unleash from a life that I'm not so sure you've been happy with or has made you fulfilled. Check this out Mom, he helped me to learn this: "The root of the SELF, the seat of consciousness. You are the conscious being who is aware that you are aware of all inner and outer things."

I sit here laughing to myself about the things we were told. I mean do you remember the whole thing about smurfs being the devil and we couldn't watch. Or sleeping with a pillow between your legs as a man could result in impure actions, tight jeans or pants could lead to masturbation and sinning?! Educating yourself was not necessary, you simply needed to trust them.

A faint voice of knowing that there was a purpose within me awakened. I felt something welling up that I need to let out and maybe just maybe it was just for me. I had a power within me. You knew it, you would always say if the world got me I would do big things, but you locked that idea up quickly in shame and guilt.

Forty years in a prison of shame, doubt, self loathing and fear. Are you still in that prison? Is it comforting? I could no longer stand it. I knew I had strength to fight my way out. I was done. It was so overwhelming, scary and exciting. That deep curiosity I've had was coming to life again. Peace was starting to settle in my body.

Shame is insidious. It was my partner, lover, friend I knew so well. I welcomed it daily. A place of comfort was found in beating myself up living in humiliation and distress. Lies, putting on a show, a facade of piety that was home for me.

Taking a deep breath outdoors I suddenly wanted to quiet the mind more and I started the 'evil' practice of meditation. You are missing out but I get it. Sitting quietly with yourself and your thoughts, ideas and finding peace within yourself opposed to through the beliefs of others would be scary. You would suddenly have to really look deeply at your life and see you didn't need them the whole time. It was all within. It was within me and I know it. I can guide myself.

When asked to think more deeply about how I wanted to live, the damn of tears came rushing forward. Dare I imagine and really look at what it is I want? Did I really have the option? I did, and this is where I've finally learned to let my anger towards you subside. The tears stifled the burning fire of anger.

It was like tasting your delicious warm bread you would make every Tuesday. It smelled so good and it was warm and comforting. Once you have tasted it you want more. I knew, just like baking a passion we both share, there is a measure of science to it for sure however the art of practicing it, honing the skill through trials and errors resulted in a recipe unreplicable. Unique to you and only you.

It's my own recipe, I'm the chef in the kitchen creating my life. Yes I can learn from others and draw from inspirations. It's the failures that I cherish and no longer look at with shame and self anger. It's the beauty of trying, learning and growing. I still have many lessons to learn and old recipes to reinvent. They were passed down from generation to generation and added to. They just do not belong to me.

Shame is there at times, guilt of course remains in moments, the desire to shove myself down in lies in order to feel like I'm being the person others want pops up. I'm not tossing it away, I'm tasting it, adjusting, growing in my knowledge of myself.

Doing it for the love of myself. That's why I called you for weeks. I wanted to come visit you. I had questions about how you grew up. I wanted to know more about you, and Dad's life too. I didn't want those to fade away without ever having asked.

The excitement to share what I was doing, learning and becoming was bursting inside me. I wanted to sit and see you look at me with pride. I realized I have a knack for working with people. Not completely sure why, but I wanted to create a new movement within the queer community to unite business owners and entrepreneurs. To help others find that self guide deep within themselves. You know I love being on stage and I wanted to share the podcast that I'm working on. I don't care what the results are, how people will take it or even if I'm worthy to do it. I just wanted you to know I have to do it, and I want your acknowledgement. Maybe I just wanted to be heard by you for the first time as an adult. To be seen.

When you finally called that Saturday morning I was excited. After the quick greeting, you said, "I'm doing better, had the knee surgery and had been home unable to go out much."

I replied, "Great! I can see you today, Sunday, Monday or Tuesday." I had set aside my time to come down.

The shock when you said, "O darling, I just don't have time to see you. I'm so busy and the friends… But I have one question for you? Are you coming back to the truth?"

Whew, I knew exactly how to respond, "Mom, that is a choice you made for yourself. I'm making different choices for myself and living my life, my way. So no, I'm not coming back."

You replied that it's too bad, you know. The end is near and this system is ending. I love you… and you hung up.

We broke up. It was clear you were done and so was I. It happened, it finally happened. I broke up from you, the past and the cult. I called friends immediately. My chosen family wanted to know how it went. Shock was the common reaction, but for me it was the most grounded, warm contented feeling within. I was absolutely okay. I stood up to you. I stood up for myself. Resolved that I no longer need to live with guilt or regret. I knew clearly where you stood and I firmly knew where I was going. My own path, charting my own course from now on. I have a life to live. That day you gave me freedom, or maybe I gave that to myself but either way I was free.

The connectedness I always wanted suddenly came to realization. I had a loving family I built by choice and they chose me. You would love Kelly, Steve, Alberto, Paul and Chris, Lori, Chris and Sebastian, Nicole, Greg, Jeremy and my siblings who have always accepted me from day one.

Just know mom I love you deeply. That will never end. One can never walk in the shoes of a parent and I know you tried to do what you thought was best for you and your family. Breaking up sucks but there is a relief when you just know it needs to end.

Thank you for everything you provided. You created a wonderful, strong, funny, intelligent man that is finally at peace and set on a journey that is of his own creation.

"I am the master of my fate, I am the captain of my soul."
~ Henley

With all of my heart,
I love you

Reflections

Reflections

Reflections

PATRICK COOKE
COSTA RICA
Podcast Host of *BEING*, Coach and Musician
https://patrickcookecoaching.com

Patrick Cooke is a transformational coach, creativity catalyst, sobriety mentor, podcaster, musician, songwriter, surfer and father. His enthusiasm, positivity, and passion for life are dangerously infectious and he is known for his innate ability to connect deeply with other souls. In 2012 Patrick left his hometown of Toronto, Canada, and headed for the jungles and beaches of Costa Rica. This courageous leap accelerated his own personal awakening and initiated a journey of profound transformation. It also represented a heeding of the call to honor and embrace his life's work – to awaken and ignite each soul to their intrinsic power as the creators of their own reality.

Chapter Seven
JUNGLE AWAKENING

I fell to my knees. Arms outstretched. Face to the sky. Tears pouring from my eyes. Warm jungle rain pelting my face. I wept. Uncontrollably. Fully surrendered. Broken. Humbled. But not defeated. I had made a conscious choice. To let go of the pain. To let go of the resistance. To let go of the fear. To open my heart and let the energy move through me. Unimpeded. And goddamn did it hurt. But it was what needed to happen. A lifetime of holding back. Hiding. Running. All pouring out of me now like an energetic tsunami. I had taken the leap of faith with zero assurance of any safety net or solid ground. I had entered the liminal zone. Of surrender. Of faith. Of trust in the universe. But more importantly, of trust in myself. This was the bottom. There was nowhere to go from here but up. Yet, in the agony of that moment, all I could was be present. To allow what needed to happen to happen. And so I did. And so it did.

On one rainy September morning I remember being dropped off for my first week of kindergarten. My mother passed me off to one of the teachers at the entrance to the school grounds and, as I said goodbye and walked off, a wave of panic came over me. Deep fear. I wasn't ready to let go of the nurturing presence of my mother, I wasn't ready to claim independence. I turned and ran after her but she was already driving away and could not see my waving arms nor hear my desperate cries. It was a moment that scarred me. I remember it taking most of the morning for me to regain my composure and ease the flow of tears. It's taken me a lifetime to heal the wound.

As the youngest of three boys born to Irish Catholic immigrants, I had a relatively easy childhood. My father had qualified as a doctor in Ireland and come to Toronto, Canada in 1967 seeking employment. As a young couple, my parents showed tremendous courage and resolve in staking out a new life for themselves in the new world. Yet without the support and guidance of extended family they had their work cut out for them. Their own strict upbringings were all they had to draw from when my eldest brother arrived in 1968 and their middle son soon after in 1970. Somewhat of an afterthought (and perhaps even a mistake although my mother would never admit it) I arrived in 1974. I was an energetic child and would always be trying to keep up to my two older siblings and their friends. No matter how hard I tried I was never quite fast enough, tall enough, strong enough to compete and feel included. It was then that I began telling myself the story of 'you'll never be enough'. A story that has stuck with me even until today as I close in on the half century on this planet.

Despite my feelings of 'not enoughness', I could always sense that I was incredibly powerful. Perhaps not in physical stature or strength, but in other ways. I could feel and sense things that others were feeling and often be able to understand those feelings better than they could. I was blessed with an inherent charm and magnetism, attractive physical features and seemed to be of above average intelligence, at least from an academic perspective. The priests of the Catholic elementary school I attended were constantly reminding us to emulate their chosen savior, Jesus Christ, in our piety and humility. Displays of ego, expression or dominance were frowned upon (except when it came to representing the school in sporting events) and so I learned to hide and subdue my powers and creative expression for fear of persecution.

As I grew I walked a fine line between a lack of self-confidence and a palpable sense of incredible power. Frankly the depth of my potential scared the shit out of me. I didn't understand it. It didn't make sense that I could feel other people's feelings and understand them even if they themselves were blind to them.

From Irish descent and with two older brothers paving the way, alcohol entered my life at a very young age. I was 12 or 13 when a friend and I stole our first sips from my parents liquor cabinet. It quickly became my perfect companion with multiple benefits – easing the awkwardness of puberty, subduing my tendencies toward 'not enoughness' and a quelling of my emotional sensitivity and empathic abilities. My solid middle class upbringing in a safe home and a lack of any significant trauma made for a fairly stable and 'normal' childhood in general. Alcohol continued to become a larger part of my life throughout high school and into university years. I was never the angry or violent drunk. Quite the opposite. In fact I was 'Party Paddy' – jolly, jovial and outgoing. Yet, like most young adults, there was an underlying tone of existential dread that pervaded my thoughts. I didn't know who I was or what I was here to do and booze was the perfect way to numb any pain I may be experiencing. It was just too easy to escape into a case of beer and a bottle of whiskey than face the agony and uncertainty of the unknown.

Romantically I was never a ladies man or a womanizer. I tended to be a serial monogamist moving from one long term partner to another. At one point I calculated how much time I had spent being single between the ages of 16 and 44 and the tally was shockingly less than 18 months in total. In other words, I had no idea how to be by myself. I was always a committed, loving and fully engaged partner but I was also prone to dependency, codependency and people pleasing. Even a 10 month solo backpacking trip to Africa in 1999 saw me hook up with three different women for extended periods of time.

"I just love being in love," I would tell myself. Yet I was not nurturing the most important relationship – the love of myself. Only in retrospect did I recognize that I had been sowing the seeds of break down early in my life.

When I first met my wife I was a broken man. I had recently gone through a messy breakup. I was homeless, sleeping on the couch in my studio and my first major business venture and partnership was failing. In many ways she became my savior, picking me up out of the gutter and getting me back on my feet with her beautiful, playful and nurturing energy. Naturally, our early relationship was wild, fun and booze fueled. We quickly fell deeply in love and her easygoing, laissez-faire approach to life was a welcome reprieve from the internal chaos I was navigating. It was far easier to simply be present and enjoy life than it was to face the pain and darkness. And so alcohol continued to be my primary numbing agent when any undesired emotions would surface.

Soon after we married our first child arrived. What absolute joy it was for both of us! For me specifically, becoming a father came with a deep sense of relief. All of a sudden life wasn't just about me anymore. I could finally shift the focus away from me and the jumbled complexity of my inner world and onto this beautiful, innocent being of light. Fatherhood came naturally to me and I loved the new sense of life purpose that came with it. And with the birth of our second child 2 years later, I felt a deep sense of accomplishment and completion – like I had successfully reached a major rung on the ladder of societal success. But I was still drinking.

Professionally I had managed to carve out a sweet little career for myself writing and producing music for advertising and TV shows. I set it up so I could work freelance from home which meant I was super present with my kids during their early years – still one of my greatest accomplishments and something I am incredibly proud of. I took parenting very seriously and was careful not to shirk my responsibilities. My role as a father and the lessons I was learning from the experience would have a major impact on my future healing and motivation to self-actualize.

As a young father in my thirties my drinking patterns began to shift. Instead of being out on the town a few nights a week, it became more of a one huge night out a week thing – typically either a liquid dinner party with friends or a big night out with the boys. Given my long history and my age, my habits were starting to catch up to me. Horrific multi-day hangovers were becoming the norm and the days in between sessions were plagued with anxiety, insomnia and chest pains. It was becoming painfully obvious that alcohol was having massive negative effects on me, both physically and emotionally, but I could see no way out. Everybody I knew drank. My family, my in-laws, my friends, my co-workers, my parents. It was embedded in our culture and in the very fabric of my identity. Was I destined to be 'Party Paddy' forever? It appeared so.

Since my early years I had always had a fascination with ancient cultures, their secretive history and the knowledge that has been hidden or lost. I felt as though there was more to the story of humanity than we had been taught in history books. My curiosity and fascination took me all over the world to visit ancient sites such as the Pyramids of Giza in Egypt, Machu Picchu in Peru and Angkor Wat in Cambodia. There was something viscerally powerful about these sites that seemed to be familiar and resonated on a level that I didn't fully understand.

Later, the events of September 11, 2001 served as a massive wakeup call. They ignited my interest and curiosity in global power structures and the politics of power on the planet. It was becoming clear that again, like the ethos that was beaten into me by the Catholic church, that what we had been spoon fed in the school system was not the full story. My already fully developed disdain for authority began to become even more pronounced and, as I investigated further, I entered a rabbit hole of seemingly never-ending depth. I spent years researching secret societies, untold histories and every conspiracy theory from Atlantis to the faked Apollo moon landings.

My world view was crumbling as it became clear to me that the system was rigged and that we, the great majority of the population, had been duped, swindled and enslaved. It also became clear that the war for power and indeed our very consciousness had already been waged and we, the vast majority of people on the planet had lost. I descended into a dark place that one might call depression. I remember feeling deeply troubled and powerless to do anything about it. And so I continued to turn to my trusty friend to ease my pain and to numb my worried mind – alcohol. It was an unsustainable solution and I knew it.

On the surface I had the perfect life – a beautiful wife, two gorgeous and healthy children, a good career in a creative field, a house in an up-and-coming neighborhood and a solid network of friends. For all intents and purposes I was incredibly happy especially when I was being present with my family and not sequestered into the recesses of my own mind. Yet, ever-present was the deep gnawing feeling of unfulfilled potential. Like I was capable of so much more and was playing small. On many levels I knew I was hiding in the shadows, too afraid to put myself out there fully. The feeling was most pronounced in regards to my creative expression. I held deep fear of being exposed as a fraud, ridiculed by my peers and mentors. Simply put I did not trust myself. Simultaneously there was a massive fear of success, of being fully seen, of shining my light so brightly that it overshadowed others. And whenever I even considered tapping into the unknown depths of my own power and potential and sharing my infinite light, the priest's words would echo in my ears, equating my unbounded self-expression with the mortal sins of pride and arrogance. And so I capitulated. I retreated back into the shadows. And whenever the pain and discomfort of unfulfilled potential reared its ugly head, I would self-medicate. Now with predictable results and ever mounting consequences.

In January 2012 we traveled to Costa Rica as a family for the first time to visit some friends. During our two week stay I had what one could refer to as a 'soul's calling'. Despite traveling extensively in the world, I had never felt anything like it anywhere else. There was a powerful magnetism that I could not explain. Superficially I was drawn to its rugged beauty and expansive natural environment, yet energetically there was an intoxicating attraction, not unlike Gollum to the ring of power. It was overwhelming. After returning home to the city, it took two weeks of sleepless nights before I finally blurted out to my wife as she was feeding our son, "Honey, I think we should move to Costa Rica."

God bless her heart as her only response was, "Okay!"

With little clue as to what we were doing or why, we packed up all of our stuff, rented out our house and committed to a year long stay in Central America. I felt an aliveness and sense of adventure unlike anything I had ever experienced before. Little did I know that I was actually initiating the first steps towards my leap of faith, toward my full awakening. Arriving in our little surf/yoga town felt like we had entered a different dimension. We enrolled our kids in an international Montessori school surrounded by nature and populated with students from all over the world. The house we had rented was steps from the beach. This felt right. Like I could finally breathe. Little did I know how much work there still was to be done.

I have always had a voracious appetite for learning and an unquenchable thirst for knowledge. Some would say I'm a seeker, unsatisfied with conventional rhetoric and authoritarian decrees, I have always sought deeper and higher truth. Synchronistically, the first book I read upon arriving in the jungle was *The Power of Now* by Eckhart Tolle. The maxim "the teacher arrives when the student is ready" could be duly applied here. I was ready to begin my training in earnest like young Luke Skywalker meeting Yoda for the first time. Tolle's masterpiece shifted my perspective in a profound way. Perhaps for the first time, I came to understand that I am not my thoughts. I am not my ego. I am not my mind. Although I had a fleeting and somewhat superficial and intellectualized understanding, I began to recognize the distinction between my truest essence as an infinite being and my forged and illusory ego identity.

Michael Singer's *The Untethered Soul* was next on my reading list and served to cement the notion. I am not my mind. I am not the voice in my head. I am the observer. I am the watcher. I am the witness. Another hugely impactful nugget of wisdom came from Singer: "If you are doing something to avoid pain, then the pain is running your life." This hit home for me. I was avoiding my pain and it was running my life.

Despite the massive change in location, our lives continued on pretty much as they had back home. As the saying goes "wherever you go, there you are." For the following year our rented beach house became a hot spot hotel for the revolving door of family and friends eager to come visit our newly found oceanside paradise. As we welcomed each new guest it quickly became clear that they were not here to rest and reflect. It was party time. Happy to indulge and oblige, I continued playing my prescribed role of 'Party Paddy', only this time I was in board shorts with an omnipresent sun tan. As the first year turned into the second it was becoming ever more clear that the path I was on was unsustainable. The physical effects of my alcohol consumption were mounting. Headaches, upset stomach, chest pains. Not to mention the mental/energetic effects – anxiety, mood swings, low energy. Despite my desire to change it, I didn't see any way out. Alcohol was ubiquitous. And even more disturbingly, it was completely intertwined in my self-made identity. I could not imagine a life without it. I could not imagine myself without it. I felt trapped. So I kept drinking.

As my life and the identity I had built was beginning to unravel and, despite my obvious dependency on alcohol, I continued my pursuance of personal growth and development. I experimented with my plant medicines such as ayahuasca and iboga in vain attempts to satisfy my desire for universal truth and meaning. My cushy career in advertising music was beginning to evaporate before my eyes. Partially because the business was changing but more so because my interest was waning. After over 10 years of selling my talent to advertisers and corporations I was burned out. And the more I uncovered about the true nature of our global macro-economic system and the power elite that control it, the less motivated I was to participate in it. Yet I had no alternate plans to earn income. As my financial position deteriorated so did my confidence and my grip on reality. I was slipping into the abyss of the unknown without a compass and I was terrified. Resentment grew in my marriage as I fruitlessly tried to reconcile my desire for deeper truth and my worldly duties as father and provider. All the while my trusty friend alcohol was by my side to put out fires and numb the pain.

As an attempt to mitigate financial losses I began performing music again. I had played in bands and performed consistently from the age of 14 to 31 but my live career had taken a back seat to my more pressing commitments of raising children and making money. Plus my desire to express myself musically was being (somewhat) fulfilled by my work. What began as simply an additional source of income quickly became something else. Performing became my oasis, my meditation, my flow state, my deepest presence. Each night I would practice being fully in the moment and letting the energy flow through me. Little did I know that I was in a spiritual bootcamp. Learning how to truly surrender for the first time. As my life entered a stage of tumult and uncertainty, music and the creative expression it afforded me became an essential vehicle for grounding and healing but also learning.

Now a few years into our Costa Rican adventure my wife and I were on the verge of making a seminal decision. In lieu of a few interesting (and drunken) encounters with other couples, we began talking about opening our marriage to external physical encounters. Initially this was a titillating prospect for both of us and, as we discussed it openly, both of us seemed to be aroused by the notion. In retrospect we were incredibly naive and failed to adequately assess the potential risks or the primary motivations for such a massive decision, but we did it anyway. We agreed that some external physical encounters could be precisely the right spark needed to reinvigorate the romance in our own relationship. After all we still loved each other deeply and had come to the conclusion that nothing could shake the rock solid foundation of our union and commitment to one another.

I was the first to stray. Although it was a very superficial and somewhat juvenile encounter, it still registered. Not that we were keeping score but there was a feeling that a glass ceiling had been compromised. Not long after my wife came to me with a request. An old high school flame had re-entered her orbit and was planning a visit to our town. As we discussed the possibility of a dalliance we both got very aroused. I genuinely felt a sense of deep 'compersion' or the pleasure experienced in the knowing that a loved one is experiencing pleasure at the hands of another. I loved my wife deeply and I honestly wanted her to have everything she wanted. There was also the other side of it. Selfishly I wanted to have a similar experience, I wanted to feel the love of another as an exploration of my deepest expression.

Soon after, with my full consent and approval, I sent my wife off to rendezvous with another man. This would become one the most difficult nights of my life. To distract myself I took the kids to a dinner party at a friends house and began drinking. My trusty elixir didn't seem to be as effective this time around as the energy and emotion emerging from me was more powerful than anything I had felt before. I kept drinking. Faster now. A few others that were paying attention noticed something off about me but I quickly played it off as nothing. Upon returning home and getting the kids safely to bed, I collapsed to the floor with a bottle of rum and large chuck of hashish and promptly drank and smoked myself into numbed oblivion...

Sending my wife off to be with another man was the most humbling and painful experience of my life. The following weeks saw a beautiful exploration of deep emotion and candid communication, a testament to the sacred relationship and deep respect we held for each other. There were both massive highs of ecstasy, love and excitement tempered with epic lows of jealousy, inadequacy and doubt. It's safe to say that the experiment had worked, at least on some levels, as the renewed intensity of communication between us translated into some of the most beautiful, connected and intense love making of our entire marriage. Then the other shoe dropped. My wife announced that she was interested in continuing to see her new/old partner and so what was initially agreed upon to be a one off encounter turned into something completely different. Something that my already fragile ego was simply not prepared for; my wife's exploration of a love relationship with another man.

With my full approval, consent and encouragement she pursued her new relationship. I have often asked myself why I did not put my foot down and say 'no' considering the deep pain I was experiencing. I wanted to be the 'evolved man'. I wanted to appear strong and resilient. I wanted my wife to have whatever she wanted because I loved her deeply. But I also wanted it for myself. So I endured.

About a month later I found myself on a solo trip back to Toronto to visit my parents. I had left my wife and our kids with her new partner at my home in Costa Rica. Alone in the city, after a particularly hard night of drinking, I had a complete nervous breakdown. I felt like I had just given my life away. I felt as if the support, love and security I had enjoyed in my marriage had just evaporated into thin air. I felt isolated and terrified. Like a lost child with no sense of direction, no home, no strength, no sovereignty, no power. I cried uncontrollably. Completely emasculated and disempowered, it was the lowest I had ever felt in my life.

Foolishly another rash decision was made. Instead of recognizing and allowing myself the space to process and heal all of the deep emotions that were surfacing for me, we agreed that what I was going through was all normal and just a phase. The solution then was simple. Let's find Patrick a girlfriend to restore the balance of the situation. That seemed like a far more palatable solution than facing my darkness. And it's exactly what happened.

As my wife's relationship with her new lover deepened, I quickly fell in love with another woman.

Problem solved, or so it temporarily appeared.

Nothing could be further from the truth. For nearly the next two years, we continued to juggle this tumultuous, volatile polyamorous situation. My relationship was a complete rollercoaster cruising to epic highs only to come crashing down to devastating lows. Only in retrospect would I uncover what had really happened. My wife's dalliance with another man had severed my attachment to her. I am not speaking of the sacred bond between man and woman, that bond is eternal and unbreakable. I am referring here to my fragile ego identity and it's need for external safety, security and validation – all of which I had conveniently tethered to my wife when she pulled me out of the gutter many years earlier. I had failed to enter my marriage as a full, whole and healed human being and the unresolved, unacknowledged emotional wounds of my past were now opened to the world once again. I was being controlled by my pain. At the time I lacked sufficient strength and self awareness to recognize what was happening, and so, instead of creating the space to do the work of healing, I simply re-tethered all of my needs onto my new romantic partner. Big mistake number two.

The instability of the situation grew and quickly reached a zenith. My new lover was demanding that I leave my wife to be with her fully or she would leave. And because I was now beholden to her for my safety and security, I was bending over backwards to fulfill her wishes and desires. Unfortunately it was often at the expense of my now declining relationship with my wife. I was stuck. Caught in a quagmire. This signaled the height of my collapse. My career was flailing, my marriage was deteriorating, my sense of identity was eviscerating, and my trust in myself was non-existent.

In the depths of my desire for resolution I resolved to consult the wisdom of the earth once again. The timing was perfect for another encounter with the live intelligence of mother ayahuasca. I entered the sacred ceremony space with reverence and humility and with the intention and request for clarity and direction. It was a beautiful experience which highlighted the depth of love, respect and compassion I held for my wife, the mother of my children but also the growth and learning I had found in my new relationship. I was at a crossroads and seemed to be facing an ultimatum. In her infinite wisdom, the sacred plant refrained from giving me a straight answer. She instead offered a new perspective. Rather than being taxed with choosing one path or the other, perhaps there was another option I had not considered. A higher path. It was in this moment that I found clarity. I needed to create space. I needed to be by myself fully in order to heal my lifelong emotional wounds and reprogram my deeply ingrained patterns of 'not enoughness' and self-doubt. It was probably the most difficult decision I have made in my entire life. I let my new lover go and she left the country. My wife and I, in numerous discussions, came to the mutual decision that it was for the best that we separate. Recognizing my need for healing and expansion, she committed the most beautiful act of love – she released me. She set me free.

I love my wife deeply and shall for all time. She is my soulmate and the mother of our beautiful children. I hold the deepest gratitude for her and how she found the courage to offer me the most precious gift. She graciously offered me the space I so desperately needed in order to truly know myself. To heal from my wounds. To begin to trust myself. To begin to fully love myself. To remember my intrinsic power and my birthright to live in full expression and abundance. And for that I am eternally grateful.

The gravity of these decisions hit me hard. It was then that I found myself at my lowest point. On my knees in the pouring rain, arms outstretched, heart wide open, fully surrendered to the universe. This was my portal into true self-actualization. This was my reboot. This was my deepest awakening. I had become a humble beginner. Raw, hurting but wide open. And so the healing began.

With new found clarity I then made the most empowering decision of my life. To end my lifelong dependency on alcohol. I knew in my heart of hearts that in order to fully heal, I needed to feel every emotion in its fullest expression and intensity. I could no longer afford to have an escape route. So I removed it. At the time of writing it has been two and half years since my last drink and this era has been one of profound transformation. Exactly one week after I made the decision to go alcohol free the beautiful, benevolent, supportive universe responded in kind. I was invited to be the guest musician at a weekend long retreat at a five star resort at the base of a volcano in the mountains of central Costa Rica. The retreat was for the Association of Transformational Leaders and for the next four days I bared witness to the powerful energy, coherence and power of their group. My search for an empowering and impactful career path had been revealed. I was deeply moved and inspired by the caliber of character and authenticity displayed by this group. It was awe-inspiring and hugely motivating.

Since that moment I have been on a quest – to heal myself, to reprogram my negative conditioning and programming, to come back to wholeness and full alignment, to feel the full aliveness of my being in every moment, to be in full, unabashed self-expression, to live my purpose, my dharma, my soul's mission. Each day I gain more and more clarity and my positive impact grows and grows. I have found my power, I found my calling, I have found my love. I have fully embraced my unique gifts of empathy, passion and creative expression.

There is one word to describe how my life feels now – MAGICAL.

Not because it is easy all the time, not because it is without challenges, not because it is free from pain, but because I am no longer running. I am no longer hiding in the shadows. I am no longer using alcohol to escape and numb myself. I am no longer owned by my pain. I have taken my power back and I am standing in it fully. In full, uninhibited creative expression of my beautiful uniqueness. And the most amazing part of it all is that this feeling is available to each of us at all times.

Life is incredible if you allow it to be. All you have to do is choose it.

Reflections

Reflections

Reflections

RENELLE MCPHERSON
AUSTRALIA
Intuitive Healer and Life Purpose Activator
Founder of Temple of Light ™ Healing and Retreats
https://templeoflight.com

They say you can awaken your intuition if you spend enough time by yourself, and this is just what happened for Renelle McPherson, An Intuitive Healer, Life Purpose Activator, Breathwork Facilitator and NLP Coach.

After spending five years in solitary confinement within a Japanese prison, Renelle knew she was born to create massive impact in the world. Her raw and real awakening has gifted Renelle the belief that 'we are not broken, just disconnected' a belief that she now gifts her clients who take part in her transformational Retreats around the world, which help them heal from the emotional and spiritual anarchy of their pasts, whilst learning to embody the Divine Feminine and Masculine in their everyday life. Renelle attracts clients from all over the world due to her no nonsense approach to life, a much needed awakening in the world of coaching in itself.

Chapter Eight
THE TANTRIC TANTRUM

And as I danced around the gathering of men, I came upon the one who would penetrate my long held wall of 'fuck off' energy.

With his intense gaze he penetrated the armor I had been wearing my entire life.

It was at that moment that I broke.

Unable to keep the mask up any longer.

I bolted from the room in tears.

My whole life flashed before my very eyes.

Like a movie montage, it played out as a sequence of photographic memories.

Memories of every moment it had never been safe to be a woman.

Every moment of abuse, physically, sexually and mentally.

Every non consensual touch, those times I was overcome and frozen with fear, instead of fighting back.

Every time I put a cock in my mouth and was riddled with disgust and shame because the memories that came upon me, washed me away.

Every time I gave over my power, dishonoring myself and my body, to fill the gaping void within.

After I came back into the room, re-joining the 20 other men and women who were now sitting in a circle, and all sharing vulnerably about their experience in participating in the Honoring The Masculine Ceremony, I was feeling like an absolute fool, and embarrassed by my own dysfunction.

I practically begged the facilitator of this two-day retreat to take me on as her client. In my desperation to get help I had assumed that she wouldn't want to work with someone who was so 'broken'.

But I was so fucking done with operating this way.

I was done with not knowing how to 'be' as a woman.

I was done with my own dysfunction, operating from my wounded feminine aspects.

I was done with showing up for relationships from my unconscious and immature masculine aspects.

And in my desperate need to be loved, I was actually killing my fucking soul, and every chance I ever had at being in Soulmate Connection with a King.

I was so committed to showing up and doing whatever was needed to heal myself and love the woman I was meant to be, that I would've walked through hot coals just to get there.

Thankfully the facilitator agreed to take me on as her client, and I invested what felt like a lot of money at the time.

But who the fuck cares, I was ready to pay whatever amount, I was ready to do whatever it took. I paid $1000 for 4 x 1 hour online coaching sessions. I didn't have the money in a savings account at the time, so I went and refinanced my personal loan.

I can remember my mom asking me why I was wasting my money on 'that stuff'. I told her I was done with meeting unavailable men, I was tired of giving my everything only to have my heart broken a few months or years later. I was done with starting all over again when things didn't work out with someone. I also told her that I wanted the skills to make relationships great! That when I got married, it would be forever.

I wanted to become a woman who valued herself. To become a woman who claimed her self worth. To become a woman who no longer sold her soul or her body, for a mediocre chance of being loved.

I wanted to become a woman who was proud of who she was.

I wanted to become a fucking Queen, a woman ready to be with a King.

Yeah I could've read a book or done some online training, but I wanted that intimate 1:1 support, because I knew that it would be the thing I needed to get where I wanted to go.

I knew I'd be held accountable and my coaching plan would be uniquely customized to exactly what I was needing in my journey of healing. I also wanted RESULTS, and knew that if I invested what felt like a lot of money, I wasn't going to fucking waste it! That I would show up and do the bloody work!

My deep dive into understanding relationships, my sexuality, and reclaiming divine feminine radiance was one of the most radical transformations I have ever been on.

The realization that it was me who had been standing in my way this whole time felt like a slap in the face, but what a way to reclaim my power!

Before I had gone to the two day tantra retreat, I had the belief that if I could just be hot enough, sexy enough, thin enough, if I could just fuck like a porn star… then a man would love me and never leave.

Ha! That is some convoluted bullshit right there, and it makes me sad, that that was where my level of self worth was at, and for many more years than I like to admit.

So off I went, to this Tantra Retreat, thinking that I would learn how to 'fuck better', maybe I might get some insight in how to give a better blow job, and yet what I got, was so much more.

Now before I go any further, I wish to share with you my experience with tantra, as I realize a lot of people have some very misguided ideas about what tantra is and is not.

A lot of people believe that the only way to experience 'tantra' is with group sex, polyamory and orgy. That anyone following or practicing it are just a bunch of self indulgent hedonists.

Now, I am pretty sure a lot of the above goes on in society without the label of tantra.

And with it, a bunch of lies, deceit and betrayal.

My experience of tantra has completely changed the way I view men and women, I'm talking about seeing the natural state of divinity that is within each and every one of us.

Tantra taught me how to create the safety I needed to show up as myself, fully expressed, leaning into my edges and vulnerability, rather than wearing a mask pretending how fucking staunch I was,

Inside I was just a scared little girl, one who had feelings, and one who wanted to be treated with respect. I knew that it was me who had to treat myself with respect first, so as to be honored by the people in my life. I also learned a whole lot about pleasure; and not just the getting your rocks off type!

Learning to live my life every day in my 'turn on'. Finding meaning in the simple things, appreciating a fine sunset, the soft grass beneath my feet, giving and receiving pleasure for pleasure's sake, not just to chase the big O.

Tantra also gave me my first full body breath energy orgasm. Walking away from that experience was one of the most enlightening times of my life, and I am forever grateful for the journey.

I also feel called to share with you that is was the Honoring The Masculine Ceremony which changed my fucking life.

During the ceremony that had me bolt from the room in tears, there was a group of 10 couples. All the men were standing in a circle, as the women danced around the outside of it, embodying the vulnerability of the maiden, and the grounded sensuality of the priestess. I had started dancing in front of the guy who I had been seeing for a few months previously, but it wasn't him who pierced my being with his gaze. It was the facilitators partner at the time, a man who had done a lot of work on himself, and with women. He had this amazing energy about him, when he looked at me, it was as if he could see right through me, into the depths of places within me, that even I wasn't aware of. He had this magnetism about him, and a deep grounded awareness, that you don't often see or feel in a man's presence.

The power of being witnessed in such a large group whilst doing this work was something I'll never forget. Being forced into my vulnerability was exactly what was needed. Had I not experienced such confrontation with my own shit, I may very well be that same old girl, operating from her wounded and disempowered aspects.

When I began working online with my coach, I was absolutely stunned to realize that it was my childhood wounds of rejection and abandonment that I'd first experienced with my parents, that had created a subconscious program and belief system, and indeed was the thing creating my reality of feeling unworthy of love and my consistent calling in of unavailable men.

And all the reasons I would emotionally shut down in a relationship never asking for what I needed or wanted.

The same reasons I continued to numb myself to pain, and in the same breath numb myself to all the joy too, never giving myself the space to feel anything, and constantly living out of my head within the prison of my own mind. Trying to control and dominate everything, because if I could do that, nobody would ever hurt me again.

I believe we recreate these scenarios, (in this case, men that could never meet me in relationship) because our souls are screaming at us, begging for us to please heal these wounds with our parents, so we can finally open our hearts, and not only love others unconditionally, but finally and truly love ourselves, to feel worthy and enough, and for once actually believe it.

After doing the hard yards of healing my childhood wounds with a number of different practices from Shamanic Aspecting to Journaling and Emotional Release Tools, my coach asked me what my boundaries were.

Boundaries? What boundaries?

"What do you mean, what are they?!" I asked.

In a nutshell, your boundaries are your markers for what you are willing and NOT WILLING to tolerate, once you know that, you can make defined decisions around who and what you will entertain in your space.

You know how when you are dating a total douchebag, and your friends are there backing you, saying, "He's an idiot, you deserve so much more than how he's treating you!"

That's basically what your boundaries are doing for you, when you're embodying them. They are your masculine protector, and a way for you to honor yourself first.

It's your ability to choose YOU, by no longer allowing or tolerating anyones shitty behavior. It's a way for you to get off the people pleaser bandwagon, and give up your caretaker role for good. It's how you quit abandoning your own needs, wants and desires, filling your own cup first.

And that is what true self love is.

But whoever teaches us this stuff? Because they sure as fuck don't teach it to you in school.

The next part of my sexual healing journey was about self touch and self pleasure.

Often people assume it is about 'rubbing one out'. Not even close, it's about rediscovering how you like to receive touch.

Have you ever asked yourself that? *How do I like to receive pleasure?*

More often than not, we don't voice our needs, because 1) we fear being rejected for it, or made to feel wrong or too much and 2) because we don't even know what we like/want.

I was also utilizing my self pleasure as a sex magick ritual, to call in my King.

It was a really delicious six weeks of healing and juicy femme embodiment.

Learning strip tease and belly dancing in my lounge room by DVD.

Looking at my yoni in the mirror and rewiring my beliefs from one of disgust to that of honor and divine worship for her.

How can you not honor your yoni?! She is magic and worth nothing less than worship.

It's where you came out of, isn't it? Is that not worthy of deep honor and reverence for the miracle of life that she gives?

I also learned the art of surrender; how to surrender into the depths of life, my pleasure and bliss, and learning how to fall into my feminine.

It was not long after this six weeks of blissful healing, that my King walked into my life.

We had known of each other for the past nine months through mutual friends, but it wasn't till this point after the six weeks that we saw each other romantically.

To be honest I had always thought he was hot, but he was a legend of a guy and I never quite thought I even stood a chance.

So the night he first kissed me I was taken by surprise, inside though I was screaming a big fat fuck yes to the gods!

Our relationship blossomed quite organically, not the kind of crazy toxic and intense charge you feel when you've met a wound mate. But with a deep feeling and knowing that this just feels right, it's light, expansive and freeing. Like a nourishing simmer from deep within your soul, that happens when you've ACTUALLY met 'the one'.

The kind of love that grows stronger and deeper by the day. With someone who inspires you, is emotionally available and brings a vitality to your life that only true love can do.

I even asked him months later, what it was that had him see me romantically that first night he kissed me. He said it was the first time he had seen me really smile.

And it's true, I can remember finally being at a place in my life where I was content, grounded, and without a care in the world. I felt switched on, connected and in touch with MY OWN happiness, fulfilled from the inside, rather than seeking it externally.

We spent the summer surrendering in love, going on camping and fishing trips, taking me to my most favorite place in the whole world, the Hill Inlet at Whitehaven Beach in the Whitsundays, Australia. Where the waters are more turquoise than turquoise, the beaches are made of white silica sand and go for miles.

Finally I had the courage to bare myself to someone, in full vulnerability. Finally I had called someone who was willing to meet me there, holding space for that and in return being able to be vulnerable with me.

Being able to stand in my truth and vulnerability in a relationship was something I could never do pre healing, as I had always made emotions weak, I also didn't have the skills in how to consciously communicate within relationships.

Having the tools to know how to do relationships was the best INVESTMENT in myself I had ever made.

To finish my healing journey with my coach, I had agreed to marry myself down on the beach. Writing my vows was a very therapeutic experience, I had cried whilst writing them, and nearly cried again whilst saying them out loud during the ceremony.

Being with Troy has taught me what it is to be a Queen in a relationship with a King, and what it means to be in a conscious relationship of growth and divine worship with another.

People seem to think that soulmate connection means it's all roses, marshmallows and unicorns, as if it is always smooth sailing.

Our relationships are indeed our greatest teachers, and a potent vortex for healing and transformation, if you have the skills and know how to do so.

My King is my most favorite person on the Earth and being with him, has me wanting to be a better woman.

He is like a mirror into the portal of my soul, shining a light onto the places where I am coming from my wounded and unhealed aspects, taking me to depths that I could never go on my own.

Calling me out on my own bullshit, those times where I am blind to see where I am projecting and bleeding my past hurts onto him; and when I have the courage to honor my own boundaries, he honors them in return.

Conscious connection always has me pinching myself, like how did I get so lucky with this dude! He came out of nowhere, and I still catch myself in awe of him.

There are those times it is as if we are dancing on an Earth made of ecstasy, with our love rolling effortlessly beneath our feet.

There are also those times where we clash heads, forcing us into spaces of radical vulnerability, because this is where the growth is, and what it takes to create even deeper connection.

Our relationship is one of equality, and we work hard together to find that sweet balance of giving and receiving in respect to each other's sovereignty, whilst consciously meeting our own and each other's needs.

I find myself bowing in Divine Worship, for the Divine Masculine and Feminine qualities that he embodies and represents, for all of his unearthed, unseen, and yet to be tapped potential. I don't see my lover as the other half of me. He is the direct reflection of where I am willing to meet the depths of my own soul.

And it is from THERE that I can meet his, loving him in his allness. Love isn't about control, but the meeting of two people willing to hold space for each other, and a commitment to grow TOGETHER.

Knowing how powerfully healing the work I had been through was, and finally learning to understand how conscious relationships work, I knew I had to further my studies so I could bring this work to my online programs, 1:1 clients, workshops and retreats.

I came to the realization that my Neuro Linguistic Programming (NLP) Coaching Certificate just wasn't enough, I really wanted to treat my clients from a more holistic perspective, so I then began studying under a Tantric Practitioner and Love Coach, and have since finished my Lightworker Certification and also trained as a Facilitator in Sacred Breathwork Practice.

I see how powerful this work is every day in my own clients, and encourage you to begin your healing journey sooner rather than later. If I could slap you over the head with one piece of advice it would be this:

Take the time to learn how your unhealed wounds are creating your reality, and also learn to understand what your boundaries are and how to embody them!

All so you can rise into your power and never abandon yourself again.

This is what real self love is, and the place you need to be to create conscious and soulmate connection.

Yours truly, in love, light and darkness.

Reflections

Reflections

JASON B. KENDRICK
USA
Communication & Intimacy Coach
www.facebook.com/Jason.Kendrick1

Jason B. Kendrick is a Masculine and Feminine Communications Specialist, Author, Speaker, Reiki Master, Heart-Core Communications Trainer and Heart Centered Living Practitioner. He offers himself to the world in Love and Service to cultivate Peace, Love and Joy within all he works with.

Chapter Nine
THOSE WHO CAN 'DO'
THOSE WHO CAN'T 'TEACH'

George Bernard Shaw is the author and theologian who is credited for the phrase: "Those who can do. Those who can't teach." He is also the author of the brilliant insight into humans with this quote: "The single biggest problem with communication is the Illusion that it has taken place."

I am starting with these quotes because they both summarize what I do and who I am in the most elegant way. You see, as of the writing of this, I am a 45-year-old Professional Interpersonal Communication and Intimacy Coach. However, had you said to me 10 years ago, that this would be my profession, much less my calling, I would have laughed in your face.

The beauty and balance of the Universe is demonstrated with GBS' quote: "Those who can do. Those who can't teach." There is harmony and synchronicity in that statement. Those who can do, because they just can, and they just do. Therefore, they aren't the ones who teach it, because they are busy doing whatever 'IT' is. By that same logic one can surmise that, the ones who cannot do a thing are the ones who desire to learn that thing and then end up teaching others, who likewise cannot do said thing, but want to learn.

This is how I came to the profession I am in now. I did not know how to connect, communicate and much less how to be intimate with another person or partner. I was woefully unprepared for the adult world, especially in regard to interpersonal relationships of the intimate variety.

I struggled through like we all do and did my best, as it were, but came up wanting and lacking at every turn. I don't believe I actually 'dated', or more correctly, had a real relationship with any of the women I attempted to 'date'. I mean I didn't really understand what it meant to date a girl in an open, honest and intimate way. I thought I was but thinking something and doing something correctly are two very different things all together.

I flailed my way through bad relationship after bad relationship until I got so fed up that I stopped attempting to have a relationship at all and only had flings and one-night stands. This lasted until my late 20s, when I suddenly felt the tick of the clock and had the overwhelming need to have a 'girlfriend' and be in a 'relationship'. As I'm sure you can imagine, going from womanizing bachelor to loving boyfriend overnight, did not go well at all.

I went back and forth from lonely and single, to meeting a girl and either immediately moving her in or I moved in with her. From single bachelor to insta-family almost overnight. This was not a healthy pattern to say the least. I kept this on and off pattern going until the fall of 2013 after I finally realized my gross errors in judgment and that I was the common denominator in each and every relationship I have ever had. I separated from my last live-in girlfriend and vowed to stay single and work on myself until I was well educated and far more prepared to finally create a healthy, balanced, open, honest, and intimate relationship.

That was my Break Up to Wake Up, and what follows is some of my story and what I've learned along the way that could save you a whole lot of time, frustration, and heartache.

I've been single for seven years now…

During that time, I have been to countless seminars, conventions, workshops, spent close to $50,000 on Personal Development and Coaching. I have given myself the equivalent of a *Master's Degree* education in the areas of Interpersonal Communication, Intimacy, Masculine and Feminine Energy dynamics, Nice Guy and Superwoman Syndrome. Along with the equivalent of a *Bachelor's Degree* in Neuroscience, Mind Set, Personality Types, Neuro Linguistic Programming, Non-Violent Communication, Hierarchy of Values and the Science of Heart Centered Living.

I was not born a 'doer' in these areas. In many other areas, yes, I was a natural at a lot of things. But, in the areas of interpersonal connection, communication and intimacy, I was as ignorant as any man raised in self-imposed isolation would be.

You see, I grew up in a Southern Military family. Both my parents served in the Army during my childhood. Plus, I grew up in the late 70s and 80s, a time when children were meant to be seen and not heard. It was also the beginning of the era of the dual income household when both parents had to work to stay afloat, so both my parents worked and worked hard.

(For those of you not from the US and may not understand the connotations of a 'Southern Military Family', here is a brief synopsis to help you. The southern states in the US are, for the most part, very conservative and religious, this area is referred to as the Bible Belt. The residents of the South tend to be very dogmatic and staunch in their belief systems. If you do not agree with them or follow a similar lifestyle you may be ostracized from the community and made a pariah. Add to that the Military influences of Order, Structure, Discipline, Chain of Command and Hyper-Patriotism and you may get an idea of the influences of my childhood.)

This meant that, in my household, communication and intimacy were not high up on the list of priorities if they were on the list at all. Both my parents were focused on providing and making sure I had all my physical needs met. However, my emotional needs were rarely if ever considered.

Don't get me wrong, my parents were not some callous evil people who didn't love or care for me. They both loved and cared for me very much. They were just modeling what they had experienced and learned growing up. They both did the best they could with what they had been given.

The 1970s and 1980s were quite different than today. In many ways I believe it was better than today, but in other ways it was lacking from today's parenting models. The mental, emotional, and physical wellbeing of children were not nearly as highly regarded as they are today. I believe that the main mindset of parents back then was to create well-mannered children who would fit within mainstream society to continue some contrived legacy of family traditions.

My father was my biggest influencer when it came to my emotional wellbeing. Having not had a father for most of his life, he was lacking a model to draw experience from. His father passed away when he was five and he was raised by his single mother, who worked, and his two older sisters, who, like most children, didn't really want or welcome the responsibility of caring for a sibling.

My father did the best he could and tried to toughen me up into the societal model of manhood. What I often refer to as the 'John Wayne' model of manhood. Rough, Tough, Stoic, Emotionless, All-Knowing, and Completely Capable. At least that's what I assume as an adult looking back on it now.

I don't believe my father felt prepared or fully capable to be a father at the time and did the best he could, while dealing with his own relationship to self and his family. He said to me a few times during my childhood, that he didn't have a father growing up and he didn't really know what he was doing.

Though, as I look back on it now, I'm astonished at how well they both did, considering they were both only 23 when I was born. The thought of me having a child when I was 23 is not only laughable, but quite absurd and probably irresponsible in the extreme. But different times, different strokes, and different expectations for all.

What I remember most in relation to my father growing up was a very, 'My way or the Highway' approach to parenting. I was expected to do as told and to keep my opinions to myself, especially if they differed from his. This wasn't too hard when I was a younger child, but as I grew into adulthood, this became an increasing strain to our relationship model. I wanted to be able to express my opinions and views, while being respected for having them. This didn't usually go well as it flew in the face of the hierarchical model of him as the father and authority figure and me as the obedient son, that was well established.

What I learned to do was to become invisible and to do just enough as to remain under the radar and not draw attention to myself. I got decent enough grades, stayed mostly out of trouble, and didn't give him any reason to turn his attention my way if I could. I walked on eggshells most of the time and did all I could to keep out of sight and mind.

This dynamic didn't foster much true connection or intimacy in our relationship and as I grew older and became my own person, this rigid structure no longer fit me and I did as most kids do, I rebelled, but in my own secretive way to continue to remain unnoticed as much as possible.

I became more and more secretive and withdrawn from the family. I only participated in family things when I *had* to and usually begrudgingly. This wasn't very different from the behavior of most teenagers, but for me there was an underlying theme that fostered much of this angst.

My teenage years went by as most others do, high school, parties, girls, friends, getting into and out of trouble. Doing all that we could get away with and trying not to get caught so we wouldn't have to deal with the consequences.

I was interested in girls from a young age, probably much younger than is normal or healthy, but that's what held my attention most of my teen years, 20s, 30s… Well, you get the picture.

The problem was I didn't seem to have any problem getting a girl's attention or even getting her into bed for that matter. But, when it came to actual dating and creating a relationship, I was woefully unprepared and out of my depth. I did everything I thought I should for each girl I fancied, but continually fell short of the mark when it came to her trust in me and my masculinity.

As my high school career progressed, I began to surround myself with women as much as I could and considered most other guys jerks or bullies, whether they were or not. I assumed the guys would either pick on me, judge me, or otherwise bully me to make themselves feel bigger and better. This was rarely the case, but it was definitely a story in my head. This, of course, increased my feelings of isolation and not fitting in.

I believe I assumed most guys would be like my father was towards me, or more accurately I projected prejudices I had of my father towards those other boys. Which meant I was harsher and more critical to my male counterparts and rarely was open and free with them until such time as I deemed them a non-threat. This behavior further exasperated my own isolation and dissociation.

I had a lot of guy friends when I was younger and when I was in the Air Force after high school, but for my last few years of high school this was not the case. Since we were a military family, we moved a lot and my last few years of high school were a trying time for me, especially my Senior year. We moved to a little country town to enjoy cheaper rent and I ended up in a tiny little country school for my final year of high school. I felt like I was dropped on Mars. I did not fit into that conservative country farm culture and that disconnect furthered my disassociation from many of my peers. Add to that the fact that I've always looked younger than my years, but ending up in a brand new school my senior year, where they screwed up my transcripts and made me take a state history class, which was a freshman requirement, this meant that half the school thought I was a new freshman in need of some bullying and the other half knew I was actually a Senior. Not my ideal expectation for my final year of High School, to say the least.

Anyway, I left this tiny Alabama town as soon as I graduated and joined the Air Force. My time in the Air Force was a blur of training, travel, and partying. To say that we lived it up during my brief time as an Airman would be putting it mildly. My four-year enlistment turned into just under a three-year enlistment and it was back to the civilian world for me.

After my service ended and as I was at the beginning of manhood, as it were, I really began to shy away from most other men and focus almost exclusively on women. I was 21/22, fresh out of the service and at a loss with what to do with my life. I waited tables, bartended, and chased women as my full-time job. There was a hole in me that I needed to fill and the only thing that seemed to take the edge off was the affection of women. So, chase women I did. Early, late, and often.

During this time, my father separated from his second wife and overnight went from being only focused on work and lethargic most of his off work time, to wanting to be my best friend and hit the bars and pool halls regularly. It was a shocking turn of events for me and one I look back on now with some guilt and sorrow. I was ill prepared and too unaware at that age to realize the importance of that time and opportunity. To this day it makes me sad to think about that opportunity to truly get to know my father as a man and as a friend.

Since I had always conformed to the hierarchical make up of our relationship, I found it hard to distinguish 'my dad' from the man who wanted to connect with and befriend me at that time. I just didn't know how to shift my perspective of him and see him in a different light at that time. He was Dad.

We did enjoy hanging out some during that time and I did learn a lot more about my dear old dad, some things I think I could have done without learning, but those things have helped me to understand the man my father was much better, even if I cringe to think of those details now.

This missed opportunity set the stage for the events that would change my life and rock me to my core in the most fundamental ways. You see that period with my father barely lasted three months. I did not take advantage of it as I should have and would now if I had the chance to do it all over again. It felt weird and awkward to relate to my father more as a peer than my superior, granted he did always manage to keep his position as lead dog firmly in place, even during those days.

During October of 2013, during the time I was feeling the need to leave my last relationship, I received a call from my father to let me know that he had cancer, pancreatic cancer to be precise and that the doctors only gave him six months to live.

This cannot be, I thought. This man cannot be dying. He's so strong and strong willed. Cancer cannot take out my dad… I was wrong.

I went to visit my dad twice in the following 18 months. Yes, 18 months, after receiving a six-month life expectancy diagnosis. Told you he was tough. The first visit was like many of my other visits. Except for his new white hair from the Chemo treatments, he seemed much as he always had, strong, determined, single minded and full of his own brand of righteous vigor. We talked, played golf, went shooting, visited with family and otherwise had a normal visit, with a dark cloud hanging over that we mostly ignored in hopes to keep things seemingly normal.

The second visit was a different story all together. It was almost a year and a half later, he called to let me know that he was done with Chemo and his treatments. His quality of life had suffered enough, and he was ready to go home. My dad was always a pragmatic man, he told me over the years that he did not want to be kept alive if he was ever hospitalized or too sick to live a normal life. He was a man who was here to live life and accomplish as much as he could as fast as he could. So, when his quality of life deteriorated to the point that all he did was sleep 23 hours a day due to the pain meds and other medications he was on, he decided he'd had enough.

I received that call like a ton of bricks being dropped on my head. I had done well to pretend all was normal in the world and that Dad would soon go into remission and ultimately make a full recovery. That call ripped my rose-colored glasses right off my face and showed me the harsh light of reality. My father was about to die.

This man that I had idolized, emulated, loved, cherished, hated, despised, judged, blamed, honored, held on a pedestal and wished more than anything I could find a way to truly and deeply connect to and share my deepest feelings with so he would know how much I loved him and needed him in my life. This man who had been my greatest teacher and opponent throughout my life was leaving me. How could he do that to me? We have so much more to share, to learn, to express, to get off our chests with one another. How could he just give up and leave like that?!

If you've lost a parent, as I know many of you probably have, you'll understand what I write here. The loss of a parent, especially the one who influenced you the most, is one of the hardest things to go through in life and something that has long lasting and resounding ramifications throughout your life to come.

My father and I were two sides of the same coin, I often say. We had the same core and heart, but with polar-opposite viewpoints. We also lacked the basic skills to communicate and connect on a deep and intimate level. A common phrase between my dad and I was, 'No news is good news.' If we didn't hear from the other, we just assumed all was well and the other was healthy and happy. So, we could go months and even years without speaking. Usually not more than a year, due to birthdays and holidays and such, one of us would give in a call the other to check in.

We held this form of masculine communicating, or lack of communicating, as a sort of badge of honor. We were men, we didn't need to talk. I'm sure you can imagine how this would lead to my lack of skill in adapting to my father as my friend after his second marriage ended. As well as my guilt and sorrow over not knowing how to have that hard conversation as he lay there dying from cancer and the chemo. That conversation we all want to have with our parents as they are getting ready to leave this world. That conversation that cleans the slate and says all that needs to be said so that our hearts and souls are free, and we feel complete.

That conversation did not happen. Could not happen. It is the greatest regret that I have to this day. How could I not get over myself and my feelings of discomfort not to go to my dad and express my love to this man that meant so much to me? How could I leave all that unsaid and unresolved?

That last visit ended without the baring of hearts and souls that I so wished and hoped for. Not to any failing of my fathers, he had enough on his plate dealing with the degradation of his body and mind in the end. No, that responsibility lies solely with me and my lack of courage to do the one thing that could have healed our hearts and freed my soul, that is now tortured by this failing.

I did not rise to the occasion and meet the challenge with courage and fortitude. No, I failed in my quest to clean the slate with my father as he lay on his deathbed.

I received that call from my aunt on July 24th, 2015, that my father had finally passed away. Oddly enough, July 24th is the day before my mother's birthday, and she happened to be visiting me in Denver at the time. I chalk it up to my father's dark sense of humor and perfect timing as always to decide to leave his body that day. When my mom was with me and I had my only other support in the world to be there for me.

I sometimes laugh when I think back on it because now both my parents have almost the same birthday or re-birthday if you will. Just like my dad to do something like that.

This painful story that I am writing with tears streaming down my cheeks right now, is the catalyst that changed the entire direction of my life and my purpose, long before I became aware of the magnitude of the impact my father's death would have on me.

Like most men, I shut down and isolated my feelings initially. I could not and would not allow that flood of emotion out right then, for fear that I would be washed away in the torrent of emotion, never to resurface again.

Over the next months and years, I found outlets to explore my pain and grief, and over the last five years found some comfort with his passing. Mainly, I believe, due to the purpose and resolve his passing created in me.

I now am on a mission in this world to save other fathers and sons from the same fate. I am committed to teach fathers how to be present with their sons and how to communicate with them in a healthy, honest, and open way. So that their sons will always know their fathers and the fathers will always know the hearts of their sons are full and free.

I am committed to healing the father and son relationships in this country and the world.

That commitment and vision has led me down the path of learning all about how my father and I failed to create the relationship we both desperately wanted but were woefully unprepared and ignorant of how to create. I have studied and studied and dug into many aspects of our relationship, the good, the bad, and the ugly. I know where my father was lacking, I know where I am lacking, and I am working with other men and women to help heal this divide that is compromising families left and right in this world.

Going through my personal development training, all my spiritual and mental practices like A Course in Miracles, Science of Mind, NLP (Neuro Linguistic Programming), Heart Math, etc. I have come to the realization that we have a huge issue to heal in the world today and that issue is the lack of healthy masculinity and open, honest, and healthy communication skills in relationships.

Nice Guy syndrome, Superwoman Syndrome, Feminism, Toxic Masculinity, broken homes, single parent households, traumatized children, loneliness, addictions, suicides and so much more can all be traced back to a lack of heart centered and intimate connections in families and within relationships. We are all dying to be seen, heard, and acknowledged for who we are and to feel safe being who we are.

I am no exception to this, in fact, I may be the rule in this scenario. I have not felt safe being myself most of my life and have strived in all my dealing with people to be the nicest, most people pleasing-est man I could be… no wonder I have struggled in relationships.

One of the first and most powerful revelations into my unhealthy psyche as it pertained to interpersonal relationships and intimate connections of any kind was the book, *No More Mr. Nice Guy* by Dr Robert Glover. This revelation in book form rocked my world to its core and showed me where my patterns of behavior began and gave me a path towards healing. Nice Guy Syndrome affects a large part of the men in the world today and, as such, also affects women, children, families, businesses and pretty much any other area of life you can think of.

I think this would be a good time for me to bring in the description of **Nice Guy Syndrome** and how that has shaped my life and my subsequent career as a Specialist in Masculine and Feminine Energy Dynamics.

Nice Guy Syndrome, by its very definition, has nothing at all to do with being a 'Nice Guy', but more appropriately would be described as wearing a façade of the Nice Guy to people please and manipulate to gain the outward approval and attention of others, usually women. This syndrome stems from the lack of healthy Male role models for most boys growing up in the last 100 years, give or take a few.

As fathers left home to find work, this left the raising of the children solely to the mothers. This continued for decades and became the norm and expectation culminating in the height of this family model of 1950s America. Men had little to no interaction with their children. They ruled as the King of their Castle with an Iron Fist and natural neglect of their children when it came to time spent with them and rearing them.

My father, in his own way, was a Nice Guy. Being raised and influenced almost solely by females in his family, he was trained to look to the feminine for his validation and place in the world. He once told me that all his life he wished he had just been born a girl, just so he would have fit in. These beliefs and experiences played out all through his life and in the raising of me as his first-born son.

"Hi, my name is Jason, and I'm a 'Nice Guy'."

I have struggled most of my life, especially in relationships, with Nice Guy Syndrome. A belief I created in childhood was that I needed to be liked by everyone to be safe. I know it wasn't my father's, or any of my other family members who had a hand in raising me, intention to teach me that being myself was dangerous or unsafe, but that's the basic message I received or most accurately told in my mind, *Don't be yourself, be what others want you to be and you'll be loved, included and safe.*

This belief that I needed to hide who I truly was and conform to what others wanted me to be, lead to many, many years of frustration, isolation, and self-hatred. I didn't know who I was or who I was supposed to be. I would attempt to be what others wanted, but I could only keep that up for a little while and then I would blow up, self-sabotage or merely just disappear from the relationship, job, or situation.

This lack of sense of self and foundational self-awareness led me down the path of the Nice Guy. I spent a lot of time chasing, manipulating, and then discarding women in my young adult years. It was all about quantity over quality. I was on a mission to fill a bottomless pit of unworthiness that I felt within myself with sex and attention from women. But, like any addiction, the cure would not be found outside of myself or in anyone else. And the more I pursued, seduced, and had sex with every woman I could over the years, the less and less satisfied I became.

Don't get me wrong, I am generalizing a bit, but for the most part that was my existence from my teenage years until my late 20s. I did have a few girlfriends over those years, but to call them a real relationship or anything close to healthy, would be absurd in the extreme. Though, I'm sure most people could say the same things about their early relationships these days.

When in my late 20s, on what seemed like a whim from the universe, I just decided I needed to have a girlfriend and to 'settle down', as it were, in the midst of the height of my partying and womanizing, I set my sights on an eastern European beauty who had just moved to the area. As I am sure you can imagine, it didn't go well.

I cheated for the first six months we were together, was caught several times and we would break-up then get back together over and over. She had to go home for almost a year due to her visa status and we tried the long-distance thing, *which always works*.

Anyway, I wanted to tell you that to tell you this, I was not always the Connection Catalyst or Communication and Intimacy Coach I am today. As I started this with; Those who can do, and those who can't teach. I am a student/teacher of Intimacy between the masculine and feminine because I could not find my way at first. That is what led me to the study of Psychology, Communication, Vulnerability, Intimacy and Nice Guy/Superwoman Syndrome.

Oh, that reminds me, I haven't even talked about **Superwoman Syndrome** yet. Well, here we go.

If you've ever been in a science class that talked about Newton's three Laws, then you've heard of Newton's Third Law. For every action there is an equal and opposite reaction. Nice Guy Syndrome was the Action and Superwoman Syndrome became the Reaction.

Women are, by nature, pragmatic and it only made sense as the Woman's Suffrage movement laid the groundwork for the Women's Liberation movement of the 60s and 70s and the Feminist Movement thereafter, for the women to take on a more controlling role in their lives and the lives of their children and families.

This put the women smack into their masculine energy, but with the added pressure of societal norms for women. They have to raise the kids, clean the house, cook the dinner, run the household and family, while working at or running a business, while looking cute doing it and not asking for help, because asking for help makes them a bad Mom, Employee, Boss or Woman in general.

If this sounds at all familiar to you, then you have either seen it and dealt with it as a man, or you're a woman shaking your head right now, because you just realized how much Superwoman syndrome is affecting your life now.

The biggest drawback to Nice Guy and Superwoman Syndrome is that it negates the very thing we as men and women both need; EACH OTHER!

A Nice Guy will not attract a Healthy Feminine woman because his people pleasing and need of validation from her, turns her off and places him directly into the **Friend-Zone**. I should know, I'm a Friend-Zone Hall of Famer.

Likewise, Superwoman Syndrome negates the ability for a woman to be open to a man and his natural desire to support her. She will demean, degrade and emasculate any man who stirs any emotion within her out of fear of losing control or being weak, because she has long ago stopped trusting men to be men and not just little boys looking for their next mommy.

Besides, not one of us truly needs the other to survive anymore. With the advancements in technology in our world, we no longer have to be in a relationship to ensure our survival or that of our families. We can all get food, shelter, entertainment, and occasional companionship all on our own now. Why do we need a mate or a partner then?

Not to put too light a spin on it, but ladies and gentlemen, the satisfaction you're all looking for comes from the relationship we're all terrified to have now. An open honest vulnerable connection to another human being that could lead to love or heart break, or most likely both/and. Relationships and human connection are vital to our sanity and happiness. We are being systematically trained away from that very connection.

It is time to Break Up with disconnection. Study ourselves and others and learn to be in connection again. You are not your belief system or your beliefs. Those are constantly changing and are not who you are. Your Ego may be attached to those beliefs, but it is trying to keep you stagnant and safe, not open, and vulnerable, which is what is necessary for a happy life.

I speak from experience here. My whole life has been one of being 'on guard', looking for the threat and twisting myself to 'fit in' with whomever I was around to ensure my safety and acceptance. However, if you have ever been around anyone like I was, you know that they don't quite feel right. They seem nice enough, but you can feel something is there, just underneath, that they are hiding or masking. This keeps you from feeling truly safe with them and in a natural, unconscious way you keep them in a surface, acquaintance type of friendship.

This surface, or more descriptively, shallow friendship feeds the fears and insecurities of the Nice Guy. It plays right into his model of the world and increases the isolation and social anxiety that goes along with it. A Nice Guy will feel he has to try harder to fit in and to make friends and connections, but that he also must hide more of himself to better fit in. He may think that they aren't responding to him the way he would like because he said or did something to turn them against him. So, he vows to show less, agree more and otherwise hide who and what he really is.

Can you see how this might have negative repercussions for the Nice Guy? This lack of authenticity is what raises the red flags and Warning signs for others. The fear to disagree with or to not acquiesce to another's point of view causes the Nice Guy to come across as fake and thereby untrustworthy. This is the root cause for all the unhealthy behaviors in Nice Guys and in many others in the world as well. The fear of judgment, ridicule, or of being ostracized from the pack has caused many of us to create these fake people pleasing personas that don't inspire trust or confidence in others.

This lack of trust and confidence from others was pretty much my bread and butter for decades. I just couldn't understand why no one would ever really open-up to me or connect with me like I saw them connecting with others. I mean, they would open-up to me about their problems and issues, and I would gladly help out because I finally felt needed. But, once my services were rendered and they felt better, it was back to the surface relationship we had before. For a Nice Guy people pleaser, this is basically our Manifest Destiny. Help others, but don't receive what you need.

On the other hand, though, there is a more diabolical aspect to this behavior that tends to go unnoticed by those in the midst of this pattern. There are loving and caring people all around us Nice Guys. People who are genuinely interested in us and our well-being, but in most cases, we don't see them, acknowledge them, or can even accept that they are a genuinely loving person interested in us for who we truly are. This does not compute for the Nice Guy.

I have ignored, dismissed, and otherwise turned a blind eye to so many loving and wonderful people throughout my years because of this very thing. It didn't fit within my narrow model of the world and therefore must be a threat or up to something. How could they really want to know me and care for me? And, if they really did care for me and got to know me, then as soon as I revealed all of me and they truly knew the real me, they'd run and leave me.

This inner dialogue is constant within the mind of a Nice Guy, within my mind as a Nice Guy learning to open-up and expose my soft underbelly to the world. Not to mention that I am also a Highly Sensitive Person or Empath, if you prefer that term, and I feel more than I should from everyone around me and it can cause me social anxiety on top of wanting to 'people please' and connect.

It is a very convoluted world I live in and one that has taken me years to even map out and get a semblance of a grasp on. I am a walking contradiction in terms. I desperately want love and intimacy in my life and yet, nothing scares and terrifies me more than love and intimacy. That naked vulnerability needed to truly know another is the double-edged sword of life. It can save your life or cut out your heart.

However, as I am writing my story to you today, I can honestly say that I'd much rather have my heart cut out by Love than have it slowly rot from sorrow. Isolation is easy and safe, but so is incarceration and the cage. You may be safe from harm behind those bars, but you're also locked away from the love that could set your soul free.

We have the chance every day to be courageous with our love and hearts. It is through courageous self-expression and compassion for others that we can create what we seek with our souls. That thing that makes being human worth it at every level. We have the chance to be present, open, honest, and vulnerable with another human being today and every day of our lives. I have that chance now with you. I get to expose my wounded heart and my scarred soul to you, so that hopefully you will feel less broken, less alone, less isolated, and hopeless because you now know you're not alone.

When we share our scars, we free our souls. My jagged edges that I have shared with you, give you a place to grab on to me and to connect with me in a much deeper way that we usually do day to day.

If I only showed you my polished armor of perfectionism and plastic positivity, you'd not have anything to attach to nor would you feel any connection or trust with me. I'd just be another plastic person perpetuating the lie of perfectionism. You would not trust me. You would not believe me. You would not see yourself in me.

I share my scars now with you. I share my story with you. I hope you'll share your scars and stories with others too. Connect from a place of open, honest, real, and raw vulnerability and you will have a friend for life. It is through our struggle we gain wisdom and it is through sharing how we received that wisdom that we create healing.

The magic formula for Healing is: Love, Courage and Vulnerability shared in a safe space with those who have earned your trust and the right to hear your story.

If you don't know anyone that you can share your story with that feels safe and trustworthy, reach out. Reach out to groups. Men's Groups, Women's Groups, Coaches like me, Counselors, Therapists, or any of the other professionals in this book or that you can find in your community. There is a place for you to heal. Take this opportunity to heal so that you can help to spread your own healing to others.

Each One Teach One. Each One Heal One. The World is One.

Thank you all who have made it this far for your co-creation of this book, these words and the healing that comes from it. You are no mere passive by-stander in this. You are a co-creator of life and the magic within, without you reading these words now, this project never would have happened. You are powerful beyond measure and eternally blessed. I Love You! Though we have never met and may never meet in person, know that I Love You just as you are now. You are the Angel of Creation and you are my Beloved Friend. I need you. I feel you. I Love You!

Be the blessing you are in the world and spread your truth to those that have earned the right to hear it. You can change the world, one open, honest, courageous, and vulnerable conversation at a time. Together we can cause a chain reaction of compassion and love that will sweep across this planet.

I'm Sorry, Please Forgive Me, Thank You, I Love You!

Reflections

Reflections

Reflections

GEOFF LAUGHTON
USA
CEO of the Evolving Man
Your Relationship Architect
https://yourrelationshiparchitect.com

Geoff Laughton is an internationally in-demand Relationship Coach, known as Your Relationship Architect, the author of the internationally best-selling books, Instant Insights on Building a Conflict-Proof Relationship and Built to Last: Designing & Maintaining a Loving, Lasting, and Passionate Relationship and a co-author of two other books. He's been guiding couples and individuals in designing and building the authentic relationships and lives they truly desire for 24 years. He's also an innovator in supporting men from all over the world in living more authentic lives of purpose through his global men's community, The Evolving Man, leading groups and coaching men ready to take their life game up to the next level.

Inspired by his marriage of 38 years, Geoff coaches people in how to go beyond the settling that so many people accept with their relationships and lives, to create a life that matches their fully authentic selves.

Chapter Ten
ALL IS NOT AS IT SEEMS

(Wish I'd Learned That In Kindergarten!)

One of the hardest lessons I have ever had to learn is that transformation is not for the weak-hearted, nor for those who prefer their lives to be easily choreographed and controlled. I've had the good fortune to learn this – in ways that completely transformed my life – twice in my adult life. Each time, there was no predicting it, controlling it, planning for it, or knowing ahead of time how I was going to cope with the impacts. What I DID know was that life as I knew it was getting radically transformed (and me along with it) to lead me to what my spiritual and life purpose was always meant to be. It also helped me develop the courage to live both of those rather than the half-dead existence I was living up to my mid-30s.

From age 22 until I was 35, I had settled for a profession that was mostly convenient, rather than being any kind of calling. After graduating from a very good University system with a degree in psychology that I thought I would parlay into a career as a therapist, I decided I needed a year off from school before grad school, so found a job as a technical editor and writer at what was then the world's largest engineering and construction company in the exciting milieu of San Francisco in the early 80s. I figured I would work there for a year, make a little money-heavy on the little! – and then go to grad school, so I could become the next big splash in the therapeutic community.

What I hadn't counted on – and was yet too young to have figured out would be a pattern of big life surprises – was
1. getting totally infatuated with the combination of a regular paycheck and more money being in it;
2. getting seduced by the whole climbing the ladder thing – which I did rather quickly; and
3. meeting the woman who I'd fall madly in love with; get married to, and be with for 38 years – so far.

All of that got me on the treadmill of striving for job security, financial stability, and status regardless of how hard I had to work for it – after all, I HAD been taught that working harder than anyone else would make me a 'good man'. Consequently, what was going to be a year off turned into 16 years of a corporate career that brought the illusion of security and value, but was completely divorced from any connection at all to my body, to my heart, and my spirit. I became a workaholic that, while very good at what I did back then, was slowly ballooning from my normal 150 pounds to nearly double that, was miserable at work, and hardly ever home with my wife and our sons. In other words, I was becoming the man that the singer Harry Chapin created in his 1970's classic hit, 'Cat's In The Cradle'. Yet, I was somehow able to brush all that off as being a problem with the perpetual rationale in my head – now seen as a really insidious machination of my ego – that this is what good men do, and aren't I noble for sacrificing myself, my family, and my joy for being a 'great provider'? All of this would lead to the first of two 'break ups to wake up' that I'd go through (to date).

When I hit 35 years of age, I weighed 285 pounds. I somehow had so lost my Self that I was able to be in total denial that being that heavy was not going to be healthy for me. I got disavowed of that fantasy when I helped a few guys move a picnic table at a company picnic and then ended up being on the ground in agonizing pain from having just sustained a pretty significant strain of a couple of my lower back vertebras. In spite of my chiropractor (who had been able to get me to at least walk) telling me to rest and stay away from work for a week, I went back to the office a couple days later because – after all – I wasn't hurting. When I set my briefcase down and reached forward to get my messages off the desk (no such thing as voice mail then!), I was suddenly back on the floor in agony and unable to move.

That began a nearly four-week period of being confined to bed in so much pain and immobility I was literally and figuratively an invalid. I quickly learned that one can do a LOT of thinking when you're bedridden and beginning to wise up to there being something dramatically wrong with me… or at least with my connection to the Divine. In the midst of that, it finally dawned on me that I needed to lose all that extra weight and break up with my dedicated unconsciousness. Now, I want you to know that my life wasn't *all* misery. My marriage *was* an oasis in all of this, along with my love for our kids. Yet, none of that was enough to solely source and feed my incessant craving for feeling comfortable in my own skin, feeling competent and valuable, and feeling joyful more often than not. I had to be *literally* dropped to my knees to begin waking up to how asleep I had been for so long. So, I thought I'd found THE answer! I'd lose the weight, and then I'd be overjoyed! Right? Well, it didn't quite work that way I discovered.

I spent a year losing 110 pounds. It was agonizing sometimes, and it required something that I had never been good at: patience and discipline. Nevertheless, with all the resistance, struggle, and challenges, I lost the weight. I discovered that I liked being thinner, felt better, and that gave me a big increase in confidence. At that point, I was thinner, had been promoted to upper management in the consulting company I was working for at that time, and thought I'd turned my life around. What I learned next was that all the external circumstances lining up to be what I thought I wanted was not the ticket. It had never occurred to me that there were internal factors that had to line up…and fast. How I figured *that* one out was hugely assisted by a kamikaze attack on me on Christmas Day 1992. The attack was carried out by my ego/mind and my nervous system in the form of a crippling panic attack that hit me while my wife and I were in a bookstore that morning, and I suddenly started sweating, getting severely short of breath, and being scared to death I was about to die.

Somehow, I got through that day with believing it had just been a proverbial existential trick of the light, as they say in the music world! However, imagine how shocked and dismayed I was a couple weeks later when I got hit by another one while just walking down a street. Not long after that, I was leading a Board of Directors meeting for my company when I broke out in a major sweat, was finding it hard to breathe, and was scared shitless... all while still managing to power through the presentation to the end! The next day, I realized that something was *seriously* wrong with me... and that I was going to need to get some help...I wasn't going to be able to power my way through whatever the problem was on my own. This began what I now see was truly a spiritual overhauling of my life that – at this time of my life – was requiring me to break away from my entire conception of who I was, what I needed to be happy, and what it took to get there – and stay there. In other words, I had to break up with my ego to actually have *any* hope of waking up. I just couldn't have ever imagined what it was going to take for me to truly get that point... until more of my life started disintegrating.

To make a very long story at least a bit shorter, I started relentlessly seeking help to heal and stop my suffering. I had done the Erhard Seminar Training (EST) Training in '81, but it really didn't do much for me. Yet, through the assistance of my then best friend, I ended up getting introduced to all kinds of really powerful avenues for healing and transformation that included experiential challenges that forced me to deal with my life-long fear of heights, dynamic meditation, deep *deep* internal processing work with Gestalt and breath work, and – in what would change my life beyond what I could imagine – inner child work. Through the inner child work, I learned that my life up to that point had been largely run and dominated by a young energy inside me that was lonely, heartbroken, ashamed, and terrified. This led me to do an inner child workshop with an incredibly gifted healer which left me utterly amazed at how different I felt the day after. In fact, I was SO transformed and alight with joy that I woke up the next day being *crystal* clear that this was work I was supposed to be doing with others.

In hindsight now (25 years later or so), this was the first of what would be several times in my life where my drive and commitment to spiritual fulfillment and peace would ignite a relentlessness in that pursuit.

Along the way of training to do that work, my mentor introduced me to a woman who was a trance channel (someone who's able to bring different Spiritual energies/presences through them), and he bought me a channeled reading for my 38th birthday. I was highly skeptical until the point where, five minutes or so into the reading, the energy coming through this woman told me things about myself that NO ONE but me knew. Not only that, but it awakened me to a passion, if not obsession, with wanting to do healing work with others – as a practitioner.

Compared to how I had been feeling about my work in the corporate world I hated, I was suddenly having the proverbial experience of eating, sleeping, and breathing my desire to become a healer. I grew totally in love with the spiritual energies of this channel, along with the inner child work. Yet, my egoic fears and attachments also had me feeling like there was NO way I could leave my corporate work and – more importantly – the steady paycheck. I was, frankly, terrified to leave my job – in spite of being SO hungry to get the hell out of it and put my family and myself at risk of being homeless. Of course, the homeless bit was where my doubting ego went first as the only inevitable outcome of me doing such a completely wild-ass thing as building a business as a full-time healer! This internal tug of war was excruciatingly painful for me emotionally. I felt trapped and hopeless, even as I was already by that time moonlighting with leading inner child workshops that were changing people's lives for God's sake. This would be one of the first times that I'm now consciously aware of when Spirit would prove it had my back... even if it was in an initially terrifying way.

The full break came when I had decided that I was going to take the risk of jumping ship and start building my own healing/coaching business, even though I had VERY little true faith that Spirit would have my back. I set a date when I was going to quit, and a couple months prior to that, I had an event at our home where I brought my teacher to do a public channeling with people I'd invited, which included one of my employees that I knew was very interested in such things. What I couldn't have known was that her drug-addicted (now ex) husband would show up in his truck with a loudspeaker telling my whole cul-de-sac that I was running a cult out of my house and had kidnapped, proverbially speaking, his wife. She left to go handle that, but the hubby then started leaving death threats on our answering machine and threats to hurt my wife and kids. That began a whole legal process that ultimately led to my bosses at that time getting subpoenaed to testify by his lawyer. That ended up in me getting laid off (fired, really) with three months of severance... before my planned date of quitting. All of a sudden, it was clear that my spirit, and the Divine, were literally pushing me out of the existential plane with a parachute.

This would seem to be a good juncture to point out that I did indeed wake up through having my life as I knew it – at least the life that my ego structure had created – radically changed by no longer having a job and having the *absolute* certainty that there was NO way in hell I could continue another day in that corporate life... anywhere! So, it was GO time. In hindsight, this would be merely the beginning of a now-24-year journey towards surrendering into full faith and trust in both myself and with Spirit. I just didn't know that there was yet ANOTHER break-up that needed to happen that, had I known in advance, I may have refused to listen to myself and go find some other corporate gig that would've left me feeling half-dead inside and numb to whatever love I had in my life.

You know how SO many movies have that expository device of doing flashbacks and montages to communicate a bunch of movement and developments in the shortest period of time? Well, I'm going to ask you to imagine a montage of about three years where I started to build a coaching business (before coaching was a mainstream thing, mind you); got my first paying coaching client that had been referred to me by a psychic I'd never met or heard of; had started leading my own inner child workshops before there was an internet to market anything on; had begun traveling to fun places to do workshops that helped me also fill my coaching practice; and then – while on a drive through a rural part of Washington state, saw a billboard that initiated what would be the next big break-up to wake up in my life: leaving California – where I had lived all my life – and move to Colorado on nothing more than a strong intuitive impulse. At that time, that was some seriously crazy shit, according to my mind. Yet, my heart and gut KNEW it was the thing to do. In fact, there were SO many circumstances that made the move doable and seemed to verify that it was indeed THE right move to make, even though I was going to leave all my friends and family there, uproot our youngest son from a school he was thrilled to be at, and facilitate my wife leaving her teaching career several years before she was going to be fully vested in her pension. Like I said… crazy!

I hadn't realized until writing this that that time was truly a break-up…I was breaking up with safety, security, the known, and the comfortable to follow my gut and heart. There were so many obstacles to pulling the move off, and yet every one of them got moved aside as if by an invisible force (hmmm!). It was also one of the biggest demonstrations of how much my wife truly loved and believed in me, because she sacrificed SO much to make that move. Yet, it looked like it was all going to be smooth sailing, so I was delighted to finally get to a state I'd been energetically drawn to since I'd been in high school.

Everything fell into place to make the move as easy as could be, relatively speaking. We only knew two people in the whole town we moved to, which was a mountain town of about 1,000 people, as opposed to the city we'd left of 45,000 people. I had several clients I was able to keep because we were working on the phone. We loved our new house. To totally sweeten the deal, we both felt good about the move because I'd gotten a lucrative consulting contract with one of my first mentors/coaches who'd asked me to be part of her team for a two-year gig that was a lot of fun. While it was hard to make new friends and get acclimated to living in a small town, I still felt pretty comfortable.

Let me make a brief aside here: if you want to keep waking up – whatever that may mean to you – be wary of being too comfortable. I've learned that, when you actually say you're committed to your spiritual growth and connection above all else, getting really comfy is going to be disrupted by some kind of circumstance that you're not going to see coming, you're probably not going to like, and you're probably not going to have any damn idea of how you're going to navigate it. How do I *know* this, besides having 63 years on the planet? Well, this was when the next MAJOR break-up to wake up event showed up and rocked everything upside down.

We moved to Colorado in July of 2000. By November of that year, two things happened that were devastating:

1. the contract that I moved to Colorado feeling financially secure with for a while, suddenly went away when our client got bought out by another massive company that then fired all outside consultants; and
2. out of seeming nowhere, my entire coaching business evaporated. I almost literally could not GIVE coaching away. All of a sudden, I was making virtually NO money, I knew only two people, neither of whom could give me work, and my wife had retired from teaching and was in massage school.

In other words, to my egoic awareness, I was completely and utterly in deep shit. During this time, nothing I was doing to try to get work was working, despite the fact that I'd been coaching for a living for 14 years by then. I was despondent, terrified, ashamed, and – by Christmas Day that year – completely hopeless.

I awoke to that Christmas morning feeling like leaving the planet was the only and best option to spare my family any more heartache. This shows you how screwed up THAT whole line of thinking was and would set them up with money from my life insurance policy. At this point, the thought of praying to Spirit, having faith, trusting that Spirit even *existed*, much less giving a damn about me, was beyond my grasp. So, I had the note written, and was ready to do it; however, something inside me practically yelled at me to call my mentor Shakti (who lived 20 minutes away) to ask for help to keep me from doing it. She summoned Sarah and I to a mutual friend's place, where she proceeded to spend all day working with both of us to help me see what was really going on with the money drying up and the deterioration of my self-love and esteem that led up to ALL of it. Through that work, I decided that I would have to find a way to build up the faith that I longed to have in the benevolence and care that the Universe and Spirit was all too happy to provide, if I'd just let it.

The first thing I did the next day was go to our local small-town grocery store, where my teenage son worked by the way, and applied for a job to be a bagger or check out clerk. This was a HUGE ego death for me, given I'd been used to making a LOT more money than a grocery worker was making, along with the humiliation of being 42 years old and having to work at a grocery store! Yet, I also couldn't ignore the fact that it felt extremely empowering to be doing SOMETHING to make ANY money to provide for my family, no matter what my ego was yammering at me inside my head.

The next day, our phone rang, and it was a person wanting to ask me to work with her as her coach! OMG!! Within another week, I had suddenly gotten three new coaching clients from referrals. It wasn't enough to cover everything, but it was the beginning of my awakening to the fact that Spirit *did* have my back (in the ensuing 20 years since that happened, I've been able to see innumerable times throughout my *whole life* that Spirit had had my back). Not long after that turn, my wife had an aunt that passed away and left her an inheritance that got us through until my business got more solid and steady. There were then all kinds of seeming serendipitous events that happened that continue to fuel my life, my heart, and my career to this day. In the 14 years since we left that mountain town and moved to the Boulder area, there's been no shortage of extremely trying times and challenges.

What I've learned – and want to leave you with – is that 'waking up' (*whatever* that means to any one individual) is not a cookie cutter or recipe-driven thing. It's largely unique to each of us that are seeking that. What I feel IS fairly common though, is that it's going to involve NO small amount of fears, doubting, struggles, and opportunities to continually face your false ego identity (which is something that I've had to 'break up' with numerous times) and allow your spirit (with the help of a connection to something greater than you that I refer to as Spirit) to transcend the far more limited ego story you have about yourself. It takes courage up the wazoo, and a huge reservoir of strength to continually work on healing the wounds of your past so you can discover the brilliance and power you've been all your life. Lastly, I encourage you to remember that awakening is a lifetime gig. It's not something you arrive at by some magic formula and suddenly achieve a life-long Nirvanic state. There's no end to growing and waking up, unless YOU say so. I hope my story gives you a sense of how determination, persistence, and a strong willingness to look at what you've actually achieved throughout your life that gives a lie to the story that's held you back can all coalesce into you creating your own spiritual journey that just keeps on giving you surprises, challenges to overcome, and a level of love and appreciation for yourself that it takes to make your own Heaven on Earth.

Reflections

Reflections

Reflections

LISA BERRY
USA

International Self Mastery Show Host and Producer
www.lightonliving.com

International show host, podcast producer and trainer creating global conscious conversations Lisa herself is an international best selling published author with a background in holistic nutrition and life coaching. Lisa breathes life into the dreams of her listener, guests and clients with her enthusiasm and positive mindset and excels in her Lightworker's role as she helps them to turn their content and books into podcasts and helps them express their message vibrantly and energetically.

Lisa is a Councillor and Founding Faculty member of IAUSM, Academy Of Universal Self Mastery, and together with business partner and co-author Tamas Garza leads the IAUSM Media Department. With a desire for wellness for all as her guiding star Lisa recognizes her passion position is to find, help and connect with those who need and want to shine.

Chapter Eleven
THE HORMONE DEBATE

This was the first time that taking a pregnancy test had nothing to do with being pregnant. The single blue line that delivered a negative result for pregnancy was, in fact, a positive confirmation that I was in perimenopause.

There was no big sigh of relief that would have been released by the fearful woman not wanting a baby, nor was there sadness that would have been felt by the hopeful woman wanting a child. There was only an intense mourning feeling as I stared in shock at the evidence on my bathroom counter. Glaring back at me was the proof of what I no longer was: fertile, useful, capable, or desirable.

In a flash, I was questioning all of these qualities about myself. Conflicting thoughts and emotions were flooding in as statements popped into my mind for me to either accept or dismiss.

Lisa, you're old!
Lisa, you no longer have value!
Lisa, it's too late if you ever wanted to have children!
Lisa, you won't ever want sex again!
Lisa, your bones are going to become brittle!

So many self-defeating, hurtful, and painful thoughts were flying at me and I couldn't find a safe place in my mind to process them.

It's not like I thought that menopause wouldn't come, it's just that I thought I still had time.

My 43rd birthday was in two weeks and I thought that I was ahead of the game. Just one year ago, I had declared my intention on Facebook to solve the mysteries around hormones. I had become engrossed in learning about menopause so that when the time came for me, I would be prepared and could transition smoothly into the next phase of my life. In fact, I had become so immersed that when I missed a period, had disrupted sleep, and noticed my jeans becoming tight that I thought I was just having sympathy symptoms but I was wrong. It was my turn and I wasn't ready for this! I had so much more to learn.

One thing I did know for sure was that my body had a history of throwing me curve balls when it came to hormones. I had started menstruating before I was ten and I remember feeling tricked, betrayed, and even angry that something so big could swoop into my life. It ripped my childhood away and plopped me into an unfamiliar territory. I can still hear my mom's voice when she said, "Congratulations Lisa, you've entered womanhood!"

She had said it with such a celebratory, loving, and kind tone but all I felt was loss and betrayal! In my child's mind, I no longer fitted in with the other kids but I certainly was not a woman! I told my mother to never say 'womanhood' to me again. I rebelled against it and I disconnected from the circle of femininity.

After spending much of that day curled up with a heating pad for unexpected cramps, I turned to my mother over a soothing cup of tea and asked her, "Is there anything else that's going to happen to my body like this? Please tell me now!"

I remember her answer so clearly when she said, "Well, there's menopause but you've got years and years before that. It won't happen until you're an old lady."

It's funny how such an innocent and simple statement can have such a huge impact on a little girl. I immediately formed a belief that menopause and old were sent hand-in-hand. The word menopause lingered in my mind for the next 30 years. As I anguished over its inevitable arrival, I built up negative feelings toward the associated symptoms. The idea of hot flushes, authoritative attitudes, interrupted sleep, and weight gain were terrifying to me. If those weren't scary enough, the thought of no longer being desirable or useful were soul crushing and these would be the first beliefs that I would need to break up with.

Clearly, I wasn't ready to gracefully accept this new stage of life when just a few days before I was wrapping my head around the idea that I could be pregnant!

For most of my adult life I've always been constant and firm about not wanting to have children. Every romantic relationship began with two things: 'must love cats' and 'must not have or want children'. It was easy to stand behind this and I never doubted myself.

When I was a teenager, I had incredible pain not only when I was having my period but almost every day of my life. I didn't tell my parents for years because there was a time when I believe my pain was a punishment from God for having sexual relations. That was a belief I broke up with after I found out that I had a serious medical issue and endured multiple surgeries. Endometriosis is an estrogen dominant condition and after the surgeries failed to treat my pain, I tried progesterone therapy. I used to joke with my mom about how she was wrong about me not having to worry about menopause until I was old because using progesterone to manage the estrogen was mimicking menopause.

Just prior to starting the hormone therapy, I was told that conceiving would be difficult. The doctor said that if I was planning to have a baby, I should try before starting the progesterone. I was 19 and had just started dating a new man but I didn't like hearing that a baby might not be in my future. I made the decision to try to conceive and after a year of ovulation therapy failed, my self esteem plummeted. I became consumed with the belief that God didn't think I was good enough to be a mom.

I remember sitting alone in my living room, in total darkness. My heart was broken and tears would stain my cheeks in a hot salty mess of pain and mascara. I needed to break up with this sadness and find a way to feel whole and worthy again. That was the last time I ever looked at a pregnancy test and hoped it was positive. At that moment, I decided that I'd accept the 'forced menopause' and go on hormone therapy.

I was now in a faux menopausal state in my early 20s, I gained weight that felt like a bubble had wrapped around me. My sex drive vanished and I couldn't stand being touched. My voice lowered making me shy and embarrassed to sing. I developed multiple food allergies and suffered from horrendous hot flushes.

The changes tore my identity from me and I became a shell of my former vivacious, lovely self. I became severely depressed and every day was a chore to live through. After a few years of wallowing in complete self-loathing, I finally said enough was enough! I wanted to be happy again. I stopped all hormone treatment, I turned to nutrition and a healthy holistic lifestyle. I began understanding the body and hormones. I graduated as a registered holistic nutritionist and life coach and ran with this new power! The new power I call Self Love – Cell Love.

I was a new person. I had woken up to becoming a healthy young woman who wanted to nurture the world and not just one or two people by having children. This knowing gave me confidence to open my heart and love the stage of life I was in. When I removed the pressure of having to find a man so that I could start a family, my entire world opened up. I felt empowered by shedding the belief that I had to get pregnant or that I was someone who was broken if I couldn't. I claimed ownership of a life that felt ageless, independent, and free! I realized that my life purpose was to study and learn more about hormone health and Cell Love so that I could connect with other women.

As I face menopause in my 40s now, it's clear to me that I have connected hormones to my identity, to my value, and to my potential as a woman. Realizing this and standing with deep love for myself I have wondered how many other women have done the same thing? Was there something that I could share to help them see that those beliefs should be flat out dumped? Could there be an opportunity to help other women break up from beliefs, opinions, and identities that are linked to low self-worth?

That sounded like I was really comfortable in my own skin, right? That I woke up to rainbows and whistled happy tunes every day but the truth was, I still had some work to do because as the day went on after the pregnancy test confirmed the onset of menopause for me, many self-doubting thoughts swirled around in my head.

Amongst the negative thoughts, there was a surprising feeling of freedom. It caught me off guard and left me feeling like I was being let off the hook for something. These were bizarre emotions because they were completely at odds with the imprisoning fears that I had about becoming old!

I sat, frozen in an emotional frenzy. Thoughts appeared in my mind and I became an observer as I let them flow through me. I realized there was no longer an expectation for me to have children. I wouldn't have to watch the calendar for my monthly cycles and I wouldn't get that darn period pimple, three-day migraine, or sore nipples ever again!

As the thoughts appeared, I found myself switching from feeling free to worried, loving to judging. I found myself in a very new and unfamiliar place because being able to have children and not wanting them was very different than no longer being able to.

This new position in life had left me feeling shaky and unsure. If I accepted my menopausal ruling, could I accept it gracefully? The truth was that I hadn't actually lost anything when I realized that I was no longer able to conceive. What I wasn't expecting to feel was the loss of control when the choice was taken away from me! I ran out of eggs; my basket was empty and I wasn't going to get a refill. I was stuck in denial and unable to believe or accept that the decision to not have a baby was no longer mine.

I've never been a fan of feeling disempowered so I knew I had to switch my thinking. In order to move forward, I needed to feel that menopause had no negative impact on my value or self worth.

In order to feel a sense of empowerment, I needed to find a way to honor each stage of my life. I imagined myself as a 'crone', living unapologetically, respected and with great experience. As quickly as the image of the little old lady showed up, the devil's advocate revealed itself next and it knocked me to my knees. The saying "you want what you can't have" really fits here.

The day I was going to do the test I had thoughts that I had never considered before! The words escaped my lips before I could catch them and I said, "I think I may want this baby, if I am pregnant!"

The idea that I would welcome a baby in my 40s while I was actively preparing for my impending 'hormonal retirement' was surprising to me. I questioned if I suddenly opened up to having a baby because I was trying to buy time for myself? Was I rebelling against menopause? Maybe my clock was ticking and I just didn't want to miss my last chance to use a good egg? Was it my last chance at creating a human being with someone that I loved? Most importantly, was it an attempt to hold onto what I believed was my worth and value in this world?

These thoughts needed to be explored, honored and turned into a conversation. This wasn't just about having a baby in my 40s, this was about way more! This was about me and how I'd brought these beliefs into every relationship I'd ever been in. That was me waking up and taking ownership of my value.

Well, talk about being nervous to initiate a conversation with my man about my insecurities, ageing, hormones, personal value and then to top it off by having to ask him if he wanted a baby, after both of us were 100% against it!

That's actually the one thing I was counting on, him being firm on his no to having children. The belief in his certainty of not willing to be a father was giving me a bit of grounding in this very confusing time. When we first started dating the baby discussion came up immediately and we were both quite happy when we established that we were both against having a family. We were in total agreement. So, in that moment when I chose to make the confession that I was 'getting old' and could be in perimenopause, but that I could also be pregnant, I felt confident that he would agree that we didn't want a baby.

I was wrong! Our conversation went in a totally unexpected direction as my loving man looked at me with his heart and said if you are pregnant and you want this baby then I'll support your decision.

My mouth dropped and again I stood in the most bizarre unrecognizable world. I now had more conflicts to resolve and the 'life isn't fair' began welling up in me! I was screaming inside. Silently accusing this sensitive, committed and loving man of abandoning our deal of no babies! I told him that I was not being left to make the decision on my own. If I was pregnant then we would make our decision together.

For me, what just got really heavy was that now I had it in my head that maybe he did want a baby and maybe I wanted a baby too. What if I took that test and I wasn't pregnant? Would we feel like we had lost something that we never actually wanted? Maybe there had been a change of heart and now he wanted a baby? If the test was negative and I was in perimenopause, then the option wouldn't be available for us to explore together. I felt like my world was crashing! My past was coming back to haunt me and all of the pressure and questions of 'am I good enough' and 'am I able to reproduce' were creeping back into my mind.

Twenty-four hours before I even considered taking the test, I was feeling rather calm about entering the next phase of my life. All I had really wanted was to know that getting older was okay. I wanted to feel accepted for fluctuating hormones and pant sizes. I wanted my lover to remind me that our hearts don't get old and our spirits never fail. I wanted to hear that I wasn't alone and that I would still fit in even if my skin became loose enough to fit another person. Now I wanted to know that I was and always would be valuable and worthy with or without a baby. There were way too many insecurities for my boyfriend, my lover and my friend to ease and comfort. It was incredibly unfair for me to expect him to smooth away this cascade of emotions.

My mom passed away when I was in my mid 30s and she was always so open and helpful about both her body and emotions. I missed her and my safety place for those comforting hugs. Feeling the void of a woman's role model, I knew I needed support and connection.

Since that post on Facebook a year ago, when I resolved to solve the mysteries of hormones, I've had the most incredible journey. I've talked with women in their menopausal years and learned from their experiences as they shared their knowledge.

My favorite comment was from a woman in her late 60s who said, "Oh, menopause! Once you're on the other side it's juicy!"

I was so intrigued by this. I asked her what she meant. She shared that once hormones settle down and you lovingly step into the new beautiful phase, things get juicy again. Your passion, your power, your body, and your acceptance of your new position is like receiving an honored position. She shared with me that connection is the key to successful menopause. Connect with women of all ages and celebrate all phases. Talk about what you're experiencing and don't be alone. Let others remind you that you're not in the waiting line for death. How you serve and experience may look differently than before but that you still have so much to offer. I fully support that lady's advice about connection because that single post, which I wrote with complete transparency and humbleness, allowed my heart's request for help to lead me to people, protocols, and techniques to support my transforming body. I've met the most amazing women at every stage of their lives! I've woken up to a world full of support! I'm so grateful to learn that as estrogen drops, inflammation rises. This is a time when aches and pains creep in and I would never have linked my sudden sore knee or stiff fingers to my hormones!

I hold the stories and experiences from other women as sacred knowledge that help me and others to feel comfortable in our journeys through menopause. I encourage women to begin conversations as often as they can and ask questions like, "What nutrients does my new body need?", "What exercises are best?" and "I'm experiencing this, have you?"

We all talk about anti-aging like it's what we had for breakfast and retail markets openly advertise their miracles cures. Quietness, shame, blame, judgment and loneliness is what I'm breaking up with! Conversation and connection are what I'm waking up to!

Hello perimenopause! Here I happily come!

Reflections

Reflections

Reflections

BRICE HANCOCK
USA

CEO, Mile High Continuing Care
www.milehighcontinuingcare.com
www.milehighsoberliving.com

Brice Hancock is the CEO for Mile High Continuing Care and Mile High Sober Living which is a treatment center and sober living company in the City Park neighborhood of Denver. He is a single dad and enjoys travelling, art, and the outdoors. He is also a realtor, musician, and is an active member of Denver's recovery community.

Chapter Twelve
LAST CALL FOR ALCOHOL

I sit on the edge of my bed just like I do every morning waiting to see if I'm going to puke. And just like every morning, I run to the bathroom and puke… violently and uncontrollably. It's usually dry heaves but sometimes there's a trace of blood mixed with water that I managed to drink throughout the night. Then I sit and wipe the tears from my eyes and catch my breath. Next, like clockwork, I put on bleach stained jeans, a beer or liquor t-shirt that a liquor rep left at the bar, and a baseball hat backwards on my head. I also slip Crocs on my feet, which are the worst shoes ever. Then I quietly head out to the garage and look behind the washing machine, behind the large shelves, and behind the grill on the patio. I'm looking for wine that has hopefully been left there by my wife. We play a game where we pretend to not know the other one is drinking. I hide vodka or tequila and sometimes have beers in the fridge. She hides wine. Then she forgets she hid it and I'm in withdrawals, so I need it. She does laundry and drinks and every time she goes out to change a load, I run to the bathroom and drink whatever I have hiding either in my sock or under the sink or behind the toilet. Eventually she wakes up and appears with our son, Trace. By this time, if I haven't found her wine, I'm totally craving booze and, make no mistake, craving is suffering to an alcoholic.

The morning game is that we're both hungover and she tries to keep an eye on me and I try to get to the bar I own; to drink. At this point, I'm completely physically dependent on alcohol so if I don't keep it in my body I feel withdrawal symptoms. I'll probably take some Klonopin that is prescribed for anxiety and immediately start making excuses why I need to drive separately to get to the bar. See if she comes with me, I won't be able to drink because it will start an argument. I usually manage to get in my car ahead of them and drive. On the way, I need to figure out how I'm going to get there first or I'll have the same problem which is she'll go in at the same time and I won't be able to drink. I'm not proud but there were times where I would hit a light just as it turned from yellow to red so I could blaze through the intersection leaving her at the red light. This would get me a few minutes' lead. Once I have this lead, I capitalize on it by driving fast and make a wide sweeping turn into the parking lot and park. As I was parking, I'd have everything I needed in my hand so I could run quickly to the front door of the club. Slipping the key in and opening the door smoothly was important. I didn't want to be slowed down because I needed that vodka. Once in, I'd sprint the length of the bar, wheel around the trash can, and slip a plastic pint glass from its resting place stacked on top of the other plastic glasses. All the plastic pint glasses are washed and stacked the night before and when you stack wet plastic glasses they tend to stick together. This made it hard because I definitely don't want to pull the stack over. Then from there I'd scoop whatever ice was left in the bin from the night before and put it under the gun. Holding the gun with my left hand and the gun with my right hand I'd squeeze five shots of well vodka into the pint glass. This part seemed like it took forever. 1, 2, 3, 4, 5 and then hold my breath and chug. Chugging was difficult because my body would want to throw up again. Seeing what was killing me was also making me well. I could usually keep it down and then I'd sit and catch my breath but not for too long because she was coming. I would grab quarters out of the register and continually scan the parking lot as I made my way across the bar to the candy machine that had Hot Tamales. I believed they would hide my breath and then I'd get a bucket by the back door, pour bleach right on the floor of the men's room and start mopping to pretend like I was diligently cleaning. Then I'd hear her and in seconds she'd walk in with Trace in her arms, accuse me of drinking and then we'd argue and then she'd leave. Obviously, I'd keep drinking for the rest of the day. At the end, I was drinking about a half-gallon of vodka a day.

This was a typical morning for me. They weren't always like that but they were close to some variation of that. See I had been drinking like an alcoholic since I graduated high school. I literally blacked out every single night unless I was doing cocaine or I was staying at my parent's house. After college, most of my friends went on to have a regular life and I moved to Baltimore and after a few years was heavily addicted to heroin and regularly smoking crack. In 1997, I moved to Denver to escape. I immediately got a DUI, continued doing cocaine, and played guitar in a band for the next 10 years. After 2007 though, it was just alcohol. All day, every day. In 2007, I fell ass backwards into the opportunity to buy a music club with no money down. So about 2011, I began having serious health problems all caused by my alcoholism.

I had what alcoholics call 'the shakes'. These are withdrawal symptoms and I had them every morning upon awakening. Physical and mental health problems. I was anxious and depressed. I was having panic attacks and on occasion fainting. I was bleeding when I went to the bathroom. I was obviously throwing up on a daily basis and I had various odd symptoms such as sores on my body, my fingernails were weak and would tear, I was losing my hair, and at one point I had a layer of fluid between my stomach and stomach lining making me look quite bloated. I also had a doctor who would treat the symptoms of my alcoholism and treat them like individual problems. He would also prescribe medications like pain killers. I was also on mood stabilizers, anti-anxiety meds, meds for sleep, etc. At times, I would lose my temper and kick things so I began to have pain in my foot. I thought it was a broken toe and it turned out to be gout. I was in and out of the doctor a lot one year. Anxiety, fainting, depression, insomnia, gout, sores on my back, I had this odd pain in my shoulder, fluid in my stomach lining, constant diarrhea with blood. Sorry, it's gross, I know.

At one point, I needed to get health insurance so they sent a technician out to my house to draw blood. A week or so later, they denied me coverage saying my liver enzymes were elevated. I ignored it and went on about my business with no health insurance. I was at the tail end of a bunch of visits to the doctor including the fluid in the stomach lining deal and we both agreed that a blood test was in order. He drew blood and scheduled a visit to get the results.

I was in the examination room and he popped his head in and said, "Hang on I'll be right with you." Something about the way he said it alarmed me and I'll never forget how he approached me with his clipboard. He sat on the desk sort of casually leaning with his leg hanging down and he looked concerned and he turned the chart around and held it for me to read and said, "You're a late stage alcoholic."

I looked at the clipboard. I looked at him and back to the clipboard. I'm a what? At the top, it said 'Alcohol abuse; severe'.

And he continued, "Your liver enzymes are off the chart, your pancreas is stressed and I'm surprised your heart hasn't stopped. I give you a year to live if you can't stop drinking."

And then silence. I mean what do you say? Are you sure about that Doc? If I drink less can I drag that out to three or four years? How bad is an alcoholic death anyway?

He didn't seem to be very hopeful either. He said, "I don't know how to help you stop." He told me about medications to help with cravings and sent me to another psychiatrist. Then he said, "I once had a patient like you. She had cirrhosis of the liver and she went to Alcoholics Anonymous meetings and came back a year later completely changed."

So driving back to the bar with thoughts of an early death spinning out in my head, a seed had been planted. He said I had a year to quit drinking.

And I drank for close to two years.

I literally couldn't stop.

I had lost the power of choice. Physically, I was totally dependent and mentally I didn't know how to stop. I knew I was dying but every day I'd think, *I'm not going to die today. I'm just going to get drunk today* – and it continued.

I can't remember the day I stopped drinking. I started going to 12 step meetings but I hadn't stopped drinking. I would go to a meeting and then drink that day and night, and then a few days later I would go to a different meeting and repeat the cycle.

Then one day, for no special reason, I just stopped.

I went through physical withdrawals and kept going to meetings and started putting together some days sober from alcohol. Now, I'm not going to delve into what the 12 Steps actually are or how they work but there's a process to the program and I didn't do it. They talk about God in 12 step programs and I didn't believe in God and I didn't want to hear about God. So when people shared, no matter how much I related to them, if they mentioned the word God I'd disregard most of what else they had to say. I also didn't want to be boring or bored, and I assumed life as a sober man would be boring.

I basically attended meetings, judged everyone and hated it. I hated myself and I hated my life. I was miserable. See alcohol wasn't really my problem. It was my solution… to everything and now that I had taken it out of my life I was depressed, anxious and miserable. So, I remember right after I got a 90 day chip, I started thinking about drinking. I mean maybe it wasn't that bad. Maybe the doctor was wrong. Maybe I'd be okay. Then an argument started in my head that I had zero chance of winning. First it was a conversation. It sure would be nice to drink. Then it was sometime in April of 2013, I decided if I made it to September, I'd drink on the backpacking trip with my friends, and then immediately I decided I'd drink when my wife went to see her parents in July. The next thing I knew, I was on my way to the liquor store. Just like that I was drunk. It made me feel guilty and mostly like a failure. So I started the pattern of in and out again. Hit a meeting, drink, hit a meeting, drink.

One day, I was in a meeting and I was sharing some bullshit and I pointed to the 12 Steps hanging on a banner on the wall and I said, "Someone explain this bullshit to me. Explain it and then I'll try it!"

Next thing I knew an old woman was yelling at me. She was pissed and was being very honest. She yelled, "You think you're so goddamn smart, well, you're not! You're going to keep drinking and then you're going to die!"

I wanted to disappear.

Then a gruff biker in a leather vest said, "Hey if you're going to be a jerk just go ahead and drink. The teacher's in the bottle man."

So I did. I recommitted to the alcoholic lifestyle again and decided to stop going to meetings. In a couple weeks I was right back to where I had been before. I was waking up with the shakes and hiding shooters in the bar. The problem was I had seen the other side. I had met people who drank like I did who had succeeded in sobering up and they seemed happy.

Then one night something would happen that would change me forever.

I was sitting in my office at the bar, drunk, surrounded by liquor bottles because my office was also the liquor storage closet. I was sitting with my head in my hands and I basically had what I describe as a nervous breakdown. I disassociated because I couldn't handle reality anymore.

Then I called an old friend who I hadn't talked to in years and asked him if he had a gun.

He coordinated with my wife to take me to rehab. I felt good about that. I felt like I needed some professional help.

I had a long uncomfortable weekend waiting to go to rehab but instead of rehab I ended up in Centennial Peaks Psychiatric Hospital. I remember sitting in the waiting room waiting for a nurse feeling very disassociated from my physical body. There was a poster on the wall facing me that had the benefits of electroshock therapy in bullet points and I remember thinking, *Maybe I do need that because I'm definitely crazy.*

Psychiatric hospitals are awful. They strip searched me and took my belt, shoe laces, and jewelry. They took my cell phone, clothes and gave me some green scrubs and socks with grip tape on the bottoms. They took my medication from the outside and immediately started giving me new non-narcotic medication like Trazodone for sleep and anxiety. They assessed my mental health and if I was actually suicidal or not and immediately moved me from the psychiatric unit to the one with the other alcoholics and drug addicts. We attended groups and therapy all day and went to different kinds of recovery meetings at night.

I was assigned a psychiatrist who was going to give me a diagnosis. I felt pretty sure I was bipolar since I'd been diagnosed that before. Usually it was a milder diagnosis of bipolar II or major depression with hypomania or dysthymic disorder, but when I saw him I really turned it on. I told him all the greatest hits and all the symptoms and stories I had accumulated over the years and then came the big moment. He gave me a diagnosis of bipolar, with rapid cycling and post traumatic disorder from early childhood trauma. I was relieved, and even excited.

Booyah!

Jackpot!

This explains why I can't stop drinking and it explains how I feel when I'm not drinking. Part of me definitely would have rather been mentally ill than alcoholic because then it wouldn't be my fault. I wouldn't really have to take responsibility and, most importantly, I could medicate myself. So they put me on a massive dose of mood stabilizers like Depakote, Lamytcil, and of course Trazodone and I was comatose. I had a decision to make. Did I want to be a mental patient or admit that I was powerless over drugs and alcohol?

One day, at lunch, my wife brought my son Trace to visit. He was about 18 months at the time. The hospital staff came and pulled me out of lunch and brought me down to a room where I sat with her and Trace. I tried to act like everything was fine and we made small talk. It seemed odd to make small talk because I still had the very real sense that I was probably going to die. So there I was, playing cool chatting and then the staff member in a blue shirt came and told me it was time to go. I stood up and before I could even say goodbye, my very small son, realizing I wasn't going home with them, began to cry. I was crushed. Many of us feel like our addiction isn't anyone else's problem because we're only hurting ourselves. It was now painfully obvious this wasn't true. My circumstances were having a horribly negative effect on my son.

My life wasn't only all about me.

The day was July 4th and we had a recovery meeting after dinner, and it was really intense. By the end, a bunch of us were crying. I don't like crying in front of complete strangers but I was straight up ugly crying. After the meeting, we went out to the courtyard where people smoke and there were fireworks going off in the distance. As I watched the fireworks through a small crack in a 15 foot high security fence, designed to keep me in, the explosions seemed so tiny off in the distance. It hit me that I wasn't allowed to be a regular person enjoying fireworks with his family. I didn't have my freedom. At that moment, I felt very alone and very sad.

At rehabs all over the world, they prescribe Trazodone for sleep. It doesn't really work that well, especially for anyone who has been passing out for two-and-a-half decades. However I believed that if I took it and then laid down immediately, I'd be able to fall asleep. At Centennial Peaks, the nurses hand out the medication prior to bedtime which is around 10 pm. After the fireworks, I was late to the nurse's station so they told me I had to miss my Trazodone. Naturally, I was furious that I wasn't going to even get any so I got into an argument that ended by me asking the nurse for her name and who her superior was and by the time I got to my room I was sufficiently angry that I probably wasn't going to sleep at all. So there I was, feeling very sorry for myself from the meeting, and missing out on the fireworks, followed by the argument with the nurse.

In the next bed, my roommate snored, and I was reading the only book I was allowed to read which was *The Big Book of AA* and there's a chapter on being Agnostic. An Agnostic is a person who believes that nothing is known or can be known of the existence or nature of God. I was reading a passage and it basically said that, as an alcoholic, I needed a spiritual experience sufficient to bring about a personality change enough to overcome alcoholism.

Okay. It also talked about being open minded and as I was reading it several things happened. I needed to know why my life was turning out so badly and the answer was clear. Drinking. At that moment, I realized I didn't have to believe in God, that I just need to be open minded.

The events of the day taught me that my tendency towards selfishness was my problem. In fact, the truth was that I constantly thought about myself, and that I had always believed that I should be able to solve my problem. I had gotten to a point where I no longer trusted my own thinking. I didn't know how I was going to save my marriage. I didn't know how I was going to save my business. I didn't know how I was going to stay sober. I didn't know, and the truth is I didn't care.

In retrospect, I realize it was good that I didn't trust my own thinking because it allowed something to help me. At the time, I only knew that I was scared and I didn't have any answers. I no longer trusted my ability to solve my problems on my own. I also realized that I wasn't the first person to have this particular problem and that many others had overcome it.

Suddenly, I was hit with a warm sensation that I can only describe as unity, love, and a connection to all of mankind.

It didn't matter if I knew any of the answers because I was struck with the sensation that everything was going to be okay. I felt like I didn't want to live unless I could live the truth and the truth is that I needed to completely change my life. I also knew that I wanted to live and that I could change my life. I surrendered completely. I no longer wanted to run my own life and I let go of the belief that I needed to do it. I had the feeling that everything would be okay if I let it, and I stopped trying to control everything. Einstein believed that we live in a friendly universe. That means that there's something trying to help me and I just had to let it.

The day I got out of the hospital, I immediately went to a 12 step meeting. I shared and told the story of my awful trip to the mental hospital. I even cried. A guy shared after me that he used to call trips to the looney bin, a vacation. Everybody laughed. They weren't laughing at me. It was the laugh of people who are in recovery. They've been through hell and are on the other side. It made me feel good. The guy who shared was a Mexican dude and he was covered in tattoos. I had met him before. He was hilarious and he loved being sober.

After the meeting, I stood outside talking to him and I said, "I don't think this is going to work."

He replied, "You don't have to think it's going to work, you just have to do it."

I asked him to take me through the steps.

I spent the next year working the steps and watched as my life fell apart. I got divorced. I sold the bar. I traded in my old identity for a new one.

It felt scary while it was happening but it's exactly what needed to happen. I needed to die in order to be reborn. I was being given a new perspective. I moved to a house in the mountains outside of Denver. For the first time ever, I became a father, a son, a friend, and a productive member of society. Like I said, I won't discuss in detail the 12 steps but I will tell you they are the most transformational process I've even been involved in. I no longer have any desire to drink or do drugs. None. I have been given a sense of freedom and I emerged from the process feeling like I was no longer at the end of my life. I had the sense that I could live my life how I wanted. I could be the man and the father and the son that I wanted. Being a member of a 12 step program has given me a way of living. It is the cornerstone of my spirituality and has been the way I live my life ever since. I've been able to find sobriety, sanity, and success. Just like the book said, I had a spiritual awakening sufficient to bring about a complete personality change.

I got a job as a realtor and stayed sober and continued to grow on my own as much as I could. When I couldn't grow on my own, I got professional help. After two years of sobriety, I was stuck. One of the toughest things about early sobriety is all the emotions and feelings I had been numbing now all came to the surface. At the time, I had been in a very unfulfilling, toxic relationship, I was working a job that was a good job but wasn't my passion, and I was living in a nice house in the mountains that really didn't feel like home. I was majorly depressed and sober. I had never been depressed and sober. I was heartbroken about the relationship and I would cry all the time. I had never felt so depressed and so I found myself in therapy with a therapist who I'd seen over the years. She had also worked with my parents as a couple and my mother individually. She remains one of the smartest people I've ever met and I'll never be able to thank her enough for how much she helped me.

I was able to tackle the early childhood and the 'family of origin issues' that I wasn't able to overcome with my 12 step sponsor. She urged me to grieve the decades of my life I had lost to the disease of addiction. Yes, decades. She helped me understand the bad parts of my childhood and how it had affected me as an adult. She helped me let go of these painful events. She helped me see toxic patterns in my relationships. I cried a lot. Like a lot. It was embarrassing and healing. She began talking to me about what I was going to do with my life. She encouraged me, and she urged me to follow the threads in my life. She was urging me to do something special with my life.

At one point I was talking to a recovery 'old timer' and I was talking about how depressed I was feeling and I mentioned that I was so depressed that sometimes I didn't want to wake up.

He asked me, "Are you meditating?"

"I'm not that depressed," I replied.

He chuckled and a light went off in my head. I needed to work harder if I wanted to get out of this depression. I began meditating. I meditated a lot. I learned how to do it from YouTube. I actually learned a lot from following different teachers, authors, and speakers on YouTube. During this time, I made major changes in my life. I gave away most of my stuff, I sold my house and I quit my job. I moved to a small condo in Denver. I began working out with a trainer. I was committed to staying single. I read books on The Law of Attraction and the power of meditation. I became vegetarian and started juicing. I started buying self help and spiritual books. I doubled up on 12 step meetings. I made amazing breakthroughs in therapy and began to realize I lacked a specific purpose. I began to wonder who I was supposed to be as a sober man in the world. I wanted to be an amazing person and I wanted to help people get sober. I redesigned my life meditating on the floor of that small condo in Capitol Hill. I became obsessed with self-improvement.

One night, I was watching a documentary called *Bob and the Monster*, about Bob Forrest, an addiction therapist and ex-rockstar, and in it he helps the guitarist John Frusciante of The Red Hot Chili Peppers get into rehab through an organization called Musicares.

It struck me that maybe I could do something like that so I looked up local meetings. The only one takes place in Fort Collins so I drove up to the meeting and stayed to talk to the therapist who ran it. I asked him, "What can I do? What can I do to help the recovery community?"

"Well we need sober houses," he said.

I didn't even know what a sober house was but on my drive home I started obsessing about it and in my heart I felt like I already owned and ran a sober house.

The next day, I was talking to a good friend from college and he said, "My buddy up here has 14 sober houses. Come on up here to Minnesota and consider it sober house school."

So naturally, I went up and learned the business. Chris Edrington from Saint Paul Sober Living taught me what a sober house was. I learned that a group of same sex individuals live as a community, and agree to be randomly drug tested to ensure that they're sober. More importantly, Chris taught me the sober house vibe and the culture, and I was amazed.

My father became my investor and we bought a large Victorian house. We opened our first sober house near 12 step meetings in the neighborhood where I lived in the heart of Denver. Whatever remained of my depression turned to elation. It was so much fun, and we helped so many people that I opened another one, and another one, and I kept opening them until today there are nine sober houses. I also opened a treatment center and I even hired several of my friends.

Today, we are able to meet our client's clinical needs as they learn to live life without drugs and alcohol. My life has become a life of service. I use my talents to help others. I work shoulder to shoulder with people

I love, helping other people get sober.

My son's story was supposed to be, "My dad died when I was two. He owned a bar and he drank himself to death."

Gone are the days of waking up and drinking vodka before I can function. I have another son now named Oliver Brice Hancock. On a recent trip to Los Angeles, I went surfing in Malibu, ate sushi in Santa Monica, and slept in nice hotels. Upon my return to Denver, my hometown, I met with a sponsee, and played basketball in the sunshine on an outside court.

I truly feel like I have had two lives.

Life isn't perfect but it's nothing like it used to be.

I know I've had an awakening. My life is so big that I simply can't manage it on my own. I'm forced to rely on the power of the universe that Einstein referred to. I'm co-creating my life with God as I understand God. I experience many moments of calm, I'm present, and I don't have that persistent feeling that I'll be happy when I get enough money, or when I get the right relationship, the right job or if the right person is president. I'm happy now. I just allow things to unfold naturally and organically. I can just be. Again, I'm not perfect but I'm much better than I was.

I'm grateful that I almost died from alcoholism because it gave me the life of purpose I have today.

Reflections

Reflections

KEVIN LOCKWOOD
USA
Intentional Life-Journey Coach
www.envoypeace.com

Kevin Lockwood is licensed as a Spiritual Practitioner. He is also certified as a Visionary Leadership & Conscious Coach, Yoga Teacher, Six-Sigma Process Improvement Black Belt, and Program Management Trainer. Evolving from 30 years of supporting transformation from the inside out for individuals, Fortune 500 companies, government agencies, and non-profit organizations in over 50 countries, Kevin's current mission is helping professionals find their way through the labyrinth of their own souls to create a movement of conscious leaders. After trying to evolve other coaching systems that were primarily head-based or heart-based, he took the best from both worlds and was compelled to create something entirely new... Intentional Life-Journey Coaching. Kevin loves this practice because the best and most empowering solutions not only involve the people facing challenges, but indeed come from deep within them.

Chapter Thirteen
ON A MAGIC CARPET

*When we have a bigger idea for life,
life begins to show up for us.*

In 1993 at age 26, my alignments, politically and socially, were left-brain logically-dominated and conservative. Less than a decade later I found my preferences dominated by right-brained creative and liberal thinking. I went from having no thoughts of spiritual awareness or emotional development to leading a life that was focused on exactly that. What happened?

The shift started with a heart-wrenching breakup and the ending of an engagement. Logically, we were the perfect match. I put my best efforts into making it work and my mind told me everything should have worked. When it fell apart I felt like a failure. My vision of a meaningful life, and belief in my ability to create one, were crushed. My foundation of how to logically get life right was beginning to crack.

All of this was compounded with a move from Illinois to Virginia by myself – leaving behind a job, friends and home I felt safe and connected to. I was emotionally numb and void, pushing into depression. The check boxes I had been given as a roadmap for a successful life didn't work. I was lost and didn't know where to turn. I worked so many hours my boss threatened to bring in a cot and hot plate. I filled the emptiness in my chest at the local watering hole. At the same time my mother, one of the people I needed to show I could do life right, was battling cancer.

Today she's well and very alive at 85, but that's her story to tell, so back to me in the fall of '93.

Fortunately, my new friends, even though they hadn't known me long, knew something was off. They must have seen a light in there somewhere worth digging out. One of my friends gave me *Men Are from Mars, Women Are from Venus*, a book by John Grey. With a smile bending its way into a smirk, she told me I was a Mr Fixit. I didn't like being labeled anything, and couldn't really understand what was wrong with trying to fix things for someone I cared about. I was inspired, or perhaps annoyed, enough to read the book.

Like the good engineer I was, I used the book to analyze the situation objectively. It may sound odd, but stick with me. I determined I needed to grow the strength and functionality of the right side of my brain. My goal was to be able to understand women – more specifically one special, yet to be determined, woman who I would meet and fall in love with and have a wildly successful and fulfilling relationship.

Don't laugh, I was serious about it, and that focus gave me a reason and a purpose to move forward. Mr. Fixit set out to try and fix something else, himself, so he would *never* get his heart broken again. Synchronistically, a woman I dated for a short time gave me Ned Herman's *The Creative Brain*. I poured myself into studying the brain – innate preferences, strengths, and weaknesses. I learned how people could grow the capabilities of one side of their brain or the other.

I started doing aerobics – me and a sea of women I was too shy to talk to. I went to live theater performances. I went to museums. I studied old architecture. I learned ballroom and country dance. I even tried some yoga, all to grow my right brain. At first I didn't like any of it. But I noticed after about a month of trying something new, I began to enjoy it.

Still being a good engineer, I periodically tested my brain preferences. After three years my brain preference shifted from 80/20 logical-left-brain dominated to 40/60 creative-right-brain dominated. Nothing I had read said this would happen. Brain preferences are less innate and more flexible than scientists thought back then. I was surprised, and intrigued. I was creating a whole new angle to experience and interpret life from.

In addition to having more creative ability, I recognized something else. Still ever the engineer, I paid close attention to my awareness of things happening, intuitively. I noticed a shift in preference to work through a challenge instinctively. At first, I would follow up my intuition with logic and reason, and gradually the logic became more of a game than a need. The skills of my left brain didn't go away, they more or less slipped into the background in preference for using my right brain.

In addition to enjoying more creative ability, I recognized something else. I would think of someone and then the phone would ring and it would be them. I would get lost in a strange city on a business trip and intuitively know which way to turn to get where I needed to go. Still ever the engineer, I paid close attention to my awareness of things happening, intuitively. I noticed a shift in preference to work through a challenge instinctively. At first, I would follow up my intuition with logic and reason, and gradually the logic became more of a game than a need. The skills of my left brain didn't go away, they more or less slipped into the background in preference for using my right brain.

In 1997, four years into my quest to fix myself, I began work on my master's thesis. I fully trusted my intuition in guiding my way. I decided to develop a business process reengineering plan for a dating service. Yeah – the failed relating stuff was still following me. I went to the regional office for what at the time was the largest franchise of the largest dating service in the world. Shirley, the woman in charge, was very leery of my intentions. They had just had some bad press and she had every reason to be careful. Still, something told her to trust me.

We became close friends and creative colleagues. Six months into our work together, she wanted me to meet someone. She wasn't a client of the dating service, so reluctantly I agreed.

It seemed like a great match. I even tried the engagement thing again, but stumbled through some of the same mistakes and some new ones too. There was more to learn about myself and relating. Tricia came and went like a storm through a MidWest trailer park…

upsetting everything, no matter how well it was tied down. As things slowly settled, I began to recognize I was perfectly on path. I always had been. She was another angelic guide helping me find my way.

The most important thing to share here is that Tricia opened my world to spirituality, to Faith, to something bigger than myself that connects all that is, all that ever has been, and all that ever will be. She put a rudder to my creativity and intuition. We created our own theories about life – which I realized later were actually common among many spiritual teachers. However, the experience of Tricia in my life was unpredictable, even erratic.

She was just the match, Shirley was the bonfire. Everything Tricia and I explored with spirituality I shared with Shirley. For months and months, she quietly listened. She didn't offer much of anything – this from a friend who was usually talkative and interactive. Then one evening, as the aftermath of the Tricia storm was still settling, Shirley invited me to dinner. I had plans, but intuition told me to cancel them. Every part of me was vibrating and calling me to go see Shirley. I felt a little giddy on my way there.

I was not disappointed. After dinner, Shirley told me about a spiritual retreat she had snuck off to over the weekend. More magic and miracles happened there then I have the space to share here. However, there's a particular highlight I can't pass up. On the first day of the retreat some woman came up to Shirley and shared insights about Shirley's past. On the second day some man shared insights about her present. You can guess what happened on the third day. It was a regular Charles Dickens story. A third man came up to her and shared insights about her future.

All of this broke Shirley out of her spiritual scrooginess. Months of silently processing what I shared with her came pouring out all at once. She shared a lifetime of auspicious stories. The spiritual concepts, thoughts, and ideas that I had been exploring burst into reality for me.

Shirley was so excited that in two weeks she was going to Sedona, AZ for another retreat. Her being expressed a light and energy I had never seen before. I felt something powerful and grounded was unfolding. I told her I was going with her! Shocked and a little hesitant at first, she finally agreed to let me tag along.

At the retreat a woman named Almine was checking people in. When it came to my turn she paused, looked up, and smiled. With energetic surprise and excitement she said, "Oh you're early!" This prompted me to look at my watch, but she touched my wrist to block the view, "Oh no dear," she said in a more serious tone and slight smirk, "You're years early." She continued, "This is going to be a challenging weekend for you, but don't worry. We'll get you through it."

Almine was right. My heart was cracked wide open that weekend, and I also felt a little lost. I heard things that made no logical sense, but my intuition was on fire and I knew I was vibrating in the essence of powerful teachings. There were things I witnessed that wouldn't make sense to me, and I wouldn't have a personal experience of, for years. In one exercise Shirley and I stared into each other's eyes and opened into each other's souls. I saw my friend really for the first time. I felt her joys and sorrows in deep and profound ways I had never experienced with anyone before.

One evening Shirley and I went to a vortex on a mountain top. As we meditated together an awareness came over me. Energy began to burn through my whole being and vibrated me to my core.

Is this God? I thought. *Yes, this is God! It wasn't something I could search for, because it is everywhere. It is everything!*

I cried. I cried hard. I felt joy in the awareness of Oneness. I felt pain and sadness in my long-traveled journey, feeling separate and alone. I felt embarrassed that I had lost faith and assumed there was no God. Well, there was no God as far as the one I had been taught about, some guy watching and judging over me. I struggled through my pain about that story.

Shirley comforted me and let me know that this was just part of life's journey. "We all go through this in our own time and way. Welcome home my friend! You've always been here. God's always been here, everywhere. You just didn't realize it."

The spiritual magic and awareness in my life continued to unfold around every corner. Once I started paying attention, I began noticing how easily everything was falling into place. I seemed to meet the right person everywhere I traveled – either they were helping me or I was helping them. The checkboxes for how to do life 'the right way' gradually washed away like chalk on a sidewalk. I began to see that my life was perfectly unfolding. I realized that even the times in my life when I thought I was off course were actually key crossroads to prepare me for what would unfold next. I felt alive. I felt at home and settled in my own body. Most notably, I felt relieved that I was on track with my life.

Meanwhile, my best friend Sam was getting married in Vail, Colorado. He was surprised that I was coming, and that surprised me because he'd go to the moon and back for me for much lesser reasons. Yes, I was heading out to the wedding for sure. I wouldn't have missed it for the moon. I even had a date… someone to go with me. Shirley had introduced me to her – trying to make up for the storm that had ensued with Tricia. I didn't fall in love with Kim, but I sure loved being with her. She cracked me up with her humor and wit. With the broken heart I had, she was the perfect healing medicine. Her friends called her "Rebound Kim". We didn't care. At the time we were good medicine for each other.

The whole week in Colorado was a blast. We were like college kids playing again! At the wedding Sam and I stood on an outdoor patio and watched three bears on the hill behind the hotel. I laughed to myself that we were talking about bears instead of bars.

Then Sam threw one on me, "You need to move out here Kev, we have work to do."

In hearing this I'm thinking to myself, *Sam thinks we have work-work to do, we have spiritual work to do.*

In saying this, Sam's thinking to himself, *Kev thinks we have work-work to do, we have spiritual work to do.*

Read that again and it might make sense the second time. Those horseshoes landed in the wrong pit. What did land, however, was I realized for the first time in my life that I could live anywhere. I could work wherever I wanted and do whatever I wanted. I was free. Thirty years old and I finally got it... actually thirty-one now. The important part wasn't when I got it, it was that I got it. In that moment, I realized I was going to be moving. I didn't know where and I didn't know when, but I knew I would be moving. It wouldn't be a move out of physical necessity. It would be a move arising out of spiritual awareness.

When I got back to Virginia I felt into what might keep me from moving:

One – I was near the end of completing a master's degree. Those credits don't transfer well. And, I would have to pay my company back for all my tuition if I didn't graduate from the program.

Two – Three years prior, my friend Dave had hired me to kick off a new contract with the Air Force. I was the systems engineer. Much of the knowledge for how to install and maintain the system we employed was stored in only one place, my head. There was no way I would bale on all my friends by leaving before handing the information over securely.

Three – I had just started A Course in Miracles group with Shirley and some other friends, and I wouldn't bale on them either.

I turned over my energetic passion for moving to the Universe – to let It do what It knows how to do best. I let it all go and I continued on enjoying life in the present. While the Universe was busy conjuring up ways to dissolve any obstacles for moving, a year later I had all but forgotten about it.

There were new things connecting me to my life in Virginia. I now had a girlfriend, a horse, and a jet ski. With the loving encouragement and space offered from my girlfriend Christine, I finished my master's thesis. Again, I was blessed with a relationship that was the perfect medicine at the perfect time. I began to see the magic of people flowing through my life for a reason, a season, or a lifetime. Perhaps the value of relationships isn't in their longevity, but by their ability to awaken the powerful flow in each of us – the creative energy of life itself?

In letting the Universe prepare for my move, I wasn't aware of things that were shifting to make it possible. While I was focused on completing my master's program, the Air Force was attempting to create training for the system we had employed. That effort failed. Then they hired the company that made the primary component of the system. That effort failed too.

They came to our team next, and contracted us to develop the training. I created a two-inch think manual for installation, and another equally as voluminous for maintenance. It took nearly nine months, and weighed in at several pounds. When I finished in November 1999, I felt some form of release wash over me. Every cell of my being felt amazingly free. I didn't realize it, but all the obstacles for moving were falling away.

I remember being in Anna's office for a moment that day – our HR manager. A warm buzz ran through my body and I had a flash of insight that she was going to help me find my next job. That was comforting. I knew I was going to move someday. I just didn't know, or have an attachment to, where or when. So I tucked that awareness gracefully away into wherever- and whenever-land.

Around that same time, Christine's horse got very sick with Equine Protozoa Meningitis (EPM). EPM was just gaining big attention back then. On a weekend retreat, at an old barn in West Virginia, we attended a presentation. Miraculously, we met a woman at the conference that was highly knowledgeable about natural remedies to help bring horses back to health.

I felt the magical synchronicity of our fortune. A few days later, my heart sank when Christine decided to go with conventional therapy. Basically, it's like chemo. It involves bringing the horse close to death in an effort to kill the protozoa, hoping the horse survives and becomes healthy again.

A challenging awareness came to me. To Christine, God was a masculine entity, separate and judging over all humanity. She saw herself as a victim to life. I see myself as part of life Itself. I feel God in and as all things, as Oneness, and this guides my choices. This existentially differing view of life and in making life decisions, caused me to pause. I would not flourish and grow on the path I desired if I stayed in this relationship.

After the holidays we broke up. With extra time on my hands, I found myself in the gym a lot more. While doing squats, I would imagine myself skiing with Sam in Colorado. I don't know why. I hadn't seen Sam in nearly two years and hadn't skied in several more. But it wasn't just easier to do the exercise this way, my whole body would fall into a vibration of ease and flow. It was like the exercises were doing themselves.

One night, in early February of 2000, I walked out of the gym and my attention got pulled to a bar across the parking lot. I had never noticed it before, but something was drawing me in. I felt like there was someone I was going to meet.

I walked over and went in. It was empty and still, but there was a young woman sitting near the windows. A few minutes earlier she had just walked out of her nail salon. She noticed a bar across the parking lot that she had never noticed before. Something was drawing her in. She didn't drink or go to bars much, but she knew there was someone she was going to meet.

I felt flush with nervousness. What was supposed to happen next? My shyness, and the perplexity of wondering what to do with my own intuition, took over. I quickly turned my back to her, sat down at the bar, and ordered a beer. Within a few short breaths she was sitting next to me. What now?

I sat almost frozen as she introduced herself as Summer, and told me I had come into the bar to see her. I didn't reply.

She told me she had been psychic her whole life, but had hid it because it was difficult for others to accept. She said she didn't have to hide it from me because I would understand. I didn't reply.

She told me I would be moving soon and we had a short time to spend together. I didn't reply.

She told me there were spiritual and metaphysical things I needed to teach her before I left, and we would meet at least once a week until then. I didn't reply.

I had never met a psychic before. I wasn't sure what to think or say.

This wasn't making much sense. But, I was the one who had walked myself into this bar looking for someone. And while my logic told me this girl sounded like a lunatic, my body vibrated calmly and assuredly with the sound of her voice. A deeper awareness within me told me I was hearing truth. I finally nodded my head in agreement.

We talked for a while. The conversation was casual but the energy was intense. I finished my beer, she finished her water. We exchanged numbers and agreed to meet later in the week for dinner. She seemed elated. The feeling that seemed more prevalent for me was stunned. What had just happened? What did it mean? Could this all really be true? Should I trust her? What did I have to teach a person who had been psychic their whole life?

As I drove home I thought through what might keep me from moving. Other than no obvious opportunity presenting itself, it seemed there was really nothing holding me back. My Course in Miracles group had been going on for nearly two years now. In weighing up the spiritual teachings I felt would be unfolding when I moved – somewhere, someday – it seemed logical to move if the opportunity presented itself. I allowed myself to feel into the vibrations of what Summer had shared with me. Still, I felt no urgency to make it happen. It would unfold in its own perfect way and time.

In mid-February my boss Dave asked me if I would like to go to Washington, D.C. to take a class and become an Essential Management Skills Trainer for our office. That sounded great. I love spending time in D.C. and I love opportunities to teach. Plus, it sounded like a smart career move. It was an enthusiastic yes!

The following week a man knocked on my door and asked me if I wanted to sell my house. That caught me off guard. Why would I want to sell my house? I loved where I lived on a lake – three miles from work and seven miles from the ocean. I directed him to the house next door that was currently being rented, maybe he could buy that one. I thought nothing more of it, but the incident created a shift in my mind. If there was one thing I feared about moving, it was how to sell my house. In that moment that fear was eased. In the stillness that followed after I turned the man away, I realized the Universe was working through a block I hadn't even been aware of. Summer's words about moving took on more validity.

On March 3rd, my birthday, Sam called from Colorado. Since meeting in college, we always got together or talked at least three times a year: New Year's Day (1-1), my birthday (3-3), and his birthday (9-9). For the past two years since his wedding, whenever we talked, Sam always emphasized that I needed to move to Colorado, because we had work to do. I always assumed he meant work-work. He always assumed I was hearing his words as work-work. Both of us were still secretly knowing that we had spiritual work to do.

After our call, I turned to my computer and opened my email to get back to work. At the top of the list was an email that said "Hot Jobs". I felt a vibrational nudge and opened it up. A link in the email took me to a site with world-wide company job postings. It had two boxes to support a search: "location" and "keyword". I didn't know what to put in, so I selected "Colorado" and typed in the simplest term for my area of expertise, "radar". I found what looked like the perfect job in Colorado Springs. I showed it to Dave. He thought it would be a good career experience to apply, but expressed high doubt I would get the job.

I spent the rest of the day at work updating and rewriting my resume. At the end of the day I tried to fax it in, but with no luck. The next morning, I asked Anna if she could help me. My logical mind must have been checked out amidst my eagerness. Why would I ask the HR manager for help with sending a fax and not our highly-competent, super-friendly, especially-attractive office manager, whose job it was to actually take care of things like this?

Regardless, Anna read the job description and then she got excited. "Hey," she blurted out, "this job is working for Buzz. You know Buzz! You and he had offices side by side for years."

Actually, I didn't know Buzz. Although we shared an office wall, we both traveled a lot and I had never met him. I sat patiently in Anna's office for the next 20 minutes while she talked to Buzz. When she finally hung up she was even more excited. Buzz knew who I was and he thought I'd be a perfect fit for the job. It was then that I remembered the flash of insight I had in November. Anna was going to help me find my next job. It all came together in my mind in an instant. It was happening now, right now!

When I got back to my office the phone was ringing. It was Buzz's office manager. She seemed confused that I hadn't spoken with Buzz, but proceeded to ask when I could fly out for an interview. Since I would be in D.C. the next week, I told her I'd fly out the following week and interview on Thursday.

Afterwards, I called Sam to tell him the good news, but he wasn't thrilled. He was adamant that I needed to work with my company in Denver and gave me the number. It happened so fast, I didn't question why he would have it so handy. The Denver office wasn't interested in interviewing me because I didn't have a top-secret clearance. So I let it go. My move was unfolding on its own.

The next day I gave Sam the straight news – no deal in Denver. He told me he was interviewing with my company, and would tell them he wouldn't take the job unless they agreed to interview me. It was more important to Sam than me that I work in Denver. I didn't yet know Denver would become my spiritual teaching haven.

Within minutes after talking to Sam my phone rang. The Denver office wanted to know when I could be in their office for an interview. My mind worked quickly and effortlessly, I told them I'd be there on Friday in two weeks. That settled that. The feeling seemed to be that we were keeping Sam pacified by setting the appointment.

Meanwhile, my lessons with Summer were happening at least once a week, as she said they would. Each time we met, I would teach her what I knew about metaphysics, spirituality, vibration, energy, chakras, Oneness, etc. Then she would channel more detailed information and make notes for me. I was astounded by the insights and synchronicities, some of it took years for me to fully comprehend. She always told me I was the teacher. In as much as good teachers are facilitators who reveal a greater genius then their own by way of their students – I guess I was.

Soon my train-the-trainer management class came and went, and I was off to Colorado. Up to that point in my life I had never really been interviewed. Like the upcoming interview I was having with Buzz, all the interviews I'd been through were with people who already knew me. Those interviews felt more like an informal conversation, required only to complete the formality of a human resources' check box.

When I arrived in Colorado Springs however, I discovered that Buzz had scheduled two more interviews for me, with people and job openings in other departments that I knew nothing about. Fortunately, the week-long training I had just completed had taught me how to interview people, and by that virtue had taught me how to be interviewed. By the end of the day, I had three tentative offers. I was too naive about interviewing to know that wasn't typical. It still felt awesome though. It felt like everything was unfolding perfectly in the hands of grace and I just had to show up.

The next day I showed up in Denver. For two hours, five people fired questions at me, and they all took notes. Fortunately my training in D.C. included panel interviews as well, so I knew what to expect. It looked more like courtroom interrogation and cross examination than an interview, but it flowed easily, even enjoyably. Yes, I was having fun with it all.

The vice president for human resources sprung me from the courtroom and took me to lunch. Ron is a super warm, friendly, welcoming and disarming guy. A welcome shift from the two hours of grilling I just had, even if I did enjoy it. We shared casual banter about hobbies and sports, and returned to his office afterwards.

He locked the door, pulled the shades, and turned on a white-noise device. This was seeming like a scene from an exciting spy movie, and Ron's James-Bondish smile enhanced the atmosphere. In a more serious tone, he told me that his people wanted to hire me. He spent the next hour telling me about different programs where I could work, and asked which ones might interest me. I put two at the top of the list. Then he asked me to change my plane reservations, they would pay for it, and stay through the weekend so we could do more specific interviews on

Monday. It sounded great to me! How terrible to stay in Colorado a few more days and get paid for it!

That weekend Sam fitted me up with a ski jacket, skis, boots, poles, hat, gloves, buddy pass – the works – and we skied at Vail. Wow… amazing, beautiful, awesome, breathtaking… trails and views. It was heaven and I was floating in it – a totally different sport from the ice-faced mountains Sam and I had learned how to ski in the Northeast. I thought back to the squats I'd been doing for months in the gym, pretending to ski with Sam with no apparent logic, and now here I was.

Saturday night Sam and I went out to play pool. I started telling him stories about how my life had changed… living spiritually and intuitively. He asked me what caused the shift. I told him that Tricia had given me a book called, *Illusions*.

Sam interrupted with the subtitle, "*The Adventures of a Reluctant Messiah*, by Richard Bach."

As I continued on, Sam tried to get my attention. Finally, I heard him, after he had repeated the same statement for a third time. "Kev, I don't read books! My cousin gave me that book and I've read it three times!"

He continued, "When I said you have to move here because we have work to do, I didn't mean work-work. We have spiritual work to do."

Finally, after two years, the horseshoes found their target. As we explored it more, we realized how many of the same people we knew. People that were part of the spiritual shifts and openings happening in and around our lives.

How had I been so intuitively sensitive to everything else unfolding and not noticed this? Well, if I had realized two years ago what Sam was actually saying, I may have tried to force it all. It would likely have been difficult and untimely, and the whole process may well have fallen apart. As it was, everything was unfolding easily and gracefully, without effort, at the perfect time.

Sam and I relished our time together through the rest of the weekend. Monday's interviews were more fun and excitement, and by the time it was all over I had a tentative job offer with the Denver office.

My first night back to Virginia I laid peacefully on my bed. I thought about my move to Colorado without a worry in the world. It would be great to stop in Illinois and visit with my dear friend and mentor, Ben. It would be even better to see all the guys I used to work with at Scott Air Force Base, but that was highly unlikely since they had moved all over to different military assignments or new civilian jobs.

The next day at work I got an email from Ben. By the way things were flowing I shouldn't have been surprised, but I was. I hadn't heard from him in a few years. He was putting together a reunion with the old crew, and wanted to know which weekend I could be there, June 10th or 17th. Elated, I shut my eyes felt into it for a moment. I would close on my house (which wasn't even on the market yet) on June 10th, spend some time with my parents in NY, and then head out to Illinois. Perfect, I emailed Ben telling him I'd be there on the 17th. No other words needed.

I shared my good news about the job offers with my colleagues. They cautioned me that job offers normally take months. Until there's a written offer there's really nothing. Their logic didn't make me doubt the process. I could feel a lightness in my body that was unfolding. A week later I had written offers for Colorado Springs and Denver. I wasn't sure which one to go with, so I called Sam. He had taken the job with my company in Denver, and that is where I needed to be as well.

Sam asked me about the salary amount. I was proud that it was a 20% increase from what I was currently making. I heard a disruptive return from the other end. Sam was insisting I needed a 67% increase. I felt a little ashamed to ask for that, but I trusted him. I called Ron and let him know. After our brief chat, he hung up the phone from me... and called Sam... to ask him if I was worth it. You can guess what Sam's reply was. Ron called his hiring team and told them to give me what I wanted. They scoffed about company policy, but after researching my qualifications gave in to the request. Sam was right. The salary they would have given me wouldn't have been on par with my peers. All I basically needed to do was show up and follow the flow.

April and May flew by quickly. It pains me to think about how hard

I worked to sell my home when it just wanted to sell itself. The man knocking on my door in February freed enough of the energy around my fears to get everything flowing. But it seems I insisted on standing in the middle of the stream anyway, trying to push the water forward. I won't embarrass myself with the details. At least the experience gave me an example of how to disrupt the flow and make things harder for myself. I think I need a sign like that in my office.

The Universe is conspiring to express your deepest desires through you.

If you choose to show up, it's easiest when you stay out of your own way!

The second week of June a moving company packed up my house. On my last night in town I put on a party at a local bar and treated my friends to food and drink. I felt on top of the world. My friends had supported me so powerfully for seven years, and now I was letting them go to welcome new possibilities. Parting was sweet sorrow. An angel followed me home that night, and helped me clean my house in final preparations for closing on the sale the next morning. By noon Saturday I was headed to New York.

I had just gotten on the road, when my newly purchased cell phone rang. It was my ex-fiancée Tricia. I hadn't heard from her in over a year, but she had intuitively felt drawn to call me. She had tried my home number but it was disconnected. So she tried my work number, where I had left my new number on the voice message.

As I was leaving a home, set of friends, workplace, and smell of the ocean I loved so dearly – it settled my heart to hear the voice of the woman who had cracked open my spiritual life. It felt like another gentle sign that I was perfectly on track. Our breakup was hard on each of us. It felt cleansing and releasing to share a short moment of deep appreciation for each other as I was heading out on a new spiritual adventure.

The time with my parents was a little difficult. We all knew that the easy one-day-drive visits between New York and Virginia were coming to an end. It would be almost two years before they blessed my move to a place so far away from home, and fully recognized me as the expert of my own life. By no coincidence, it would be about the same amount of time before I fully recognized and honored the gift of choosing my parents for this lifetime. You can't fly a kite without a string, and my parents had given me the left-brained grounding from which to experience right-brained flight.

Hitting the road again, it was a magical reunion in Illinois. All of my old work buddies were there. These guys are the best of the best at what they do. They taught me a ton – not just about work – but more importantly about taking care of each other like family. My mentor and dear friend Ben had believed in me in ways I had never believed in myself. He put his own reputation on the line time and time again by setting me free to learn from my own mistakes. I couldn't have had better teachers for that point in my life, and I was happy and grateful to see them all again.

I squawked when they didn't give me the award for furthest traveled. I might have been their boss at some point, but once again I wasn't really in charge. They based their case on the fact I was currently living out of my truck. Instead, I got the award for the least changed. That made me laugh on the inside. Yes, I suppose on the outside my boyish look hadn't changed much. But on the inside, I was a totally different person, with a passion for spiritually auspiciousness adventures.

Even the drive the next day was a mystically guided experience. Without much thought I chose the more-casual northern route on I-36 through St Joseph, instead of the quicker route on I-70 through Topeka. You might remember, we used paper maps back then. I hit some horrendous storms about halfway through Kansas. When eight black Cadillac Escalade storm trackers passed me with equipment poking out in all directions, I knew something serious was up. Tuning into the weather station, I was relieved to hear that tornadoes were touching down well south of me, near I-70.

My first three weeks in Colorado I stayed with Sam. Since I was waiting for my security clearance, I spent little time at work and most of it looking for a place to live. The first weekend Sam took me to a party on Clarkson Street. I remember because he pointed out the window at the street sign. He and I had met ten years earlier at Clarkson University.

The second weekend Sam was out of town, and his wife took me to a party on Cook Street. I remember everyone thinking I was 'the husband', and they were excited to meet me. It made for easy conversation, and I felt like I belonged. In some ways I look a little like Sam – we're the same height anyway.

To bring the story around quickly, I rented a house on Clarkson Street and later I bought a house on Cook Street. Within a week of living at my house on Clarkson I found A Course in Miracles center eight minutes away. When I moved to Cook, the Center was only three minutes away.

Within months of being in Colorado, my Course-in-Miracles friends thought I might like checking out a nearby Center for Spiritual Living. I've taught youth classes on and off there for nearly 20 years, I've served on their Board of Trustees, and I currently serve on their Business Honoring Spirituality board. The Center also sponsors my license as a Spiritual Practitioner.

Within a few more months I was introduced to the Dances of Universal Peace and a wealth of friendships and peer mentors that continue to support my spiritual path beyond compare. Within a few years I became certified as a Jin Shin Practitioner and as a Yoga Teacher, and I joined the Institute of Noetic Sciences.

Teachers and teachings continue to flow into my life. I continually feel blessed to have landed in Colorado twenty years ago. It truly is my spiritual teaching haven, and I still have spiritual work to do here. When people ask me how I ended up moving here, I simply tell them I flew in on a magic carpet. If they look at me oddly, I twist my face and try to emphasize that a magic carpet really is the best way to describe it. If that doesn't scare them away and they still want to know, I tell them this story.

I'm still learning and trying to understand the feminine, and people in general. Relating really is a verb and not a noun. It's a lifelong journey – self, others, Source. I found her, by the way – a woman willing to walk the journey with me, accept me when I show up as less than the best of who I am, help me when I get in my own way, learn and grow, and find a flow together in this ever-moving stream of life.

I have witnessed people awakening to a deeper meaning of life and designing new lives for themselves without moving, getting a new job, or letting go of any relationships. I have also seen the opposite; big life changes leading to entirely new paths and new ways of being, doing, and experiencing life.

Sometimes life changes feel easy, and sometimes they feel difficult. They might seem big or small. They might unfold slowly or quickly. In all of the cases I have witnessed, they have included a willingness to try something new and a faith in something larger than the self. These are also the elements that have held me up and kept me moving through changes in my life.

Life is always in flow; the magic is in allowing it to move you.

Reflections

Reflections

GURLEEN KHOKHAR
INDIA

Renowned Psychologist, Founder of Windsor Pre-school, Transformational & Motivational Speaker, Former Model, Writer & Editor

https://www.facebook.com/gurleen.khokhar.982

A Psychologist, Celebrity and an Inspirational Public figure, Principal Windsor Pre-School & Daycare, Writer, Transformational Speaker, Ex-Model. Belonging to a defense background I am inspired by my dad Wg Cdr BD Shaurya Chakra, Gallantry Awardee and mother Amrit Kaur raised and brought up in east Africa whose a master's in English. Have been published in various social magazines and awarded the women of a substance by peep India English weekly newspaper. I have written report work for students making them win a national award and also walked the various events as a great speaker and chief guest. I have to my account of knowledge Soch Ki Udaan Desh Ke Naam & Deep Talks a platform for curbing depression and breaking barriers to speak up for the betterment of humanity. I have edited a book named *How to Live a Tension-free Life* published in the United Kingdom and acknowledged as a psychologist in *Million$seconds* a book by Brig Sushil Bhasin. To my account of achievements, I have been featured in Pinkishe NGO's magazine for women empowerment as a single woman setting standards high and also have featured on various talk shows as a relationship expert on mental health wellness including educational programs.

Chapter Fourteen
THE INNER CALLING: WINGS OF A PASSIONATE LADY

The year was 2010. My heart was blossoming to receive the enchantress of all young life – love. I was young and glimmering under the sunlight of romance yearning for perfect love. I clung to the window, looking out into the open nature, yet my eyes were vying for the hero of my life.

The inner calling was to meet a man in uniform who could turn my fantasies of having a quality life and some adventures into reality. The fuel of love was raw at the age of 27, where my hormones were at a peak, and I wanted to witness the full play of love. So, I took the call of preferring a man with a versatile personality.

As was fated, a blooming captain of the Indian Army found me on a social platform – 'Orkut'. Impressions created by the pictures on my Orkut profile yanked the attention of this Officer, and the heart was roused with a curiosity for the seemingly flowering love. The ecstasy of love-fire within me also kicked the synergy of thought, coupled by inquisitiveness to check out the mutual friends on our profiles.

With the increase in the tête-à-tête, the music of love began. It even got more inflamed by his vocabulary and proficiency in the English language. The thought of a man of uniform, not only honorable but also knowledgeable, turned me on. To quieten my puffed-up emotions,

I turned to build wild fantasies where I would often imagine love scenes and read sensual books. Apart from that, the feeling of being in true love kept the phone lines busy for days. So, being in the Army, he was at an influential position to control the cord of connection with me.

As a young virgin girl, I was bereft of the fun and frolic that girls of my age usually experience. My thoughts, therefore, were roused by the sensuality of this love relationship too. The passion of love flame was burning, and mumbling love notes were being exchanged over frequent calls. From a mutual friend, he started exposing his curiosity to seek information about how Miss Gurleen appears to be as a person.

I was also a meritorious girl, so I prioritized my schedule for studies and not forgetting the deadlines. The exchange of dialogues from "Hi" to lengthy conversations made me melt away, putting me upfront before the screen of my computer waiting for his messages at length. Like most love birds, our calls extended till the wee hours of mornings. His friends rejoiced and celebrated the fact that their fellow brother-in-arms was finally hooked to a lady who was also a Psychologist.

When parents were not around, a secured expression of thoughts and feelings were exchanged comfortably. Even so, when the thought of revealing my bond with the Captain before my parents surfaced, I felt no inhibition to do so. I was groomed in an open environment and grew up in a mixed cultured family where Amrit Kaur, my mother has her origin in Zanzibar, Africa and my father from Punjab. The strong discipline and fearlessness instilled in me by virtue of being the daughter of an officer from the Indian Air Force made it much easier for me to share the details of the budding romance with my heroic father, an Aviator and a Gallantry Awardee, Wg. Cdr. Bd Singh (Shaurya Chakra).

As I was about to graduate, this man in uniform became more eager to meet me and know me better as I was still a mystery girl to him. Although I also had such profound fondness for him, I still took much pleasure in checking on the seriousness of his intent with which this young lad was falling into a deep dark romance with me.

One day, his introverted nature drew my attention to ask him a question, "What if you get a chance to be alone in a dark room, what would you do?"

To which he replied instantly, "I wouldn't let go of the opportunity to grab you by your waist and smooch you, as you have full luscious lips and you mesmerize me to a large extent."

With this answer, my blood warmed, and I blushed. The play of hormones was witnessed to a level that I felt hot and wet, so I told him to hang up and talk on another day. This sudden demise of the conversation was aimed at bringing his loyalty to the verge of a proclamation from Patiala to Chandigarh.

While my love life was on full swing, I also suffered a big setback. My loving grandmother died in the year 2010.

The Captain's desire to meet me on Valentine's Day had to be rescheduled due to the untoward call of the Almighty. As the phone rang, I rushed to it to inform him we would not be able to meet. When I told him about my grandmother, the situation fell into despair. However, he told me that he had managed to come halfway and asked me if he could see me. With much pain, I had to deny meeting him. Due to the loss, my family was suffering; I placed the love for my grandmother and the family much higher than my predicament I was facing.

Although we could not meet, I tried cheering him up and enticed him by saying, distance lends enchantment to the view. Having understood the situation and to maintain the boundaries, he drove back on his motorbike with a heart full of love.

But a day of hope came again when we decided to meet in Café Coffee Day finally. He was astonished to greet my mother in the first place, and while I stood behind her, I quietly exchanged a hello with him. I could see a sigh of relief when my mother exited Café Coffee Day, and we ordered for coffee, devil's own being my favorite.

Meekly but patiently, a conversation ensued between us. He expressed his liking for my Punjabi attire, but I intended to use the opportunity to have a deeper understanding of his underlying thoughts and feelings for me. Half of the time, I was the one chatting and asking him questions on why he would marry or date someone freaky like me. I well appreciated the beauty in his answer.

He said, "Your educational achievements, your background, your way of dressing up, and the way you hold conversations take a fair call in bringing life to a full circle."

With a badge of honesty and integrity, he served me coffee passionately. The battle of love kicked off when the courage side of his personality started romancing the psychological side of mine. For that moment, we came outside our comfort zones, sharing the trivial joys.

This love journey engulfed me, and I was filled not only with joy, but I dreamt the prospect of my happily-ever-after. We took a more serious step towards pledging our feelings and commitment for each other when we decided to party on my birthday in Pathankot at the Army guest house where he was positioned. My creative wild side came into play when on my birthday, I gifted him with cool lingerie representing the impressions of my irresistible love for him. My unlived desires of being truly, madly, and deeply in love with him took a flight that night. He, having taken the call of service to the nation, was in the uniform and he was fluently managing the hellos and goodbyes of the evening's greetings. This is an indeed special occasion for us as we geared up to welcome the New Year and my birthday. Little did I know that to add to all the romance, there was a beautiful surprise in store for me.

Just after the birthday cake was cut at 31st midnight, we landed up romancing the night until the next day; he popped up before me in his olive green uniform holding a tiny box that bore a diamond ring inside. I could feel the emotions from the moment running on his face as his love for his dream girl was coming true. Somehow, this was like déjà vu. The conversations of love I have had with him somehow had always gifted me with the spiritual insight to see him bending on one knee to me and offering his heart with an undying love for me with a smile. The road ahead, however, was going to be challenging, I knew. To be a lover girl of a man in olive green is never an easy job.

After much time, since the birthday bash, I could not wait to reach

Roorkee, the next station of his Army unit. The plan was well crafted to win him over and spend some relaxing time with him. My sister, with two of her friends, took charge of planning for a camping and water rafting trip nearby Roorkee. When he booked a room in one of the hotels for our stay, I landed up being a fool in front of the receptionist.

How? Here is how.

Instead of simply asking for a room, I asked the receptionist, not just for a room but also gladly informed the desk that we needed the room for only three hours. Although the queer stares and awkwardness in the atmosphere after I blurted those words didn't hit me immediately, I entered the hotel room with a wink from my lover to know the other interpretations behind my words. I gravely thought of myself as so naive that I couldn't comprehend the duality of meanings in my words. How very innocent I was in dealing with the outside world, but in that precious moment, nothing mattered more than the togetherness I was experiencing with the man I loved.

The expedition was planned to explore the hidden facets of his true nature. Having studied psychology, I always feel there are two sides to a coin, so I wanted to know both sides of his personality very well. Fulfilling my wildest adventure on Earth Day, 5th June, we thoroughly enjoyed our time together like Cupid struck lovers holding each other's hands, staring away at the starlit sky, near the Ganges and warming our bodies near the bonfire. We exchanged vows, making ourselves warm enough to brave the chilly night ahead. I always had an ardent desire for a lover who would be an audacious man and could bring the kinkiest romance out on the table. The crazy heart wanting to make love died a cold death very easily when the alarm of my menstruation cycle kicked in, and the challenge moved to arrange sanitary napkins. The maturity with which he handled the situation was highly appreciated. For the next couple of days, I was fed every healthy food that could exist under the sun and was taken care of like a queen.

I never felt awkward about speaking on bold topics in front of him because that made the relationship catch fire every time we met. Our relationship was a sum of all the fantasies that could be explored in reality. Our love talks which took place at lightning speed made us feel that we were thunderstorms in the lightning. In no time, questions were being raised about our background, culture, religion, and lifestyles. It seemed like we were entering a war zone. The spirit of love in me continued to raise a bar higher. He came from a Hindu Rajput family and me from a typical Punjabi family with a defense background. My dad had flown the Chief Ministers and Prime Ministers of India, including the current Prime Minister of India, Narendra Modi, and he has always been keen on getting me married to a gentleman who could afford a luxurious life for me. As a father knows his daughter well, he guided me to date more men before choosing him as my marital partner. But love is indeed blind. Having lived a life full of struggles, my lover from Ballia in Uttar Pradesh appeared to be the best man for me. I assumed he knew about the harsh realities of life and dealt with life maturely and responsibly.

Before making the final decision to get married, my lover and I decided to take a mature call of seeking guidance from our elders. I took the Captain to meet one of my friends, a renowned theatre personality, who guided this man through the pros and cons of marrying a well-off lady. She, being a divorcee, gave the example of her own experiences with her failed marriage as lessons from where we could learn. After much bonhomie and blessings showered on us, we moved on to meet a Senior Officer of the Indian Army who also guided my lover to be careful and attempt in maintaining some stability in our relationship. To my surprise, he specifically guided the Captain to be loyal to the relationship once committed. Years ahead now, I realize all the good words of counseling must have fallen on deaf ears.

The Senior Officer was particularly very helpful in awakening in me the true essence of the real purpose of marriage. The idea behind one of his sentences still haunts my mind – 'stick by rough ends, never give up'.

To further our resolve in getting married, we got determined to know each other even better. To this aim, we decided to put up in Sarath Garuda Mess of Delhi, where we were determined to undergo a live-in for approximately 10 days to know each other and spend some quality time together as well. During this time, we encountered several romantic moments, one of which was having the pleasure to see his awestruck face when I wore a red chiffon saree of my grandmother and appeared in front of him.

Over a couple of drinks and light entertainment, we cracked some light jokes and shared notes of a healthy discussion. It was then that I asked him to fix a meeting of both of our parents if he really wanted to win me over and take me home as his bride. A consensus was reached, and we continued enjoying the evening. The temperature of the evening was rather high, so we could cuddle and enjoy oral sex, blanketing the secured feelings between us until I was made aware of the aerial view of his house in Ballia. The magnanimity of his description gave me a little blow. My thoughts of passion turned into those of anxiety that made me wonder if I would be able to walk into the lifestyle they had. The queen size life provided to me by my superhero – my dad, seemed really king-sized at that time. But I felt that was the moment of my calling. When I was required to grow from being a lady to becoming a woman, it was a decision I was required to make to venture into the real world of knowing the person and getting into his shoes to live life alongside him. I also observed he appeared to be anxiety stricken too, especially when I suddenly saw his parent's picture on his laptop.

Our staying together worked. It made me realize that despite any differences between us, he did not hide any of the facts about his parents, their lifestyle, and their background. The relationship motivated me to be confident and take up courage and win over any of the challenges ahead. I was prepared to brave the conversation at my home front too.

At home, however, my dad again insisted that I should date more men to understand what was the better or right choice for me and find myself a good partner in life whom I could marry before giving my complete commitment to the Captain. Even back then, my dad could picture that my lover might not stand by my side in the coming times. I never disobeyed my parents, but I took the call of my heart and requested my dad give me a chance to meet his family before any final decision. To this, I also highlighted that we had been educated to know love knows no reasoning and religions should not be questioned. On top of it, the milk of human kindness teaches us all to unite in the name of love. In the end, I stated that the final call would be a parental nod.

Soon, the day came when the meeting was rolled in like a battleground prepared for the lovers who were madly in love to decode their feelings in front of everyone. So, we were prepared for the firing of questions from everyone. The journey from my sweet abode to the Airforce Institute was a ride of life. Time was flying fast, and my heart was beating faster. We were all getting decked up for the big evening to meet and greet each other's families.

It all seemed like a new door full of hopes was opening up.

Before this particular day of meeting our parents, he had stayed at our home, and my father never liked that gesture. Not to be taken on the wrong side of matters, my family has always been very cool and open-minded in welcoming and helping my male friends to stay over at our place during any emergency. But his stay-over at my place with my mom's permission wasn't taken in a good light by my dad as he was an officer and my dad believed in some decorum between officers.

As fate had it, the special evening went well, but my dad acted as a villain who was shooting out tough questions and putting up practical statements to the boy's family. He was unequivocal to state that 'my daughter is expensive for me as a pilot and to hold her for life would be a drill for your life'. He further highlighted a tougher scenario by adding that 'gentleman you need to curtail your desires and be able to manage her being a spendthrift as well'. As far as other usual Indian weddings are concerned, everyone in both the girl's family and the boy's family exchanges many niceties and are quite manipulative in their dealings. In our meeting, the clarity of thoughts was of prime importance where everything was brought to the table and discussed openly.

On top of it, what brought the completion circle on the embarrassments was me walking in the garden to showcase my whole body so that no one would question my physique after the wedding. No one complained rather complimented on my looking fairer than the moon. My dad's goals in bringing every single matter to the table were to have a clear understanding of their orthodox thoughts that could chain me and render me unable to take the flight of my dreams in the future.

By the end of the meeting between the families, hugs and greetings were exchanged, and the tense atmosphere changed to smiles and conversations quickly. In a fleeting moment, I became aware of the presence of a sweet box with a token of money in my lap, and I was called a booked bride. My mom's apprehension was very right at that moment, and she thought that she wanted to take some time off to accept this marital proposal.

While on the ride back home, my mother reaffirmed from my father, "Honey, I hope she stays happy. Are you happy?"

My father reverted that, "My daughter is happy, and so am I."

Once the brakes were applied, the car parked, and we finally reached home, there was something new stirring up inside me. I felt like a new bride was opening the door even as I was breathing a sigh of relief. My mind was quickly moving towards preparing for the future while excitement bubbled inside me. In my own happy world, I took to imagining my soon-to-be wedded groom joining back his duty and taking leave for the marriage. One day, I received a call from him, and he broke down the news received from the Regimental Center of the Indian Army that he could afford to have only 10 days for the marriage and the plans for the marriage had to start immediately. He was a captain when we were courting each other in the year 2012.

On 21st April 2012, I donned the red lehenga selected by my parents, the fabric of which was passionately interwoven with the hopes and feelings of a new bride. It was a busy day; the bridal grooming occupied much of the day while my thoughts were on when I would lay my first sight on my groom dreaming about a fairy-tale and blissful marital journey. I could fantasize the kinky romance, the whispers under the pillow and I could feel the blush on my cheeks when I would rub mine against his. That evening, I was drunk from the prospect of such a love-filled life, of being able to hold his hands for the rest of my life, that my attention turned into how I would become his perfect wife. The wedding took place in a Sikh Gurudwara; it was a lavish ceremony attended by many big shots and media personalities. It was a very hectic day as the reception was also on the same day.

The reality of being married to the true love of my life bewitched me. During the reception, the glow on my face was lighting up the stage well with the overview of the glittery sky and joys in the parental eyes. I was enjoying the foot-tapping music as a newlywed bride. As the guests came up to us, and we greeted them together, many compliments showered on my husband for having a brave lady like me in his life.

The much-awaited first night flagged off in a five-star luxury hotel. Our walk from the entrance till the room was a walk of relaxation as we had won the war of two years of courtship and the firing of questions from society and parents. The battle of challenges on both sides of the families were won, the apprehensive outlook was no more questioned, the wildest love came to the fore as he asked me a question in the room, "Are you comfortable?"

I politely smiled and replied, "I am fine; I just need to shed my heavy attire and ornaments for nightwear, and may I with your permission, do so?"

Like a Knight in the shining armor never leaves his prey, he grabbed me to the glory of being Mrs Singh, and I gave in to his love.

We stayed in Delhi for over two months, met many of his relatives and got done with the ceremonies from his parental side. The trip to his hometown was planned and scheduled for a later time with mutual understanding. The stay in Delhi was also a time when we, as husband and wife, took to marital merriment by exploring all the sexual fantasies. By this time, it was established to his family that he had married a strong woman with a bold outlook. This paved the way for the coming of some consternation in our married life. Signs of jealousy became apparent amongst his relatives when we visited them but never did I sow any negative seed in his mind. While I was staying with his relative's home, I was clear to refuse what I did not like politely. That was taken as a rude expression instead of understanding a lifestyle I came from. It seemed to me that I was not received with open arms despite my husband's full cognizance of everything.

In a society where everyone dons a manipulative self, I only knew to be truthful and honest. As per the Indian traditional society is concerned, a woman is expected to subjugate to the needs and desires of a man. Not surprisingly, I was coming off as a rebel. Having said that I was also educated enough to resolve the pervading issues and strike a chord with his kin.

This was an important phase in my life. From here, our relationship transitioned from the passionate romance to making me enter the realities of being an army wife. I was 'dined in' officially as Mrs Singh in Ahmednagar. The night of my dining-in was a remarkable evening where the commandant's wife expressed, 'Oh my god, she's beautiful'. I entered the lush green gardens decked up in my beautiful reception saree, like a shiny disco ball that could light up everyone's life. The attention from all the officers was quite appreciated as I was given a remarkable honor to be an asset for the regimental center.

My husband was always eager to express his love in a code word, as the humor in uniform was that Junior Commissioned Officers could hear and understand those code words. As a newlywed bride, I imagined and always welcomed the emotions behind his homecoming with a kiss and a quick session of love wherever it could be possible. The adventure of my marital journey had just started. or so it seemed to me then. It turned out that my husband was appointed as an adventure head of the MIRC team. The biggest blow came when an understanding dawned upon me that we had to live separately as he had to take the call to leave for Arunachal Pradesh. To this news, my husband chuckled and said, "Ask more from God to give you more adventures, and now you take to playing cricket at your home."

Whenever I have thought about marriage, the picture of a jovial relationship with a naughty side came to my mind. To my delight, every note of love in the morning when we were together in the initial six months of marriage was remembered in the drape of sarees to winning the crown as a well-dressed lady. Be it being called the mistress of spices to the monsoon queen and even the safari rides with the Generals and high lunches to evening teas, I was appreciated often. He was also always appreciated for having a lovely wife as I was becoming the talk of the center. It was not a surprise to me that our house was also the eye candy for people due to its beautiful interiors. It was named 'THE PARADISE P-47' by me. So, P-47 became an abode of the souls who were celebrating the bond of love while bachelor officers dropping in named me a baby doll.

Our house was hitting the headlines among my husband's colleagues for our love and passion; our pictures adorned all the walls. The *Fifty Shades of Grey* was happening for real in my life. We expressed our love for each other whenever and wherever we could get an opportunity – we smooched, kissed, opened up our hearts to each other, to making out on the dining table to skipping the welfare calls, and everything was so freaking awesome to me. We became the epitome of a love engineered marriage.

I lived the best romance with this hard nut who knew the best ways to learn to communicate. The creative side of us from exploring the home corners to leaving love notes everywhere was explored by us to keep the fire burning. We celebrated the game called life with tremendous joys, and the time came when I had to travel back to my parental home, and that was the time when his voyage had to begin. The period of two months enduring separation from my husband while he was away at work was a hard cry for a newlywed girl like me.

Time passed by, and one day, he gave a surprise by landing up straight to my room in the wee hours of the morning with the help of my sister. The tears of happiness started rolling, and the warmth of his hands reassured a love that was so true. He had put up with us for two months at my parental home where he was pampered being the son-in-law, and we enjoyed the quality time together before heading back to the regimental center. Everything was going smooth till the real danger alarm of breakup was planted on our first marriage anniversary.

From the fairy-tale love story, my marriage was suddenly taking a plunge into the abyss of changes and misunderstandings. I noticed him breaking off from his normal behavioral pattern. I was experiencing the rising insecurities brought on by his untimely irritation, the cause of which was pointed out to be me. This was becoming a nightmare. The period from January to April 2013 was a call of my breakup journey. The shocking reality crept into my life like the horrifying ghost of a horror genre. I began to observe his self-centered obsession to pursue his career and the actual love between us withering away.

When I recall the incidences that deteriorated my trust in him, the first account that comes to my mind is when he slapped me for the first time in the guest house. This was a crucial point for me to realize how frustrated he was over his financial dealings. His apologies offered to my mother for hurting her daughter were considered, and he was forgiven. Even I took the incident with a pinch of salt. Dark clouds started hovering over my mind when he planned a trip to Goa for our honeymoon.

Another shocking news was waiting for me during this trip when he revealed to me on board the bus from Pune to Goa that his parents would join us to live with us after the honeymoon. This raised a lot of insecurities and mixed feelings in my mind for not being in a clear picture. The honeymoon turned out to be a sour episode of love where I was deprived of sex. The breakdown was heart-wrenching, and the trip transitioned from being a honeymoon to the dull and dry romance it was becoming. This was another breakup point for me which I was beginning to realize with some fear in my mind. The decision to welcome his parents in our home where disturbances in our marriage were already stirring up was the worst phase full of insecurity in my life. Without a surprise, when my mother-in-law arrived, she confronted me with an unpleasant note. They came over to judge me is what they stated.

Our happiness had come to a standstill, and it faced the danger of extinction as I began to my husband in a new avatar. He became a devil in the uniform. His parents did not accept me, and they were finding each opportunity to belittle me. I suffered from emotional breakdowns. There were times when they excluded me from their conversations. I felt a sense of total alienation as I belonged to a different religion and background too. My background of coming from a rich family was proving a barrier to their mindset.

When I was growing up, my mother was very instrumental in teaching me the role of the in-laws in family life. But whatever lessons were imparted to me, I was facing issues I had never imagined. The sad story of my life took a further twist when even the financial baggage was also thrown on me, and I was deprived of the right to be a wife. The revelations of the house help named Gyanma and Biju made me cry in the night. They stated that my mother-in-law was into witchcraft practices which caused disparity in our marriage. The disturbances of energies could be seen all around despite my ignoring the same.

Initially, during our courtship days, it was an agreement between my husband and me that we would never take our problems to the bed and believed in resolving every issue as early as possible. My saddest breakup call is horrible enough to mention that a male ego was resting in the garb of my husband, and it deprived me of his love. The wings of our love were clipped, and it bore the testimony of a downtrodden relationship for everyone to witness in the Army unit. The only blessing in disguise during this time was Romeo, a stray dog who always accompanied me around. It seemed he could sense the evil things that perpetuated on me and his soulful glance and voiceless sympathy soothed me. Even the servants of the house gave me some respite as I kept myself occupied in serving them tea and chattering about their welfare.

After some time, the unfortunate incidence of loss of love and more arguments made my parents bring me back from the center after which I re-joined my husband in Roorkee, his next station. The saree that aroused fond memories of our love was never worn for dining out again, and it remains packed up, never opened till today. The day I decided to re-join him to give the marriage a second chance and see if there was a scope to revive it, my parents appreciated my intentions to work on the relationship. However, to my utter surprise, I found out later that some of the Senior Officers were also guiding him to leave the marriage and to choose what was better for him. This turn changed the way in which I wanted to work on the relationship. I intended to put in my efforts, not just as a wife, but foremost as a friend.

The biggest boon during this time, which also helped me to overcome the challenges and boost mental strength was my spiritual vision that could very well predict the outcome of the marriage on the D-day itself. My younger sister gave me the greatest strength in letting me know that life has not ended. Both of us treasured the principles of being raised by a thorough gentleman who knew the importance of walking with strong women and whom he raised very well. I was born in the National Defense Academy, Khadakwasla, Pune. This fact alone made every cell of my body speak the power of courage and valor.

My mother-in-law proved to be a crucial factor in breaking this marital bond wherein her greed for acquiring the property proved a major role in winning over the mindset of my husband. Initially, I was never doubtful to walk with a less privileged man. Rather I was confident to work out the situations for a better future. Where a man gives up, a woman rises – is what I believe in. While my husband was making headway in his career, mine took a step back. What added to my disappointment was the fact that my choice to put my family first was naturalized in such a manner that they came to the point of ignoring all opportunities that came by me.

One day, I was sent a circular to join as a teacher, but it was signed and sent back without my due acknowledgement. Who knew the blame of not being able to strike a connection financially and manage house-hold affairs was coming all on me? Above all, my profession was rebuked and stigmatized in the family by being labelled as a psycho. This increased my sense of disgust against them for every waking minute of my life with them. On top of that, I was body shamed by my father-in-law, who himself is a professor. The water rose above my head when my mother-in-law made a statement that my mother has not given birth to sons. It was too much for me. I broke out in tears and gave back a befitting reply that only a shallow mind can speak such dirty words and women like her are detrimental to not only the mental health wellness but also for the progress of the nation. It was then that my mother-in-law confessed her evil doings and I had recorded her confessions, but my sad fate, they were deleted by my husband without my knowledge when I left for an evening meeting to the army mess.

My husband was mindful of appearing as sweet as possible before the others and played a victim by virtue of being from a low-income family in this breakup battle. It was a shameful act from one of the most respected men in the uniform of the nation pursuing such a gesture. At that moment, I felt he was undeserving of the uniform; he fell short of the valor and the commitment that the uniform demanded, he didn't have a specter of the love and courage of the uniform that bound the nation and family as a complex whole. By writing my story, I am projecting the dark side of the Indian Army Officers where some officers are playing with the emotions of the girls and yet are being supported by the same men in the uniform. I have to say counselors should also assist the plight of officers who are trained for fighting wars in respecting the families and giving them due importance. When I was physically abused, I took the call of not making it appear as a revengeful game by putting his family behind bars, but supported the idea that he realized his faults.

My last flight as Mrs Singh was from Girinagar to Chandigarh, where I relieved myself of extra mental baggage and was prepared for braving the court battle, all alone. I was being encouraged by my self-driven inner goddess that was waiting for a spiritual awakening. I donned the look of a lawyer to fight against the injustice as it was my responsibility to deal with the consequences of my choices. I learned that a beast could not be turned into a gentleman if he is unwilling to change. I also learned that you do not seek validation for the psychological freedom from others to be who you are in the game of life. My spiritual awakening was rising and shaping towards a whole new different outlook as I pulled through the court battle. Little did I know, the power inside made me not rely on anyone for gaining the strength to pick up my shattered dreams, compelled to look for the dawning insight, towards new hope and aspirations.

During this struggling period, what blew me away in truth was my husband's one sentence that woke me up, he said, "Who told you to walk with your virginity in this wedlock?"

The inner transformation that took place on coming beyond this relationship made me slap him six times and warn him against ever challenging the integrity of a woman whom he had loved in the first place. I was truly empowered to be a woman of substance. All this while I regained my confidence to kickstart my career again and my story began to hit the papers for my work, as I started working on relationship issues wherein I managed to patch up many souls while undergoing my challenging battle of love and marital breakup myself. There was enough courage which was growing inside me and still a lot that life had to offer. The only walk that transformed Mrs Gurleen Singh to Miss Gurleen Khokhar was the call of the Lord above, and that was a wakeup call.

All this while, I had thought of my marriage to be an eternal walk, of an impeccable bond which turned out to be a disaster initially but later on a winning flight of transformation. I wear this hurt and pain as a badge of my courage and triumph. I relate to my story as the daughter who was brought up by an Officer, born in a Defense Academy and supported by the men in uniform. Uniform still holds a lot of value for the nation, and the officers serving in the courtship should respect and act to their commitment. My breakup call was my husband's misconduct and disrespect towards my family and me for his own selfish interests.

The desire to make this real picture play in the mindset of everyone is to believe in the inner voice and the wonders of our own true self. The idea conveyed in the story is not to purport a sense of revenge, neither is it to belittle the man I married but to awaken the souls in true love not to tolerate toxic relationships. The supreme message is to provide the readers with a base to celebrate their original worth. My profound knowledge states that never take anyone for granted in love. A tip by a psychologist to all the people in relationships is 'Go by exploring ways to mend the fences rather than looking for ways to move out easily'.

The Indian Army is a great organization serving the nation, and officers need to value their duty and respect their respective partners too. They usually give up on not being able to strike an equilibrium between the home front and the battlefront, and that stands as a breakup point for many divorces.

On the 6th February 2016, a day with mutual understanding, I signed the documents of divorce and finally became an independent, dynamic lady. Being an inspirer to wear my heart on the sleeves, loved by my parents and spiritually blessed, I promised myself to own each stage of my life by raising the respect for my parents even higher. The fire of passion to live and be loved always held me stronger as I experienced not a failure in love but raised a bar higher by winning a trophy of learning that never fall in love by giving up on yourself or your dreams, but rise in love by inspiring many.

I dedicate this story to Lord Shiva and Guru Nanak Dev Ji who are the supreme source of my life and who have given me wings to have my mother alive and healthy, a father who is proud of my achievements and my sister who is very close to my heart. I wish that whenever this story is read, it becomes a testimony to love so that you can give more love without expectations in return rather than being a doormat to physical abuse and mental harassment. I want to point out that love is the key to adapt to any situation, but not to be rigid. Love to live in the present and not for over assumptions in the future, love to respect individual differences and not for mere pity only. The initiation of the essence of my strength was already made by my husband's grandmother, who named me Gauri (wife of Lord Shiva) as she could never pronounce my name correctly.

Today, I truly evoke the power to fight for truth but not tolerate the injustice that was done to me. I took rebirth as a new lady for a walk of life that would enlighten many souls, who are dying to know the facets of true love. Herein, Miss Gurleen Khokhar, a Relationship Expert, known Internationally, having etched a mark of her own through a transformational platform – Soch ki Udaan Desh Ke Naam and having owned the privilege to be the Principal of Windsor Pre-School and a Public Figure as a Transformational Speaker, stands upright to wake up for all the positivity that the universe has to offer. Last but not least, having donned the tag of a model too, now I conspire to be a bold role model for the world and set on a higher spiritual course by healing many souls stuck in relationship issues.

I would sum up by saying:

Who said you could marry only once? Or who said that marriage is the only best bet left in one's life? Let time unfold, and the real magic will take place. Jai Hind!

Reflections

Reflections

ARLENE WALLACE
CANADA
Intentional Parenting Advocate

Arlene Wallace was born in Jamaica and now resides in Ontario, Canada. She is the proud mother of Noah, aged 23, an Educator, and a passionate advocate for all single parents and their children. Arlene appears as the featured guest on the podcast series *Intentional Parenting with Arlene Wallace*, set for release in the fall of 2020.

Chapter Fifteen
BREAKING UP WITH BEING A BROKEN PARENT

I was the loudest parent in the auditorium. I couldn't sit still in my seat. People turned around to stare at me but I didn't care. Noah was graduating. Despite all the difficulties, despite the obstacles, my son was graduating, and I was proud, so proud!

And I still am. This has been a journey, a long and sometimes twisted road, but we are here, both of us so much stronger and wiser. Noah is now my biggest supporter, as I am his.

This was never easy as there were many challenges but Noah made the decision over and over to live even before he came out of my womb!

From living in an incubator for the first four months of his life to being bullied at school, to not feeling safe and secure in his own family unit, and yet together we have managed to overcome it all.

I tell my story because my son has inspired me, molded me, and caused me to be a transparent, trustworthy, open and responsible parent.

I have become, with his help, an Intentional Parent.

These have been difficult lessons to learn, but they are so worth it.

I began my life in a large family in St. Ann, Jamaica, far from the life I am living now.

You may recognize the name of this town as the birthplace of reggae singer Bob Marley. I was born in the rural area of Saint Ann, countryside, called Shawberry. It felt more like a village and I guess that's why everyone felt like family. The beach was only ten minutes away by car but we all enjoyed walking barefoot to these beaches; no one minded the 45 minute walk. I was a little girl with her family enjoying the sunshine, my favorite fruit called Naseberry, and the carefree days of the Island.

I was very young when my mother emigrated to Canada, though my father lived in Jamaica with his mother, I was raised and lived with my maternal grandparents. This felt very natural and I loved them as if they were my parents. When I did go to visit my father, I remembered that I never wanted to go. I felt estranged from him. I was told he was my father, so I believed this. However, I did not have any feeling of a bond with this man.

I never formed a bond with my father's side of the family either. They were distant, cold and so unlike my mother's side. Growing up with my maternal grandparents, I felt loved, nurtured and that I belonged to a family unit. But with my father's side, I never felt truly comfortable with any of them.

But all of that changed when I was six.

My mother had made arrangements and sent for me to move to Canada to live with her. Though I was excited, I was also very nervous. I was excited to be united with my mother. I didn't quite know what to expect. However, having felt so loved by her parents as if they were my own, there was a natural warmth that filled me from within and a curiosity of knowing this woman. I was a young girl, and Canada seemed so far away. No one took the time to explain to me where I was going, why or what my new role was going to be.

It was more than just my family being different; my entire world changed. I'd never seen snow, nor felt the cold bitter winds. Gone were the days of running barefoot as seasonal footwear became a part of daily decisions. Rain-boots, sandals, winter boots, running shoes, and I'd never been asked, "What size is your foot little girl?" before.

It wasn't just about not being prepared.

I felt ripped away from the family I knew, the people I felt love for as my parents. When I arrived in my newly adopted home, I felt like an alien. I was suddenly living in a new country with a strange woman who I was supposed to call 'Mom'.

I couldn't.

I couldn't because I didn't know her. I didn't grow up with her. She had left when I was very young. My grandmother was my mom – I called her Mama. My grandfather was my father and called him Daddy. I was their little girl.

I have distinct flashes in my mind of the times that my real mom, my birth mother would get stern with me. She raised her voice or set strong boundaries to force or coax me to do something.

My inner dialogue running rampant, *Who is this woman? Why does she think she is trying to tell me what to do? She's not the boss of me.*

Each time I would hear her demanding tone of voice I would think this. Who was this stranger, anyway?

I was so confused. I was so out of sorts during this very delicate time in my life.

It was in these moments that I SWORE to myself that one day, when I became a parent, I was NEVER going to treat my child in the stern and authoritarian ways that my mother chose to do so with me. I promised myself I would break free as a mother. I was going to break free from this demanding and soul-crushing impulse, which was all I had ever known.

I was going to be better. I was going to break this chain of harshness and mistreatment. I was going to be honest and open with my child. I was going to show up in a different way.

The uprooting to Canada had me quickly become reserved and always questioned things. This was a far cry of the child I knew myself to be in my birth home of Jamaica.

Not the curious, inquisitive, confident child, but rather the distrusting, unsettled, insecure new girl in my adoptive home.

In addition to feeling different than everyone, I looked different. I was Jamaican but my skin was lighter and my hair was straight and brown. The kids at school thought I was Indian. They called me racial names like Paki. This further alienated me. I felt so alone, so hurt and so distant from anything that felt like comfort.

I'll always remember my grade one teacher, Ms Achey, who was Indian, and she was so kind, so nice to me. I felt a connection to her. In retrospect, it was because I think she too felt like an outsider, and I could relate to that. Due to her nurturing ways, I looked up to her. I began building trust in others and as that grew, I began to make a few friends.

A few years passed, and I became more accustomed to the new ways of life. Little did I know that my world was about to change for the second time. And once again, my trust in my parental figures was shattered.

This time it was adding my father to the family unit. Unbeknownst to me, my mother had arranged to sponsor my dad from Jamaica. Suddenly, he was with us in Canada and from the outside world – our family was complete. Mom, dad and daughter all united under one roof. For me, though, this was just another stranger in my newly acquired 'safe space'. And, once again, I had to adapt. No one had asked me about this. No one had told me about this new change. It was just here. My new reality. It was in this time that I experienced some of the darkest days of my childhood all over again, only as an older child, which meant I knew more. I saw more too.

I had known my mom was abused, physically. Sometimes I heard her cries and one day I saw it happen. My father was always a dominant man.

The day I saw my mother being abused, I asked myself why she allowed that to happen. Why? She was a grown-up, she could prevent it, or stop it, right? So why didn't she? If she couldn't, or wouldn't stop it from happening to her, she couldn't or wouldn't stop it from happening to me. And she didn't. I experienced this too.

Again, just further evidence to fuel my absolute desire to break the cycle and be a better parent to my own child than the childhood I had experienced.

When I did finally become a parent, my father had passed. I wouldn't have the stress of his disapproval, but as I was soon to experience, parenting was stressful enough.

It came as a surprise to me, even a shock, that I was pregnant to begin with.

I had been told by our family doctor that my chances of ever getting pregnant were very slim because my hormones were out of balance.

I was thrilled to learn of my pregnancy. I promised this baby boy that I would be the best mother ever. I wanted to break the chain of authoritarian parenting and abuse more than anything. I wanted him to have it better than I did. I would do anything in my power to make this happen.

And yet I wasn't truly prepared to be a mom. My son's father had left the picture before his birth. This started a chain of awful thoughts I had about myself and my unborn child. I didn't feel confident, worthy, or even deserving of this precious baby. Because of this I was petrified of losing Noah from inside my womb during my pregnancy.

My biggest fear came true as I was feeling very off one morning. I had left for work and felt a twinge of pain. As the hours passed, the pain increased. It was unbearably strong, so much so that I struggled to speak.

Work took me off my shift and instructed me to sit in an empty office; and that is what I did, for hours, sitting on the office floor until the pain subsided enough that I could safely drive home. It was a long grueling two hour drive in a Canadian snow storm home that night, and when I finally did arrive home, the pain was excruciating. At the time, I thought perhaps I was constipated as I was only five and a half months pregnant; nowhere near my due date.

If it weren't for my mother insisting that I call the doctor as opposed to spending time in the bathroom, my son may very well have been pushed out into the toilet!

Met by biased, judgmental and non helpful nurses at the hospital I arrived only to find out that I was in fact in labor and already 4 cm dilated!

Scared and alone, not knowing what to do and the nurse's ignorant direction to "call the baby's father" only made me feel more scared as I didn't have anyone. I was about to become a single mom who wasn't prepared for less than six months along her term.

The pain was relentless and this baby was coming!

The situation became critical and intensified the event. There were no rooms at any nearby hospital! I was about to be air-lifted to a hospital in another city to deliver a baby.

I desperately thought that he and I might not make it. Moreover, I was fearfully questioning God. How am I supposed to see my baby if we are so far apart? If he is born and kept in this other hospital so far from home, how will my baby live without his mom to help him?

I felt the panic with every moment that passed. The helicopter had landed, I was prepped and on my way to be loaded in and ready for take off. As they were wheeling me onto the helicopter pad, the call came in that a room had become available. I was to be redirected and able to give birth right there in my home city.

Overcome by relief, but only for a moment.

It was time for Noah to enter this world. I'll never forget the doctor's faces.

Noah might have been four months premature but there was something beautifully unusual and special about this tiny baby. He wasn't born like most preemies, whose eyes are usually sealed shut, motionless and weak.

Not my Noah, he came in this world eyes wide open. Strong and vibrant, arms and legs stretched out fully expressing the life that he brought with him. He was breathing on his own for the first three hours, again something unusual but It would be 72 hours before the doctors could give me a full assessment and any assurance.

This was by far the scariest time of my life. While Noah stayed for what seemed an eternity in the incubator there were so many life-threatening moments for him. Doctors provided little news or reassurance.

This was agonizing.

Noah struggled so much and so often and there was nothing I could do. This is absolutely the worst feeling for any parent. All I wanted to do was to release my son's suffering. I wanted to assure him, to make everything okay.

But it was not okay.

I can remember asking God, "Are you ever going to give me the chance to be a mom?"

Here was my opportunity, and with it, I dedicated Noah's life to God.

By this point, my maternal grandmother was living with us in Canada – my first mom. I used to go to her room and sob in her arms. She reassured me and often asked if I had prayed that day.

I would reply, "Yes I have been praying, all day."

And she would say, "Then God has got him; he will be just fine."

This always felt like a tremendous burden lifted.

While Noah was still in the hospital, my best friend came to visit. She took one look at Noah tugging on his ventilator cord and said, with total conviction, "He's a survivor. He's going to be alright."

This gave me the hope I needed for us both to get through the next four months while Noah grew and became healthy enough to come home with me.

It was this spirit that Noah carried with him from that moment on and needed as we still had some difficult challenges coming our way.

I wish I could say that our experience turned out perfectly from then on. However, the truth was that I did not feel deserving of Noah.

I felt deep down that I really didn't deserve this precious gift. I felt that way because I didn't like myself back then. At the time I didn't know it. In the moment, we never do. I didn't know how to handle being an intentional parent.

I was an attentive mom, some of the time.

I often would leave Noah behind with a family member and go out to party. Between the ages of two to eight, I neglected Noah. At that time, I believed I was the best mom I could be for him. It was all I was capable of, and no one can do more than they have the capacity to do. One has to grow first, and grow I did.

I decided at one point to go back to school, where I took a few child psychology courses. I hoped to obtain some tools that could make me reflect on the type of parent I was and the type I wanted to be.

I felt a tremendous amount of guilt. The sad reality was that I was just like my mother and father. I had become strict and domineering. Noah's personality resisted this. We clashed often.

I was also very disengaged. I was disengaged in the sense that Noah's feelings and experience didn't matter to me. Everything had to be my way. I wanted to break my own family cycle of abuse so badly that I overcompensated. I stressed myself, and thereby caused him a tremendous amount of stress.

In addition, I became both verbally and physically abusive. Once again, repeating patterns from my own childhood. I was always quick to criticize. Every little thing he did was wrong to me and set me off.

Every. Single. Little. Thing.

I created an environment where he didn't feel safe, making him deeply uncomfortable. Noah's self-esteem suffered; it got to be very low, and it showed. When he walked he would always have his head down, looking at the ground. I know he would have rather been anywhere but at home. Through it all he yearned to gain my love and would try desperately to please me, but I just wasn't reachable. Noah felt inadequate and insecure; he sank into a state of depression.

From daycare and into elementary, Noah struggled in school. He was easily labeled based on his academic performance and there was so much misunderstanding and miscommunication, both at home and at school.

Noah and I had some difficult conversations years later about how he felt during these years. He broke my heart when he expressed to me that the biggest thing he felt was loneliness. He was alone and he didn't feel wanted. He said he wasn't able to meet his milestones in school because he could never do anything right.

Noah's struggles continued into high school. This was largely because of me. As much as I hate to say that, it was because of me. I was playing the part my parents all over again. Abusive, strict, stern, unloving, closed – I was all of those things to my son.

Although I'd sworn that when Noah was born that I would break the cycle, I hadn't yet, and I was a broken parent.

Broken.

I was so hard on Noah when he wasn't performing well in school. I became so angry at him and I was harsh. I feared for him, in all honesty. I feared what his outcome in life would be. Would he always struggle? Worse still, would he grow up and be a father and continue this detrimental cycle?

In response to these questions, I panicked.

I thought I had to push harder, to drill things into him. I didn't realize the damage this caused him; I wasn't even able to think about it. I was exasperated as Noah retreated more and more. By the time he reached high school, he had taken to suffering in silence. I was not able to talk to him: when I would try he would make up stories to try to please me or just shut down to try to cope.

My militancy was seriously damaging him. I placed guilt and pressure on him. I piled it on and it was costing him. I knew I had to stop this; it wasn't fair to him. He hadn't even been given a chance.

I absolutely had to break the cycle, but how? Even though I had taken some child psychology courses and learned a few new tricks, I really didn't know how to do it. Up to that point, I hadn't been given the tools. So where would I find them? Where would I find all this and begin to turn this broken situation around? I didn't want Noah to turn out like me.

Like many parents do when they realize they've been doing things the wrong way, they overcompensate. They try to become a super parent. This happened to me, too.

At the time, I was a teacher. I began to notice that I treated my students differently than my own son. I took care of them; I showed them compassion and empathy. I was open to teaching them. I was patient. I was kind. I allowed them to falter and guided them gently. Everything I employed with them, I did not do with my own child.

I found myself staring at my reflection in the mirror and it dawned on me, I was a hypocrite. I knew I had to treat Noah the same way as I did the other kids. I felt sick.

This was a deep and gut-wrenching wake-up call, and other wake-up calls soon followed.

One day, I don't remember exactly where I was or what I was doing, the realization came to me that although Noah was still a child, he is a human being and would one day grow to be a man. His life was still in my hands, and if I could somehow turn things around, his life would go on to positively impact others.

I could still teach him. There was still time, no matter what I had done wrong or how much harm I had already caused him. There was still time.

In order to improve Noah's life, maybe even to save it, I needed to change my mindset. Knowing this was what I had been missing, I made the choice to change and transform.

Without this, how can anyone unlearn and readjust their behavior?

I began one day by asking Noah to sit down and have a candid conversation.

This was a difficult conversation to have. I was nervous, very nervous. I was about to open an entirely new dialogue with my son. Level with him. Share with him that I didn't have all of the answers, but I was willing to try. I was willing to learn. I was about to open up and share that I wasn't perfect and really own this.

I didn't know whether to cry or to break down into a ball on the floor, so I simply kept breathing.

I started by explaining the reason for our conversation. I wanted to make things right. In elementary school Noah had cried out for help through his behavior, and he was labeled a behavior child. I felt that label was placed on him because of me. I neglected him in his formative years.

He is still paying the consequences for my neglect, I realize, however on that day when I sat him down, I asked him, "Noah, is there anything that I have done in the past that still causes you pain when you think about it?" I braced myself for his response.

He told me of one time when I was deeply angry with him, I very nearly caused him severe injury. In a fit of rage, I nearly caused him to fall down a flight of stairs. So much chaos comes with unmanaged, untamed emotions and our stable footing can be easily shaken.

Noah was a teenager when we had this conversation, and to this day I am amazed that he had the courage and the patience with me to sit down and have it. This is the type of person Noah is: he is quick to forgive, he doesn't hold a grudge. I believe this is how his vibrant spirit that he came into this world with, keeps showing up. I sincerely apologized to him that day.

We hugged, then he went on his way. This, though, was a pivotal moment for us. The dynamic changed. I opened a dialogue with him in a way that I had never done before. Instead of being authoritarian, I listened. I listened to my son, to his thoughts and feelings, and this shifted our relationship into an entirely new space.

This is the day I truly chose to become an intentional parent. I have not looked back. I dove in. I began learning even more about how to engage my son in active parenting, how to open dialogue. I learned how to embrace my son differently, how to encourage his growth, how to be a positive influence in his life.

I chose him. I chose me. I chose to be a better, more vibrant being.

I realized that day something that I embrace now: Noah has been one of my greatest teachers of unconditional love.

This conversation drew us so much closer, and I promised myself that I would always do whatever I could to make him feel safe and secure.

I felt blessed that day to be Noah's mother. I felt like I was given a new opportunity. His open heart and forgiveness propelled me to want to change.

But I was not through the hardships yet. Not by a long shot.

After making my decision to change course as a parent, I became severely ill. The symptoms presented themselves for about six months before I went to the doctors.

I didn't want to be a bother to anyone and I didn't want to slow down, but my body was leaving me no choice. I was diagnosed with kidney failure, and my health deteriorated quickly.

For a while, I was at death's door. Noah became so scared that it actually drew us much closer. It's now two and a half years later as I continue with my dialysis and Noah and I remain close; we communicate all the time. He's so attentive and caring and is always asking what he can do to make me more comfortable.

My health remains an issue, but I know I will overcome it. I know I have God's help.

Perhaps the main thing I have done in all this transformation is, once I made the decision to change, I submitted my life to the all-knowing Creator. I made a commitment to myself, to God, and to Noah that I would break the cycle.

Through dedicated prayer and meditation day and night, I was determined to elevate myself. I realized I needed to be whole first in order to truly help Noah, and I was broken. I acknowledged this.

Once I became whole, I could then help Noah to restore his life. Along the way I decided to seek help; I found myself a mentor.

My life began to transition and transform. I knew that Noah developed low self-esteem and feelings of inadequacy as a result of my broken parenting, so I found him a child psychologist, and Noah opened up. At this point he began to take his own steps to start to change.

And we both realize it is a process. Clearly it is not easy to overcome generations of unhelpful and abusive behavior. These so-called 'generational curses' keep feeding themselves until someone finds the courage to break them. All too often, this person doesn't find the courage until they have sunk far into the behaviors themselves.

Sometimes you have to hit rock bottom in order to bounce back up.

This may look like kidney failure. This may look like you staring at your reflection in the mirror and knowing you are a hypocrite, and that you had better do something about it while you still have time.

Who knows how much time we really do have? All we ever have is the present moment, so if you are considering a change, you can't make that change tomorrow, you can only do it now.

Right now.

If you know you are a broken parent, break up with being broken. Know you can be whole.

If you know you are continuing a cycle of violence, know you have the power to stop it, no matter how difficult it may seem. Yes, life is difficult, but it is purposeful. We are all here on earth for a reason; embrace all of you and leave your mark in this world.

Purpose lives within you. Life doesn't have to be flawless to be beautiful. I have come to learn how valuable, precious and uplifting a positive relationship can be.

Master yourself. Inspire that mastermind living inside you. You do not have to be broken. You can choose to be healed and whole.

Reflections

Reflections

If you have purchased a copy of this book, we would love for you to send us a selfie of you and the book on your preferred platform:

facebook.com/RealDawnBates
instagram.com/realdawnbates
twitter.com/realdawnbates
linkedin.com/in/dawnbates

…so we can thank you in person.

With love and gratitude,
From all at Dawn Publishing

www.ingramcontent.com/pod-product-compliance
Lightning Source LLC
Chambersburg PA
CBHW021430080526
44588CB00009B/484